DISARMING DIPLOMAT

The Miller Center's W. Alton Jones Foundation Series on the Presidency and Arms Control

Presidents and Arms Control (1994), Volume I

This volume draws on scholars and practitioners who had experience in policy making and decision making. They examine how presidents make decisions on nuclear weapons and the context in which choices are made. Three topics constitute the core of the volume: negotiating arms limitation and ratification of treaties; the presidency and the arms control and disarmament agency; and the future of arms control.

Presidents and Arms Control (1994), Volume II

The attention shifts to patterns and approaches in volume two: reviewing the facts; strategy, budgets, and politics; and processes and contingencies. One writer discusses arms control in the Reagan administration. Two ambassadors evaluate organizing for arms control in the U.S. government. Finally, a leading analyst considers lessons from the case of the Soviet Union.

Disarming Diplomat: The Memoirs of Gerard C. Smith, Arms Control Negotiator (1996)

This volume is, in effect, a summation of the first two volumes. Ambassador Smith, from the standpoint of his personal experience, examines most of the questions previously addressed. He provides a portrait of the factors that enter into the actions of a *disarming diplomat*. He introduces the reader to leaders and diplomats with whom he has worked over his long and productive career. The book helps us understand the little-known practice of contemporary diplomacy.

DISARMING DIPLOMAT

The Memoirs of Gerard C. Smith, Arms Control Negotiator

Gerard C. Smith

Foreword by Henry Owen
Introduction by Kenneth W. Thompson

MADISON BOOKS
Lanham • New York • London

Published by Madison Books
4720 Boston Way
Lanham, Maryland 20706

3 Henrietta Street
London WC2E 8LU, England

Distributed by National Book Network

™ The paper used in this publication meets the minimum requirements of American National Standard for Information Sciences—Permanence of Paper for Printed Library Materials, ANSI Z39.48–1984.
Manufactured in the United States of America.

Co-published by arrangement with
The Miller Center of Public Affairs
The University of Virginia

The views expressed by the author(s) of this publication do not necessarily represent the opinions of the Miller Center. We hold to Jefferson's dictum that: "Truth is the proper and sufficient antagonist to error, and has nothing to fear from the conflict, unless by human interposition, disarmed of her natural weapons, free argument and debate."

Library of Congress Cataloging-in-Publication Data

Smith, Gerard C.
Disarming diplomat : the memoirs of Gerard C. Smith, arms control negotiator / Gerard C. Smith.
p. cm.
Includes bibliographical references and index.
1. Smith, Gerard C. 2. Diplomats—United States—Biography. 3. Nuclear arms control—United States—History. I. Title.
JX1974.7.S482 1996 327.1'74'092—dc20 [B] 95-47025 CIP

ISBN 1–56833-062-6 (cloth : alk. paper)

Contents

Foreword

Gerry Smith and I worked together as colleagues in government, as co-workers in the Trilateral Commission, and as business partners in the Consultants International Group. In each of these different roles, he showed the same qualities of intelligence, innovation, integrity, common sense, kindness and persistence in good causes.

Among these causes, one was preeminent for him. He first became aware of the dreadful force of nuclear weapons from reading about them when he was working for Commissioner Murray at the Atomic Energy Commission. Later, he went to the Pacific and saw a nuclear weapon explode and virtually devour a Pacific island. After that there was no turning back for Gerry. He saw his supreme goal in life become limitation of the threat that nuclear weapons posed to God's handiwork on this earth. This goal, like most things in his life, was partly rooted in his deep religious faith.

Gerry Smith is well known because he negotiated the nuclear arms agreement, SALT I. That task was important, but it was only part of a wider strategy, which Gerry followed with considerable success.

The first part of this strategy was to use patient diplomacy and other forms of communication to defuse crises that could lead to military conflicts, in which there would always be some risk that nuclear weapons might be used. To this end, he invented the U.S.-Soviet hot line, for which President Kennedy wrote him a gracious letter of thanks.

The second element of Gerry's strategy was, paradoxically enough, to build up U.S. military forces–so that if there were a war, it could be fought with conventional, not nuclear, weapons. Soon after he became head of the Policy Planning staff, he went to the Pentagon to lay out his views on this point to the Joint Chiefs. Working for him at the time, I doubted that the Joint Chiefs would heed these views, coming from a civilian who never got to be more than a lieutenant in the wartime Navy. But they took Gerry seriously; they sensed that he knew his facts, and they listened to his reasoning. The military respected Gerry, and he respected them. He kept pressing for a conventional buildup throughout his term as head of the Policy Planning staff. At the end of that term, there were more infantry divisions with wider conventional capabilities than at the beginning. So the threshold for using nuclear weapons was raised.

The third element of Gerry's strategy was to control nuclear weapons, and there, as indicated above, he played a key role in negotiation of the SALT I agreements. Now we take strategic arms limitations and reductions for granted, but when Gerry started out on this course, there were few people who agreed with him–in the armed forces, the Defense Department, or the White House. He kept on pushing, however, and he kept his potential critics in the Defense Department and the Joint Chiefs fully informed of what he was doing. He played it straight. When at the end of the SALT I negotiations it became clear that this effort would succeed, there were many people who wanted to join in the effort and in claiming credit, but at the beginning it was a pretty lonely business.

These three courses of action related to the central U.S.-Soviet relationship, but unlike most of us, Gerry saw further ahead than that. When he was recalled to duty by President Carter, he focused on an altogether different nuclear problem: the threat of nuclear proliferation. To say that he did not solve the problem would be a vast understatement, but his work underlined its importance, and the fact that, if we wanted to prevent the proliferation, we could not always expect to have trouble-free relations with the countries that we didn't want to see develop these weapons.

Gerry's four-point strategy succeeded, in the sense that in forty-five dangerous years of Cold War, nuclear weapons were never fired in anger. Of course, he was only one of many people who worked to this end. But, as one who worked in the government during those years, I can testify that there were very few people who contributed to this success as much as Gerry, and none who contributed more.

His work reflected the qualities mentioned earlier, but it was also due to the fact that he was not seeking fame or power for himself. He remembered Jean Monnet's saying that "there is no limit to what you can achieve if you will give others the credit." As the fact that he felt this way became clear, his influence grew. Both the people who agreed with Gerry and those who disagreed with him appreciated his character and his integrity, and so they paid attention to his views.

All of this gave the impression that Gerard Smith was the sort of solemn person that his photographs in the newspaper sometimes suggested: the Irish hangman. But he wasn't that at all. He was a kind person, good-natured, and with a great sense of humor. He had a questing mind, always searching out ideas, and reading new books, which I hadn't heard of and which he wanted to discuss.

These are among the many reasons that his friends miss him and that the readers of this book will learn, as I did, a great deal from him.

–Henry Owen

Introduction

Ambassador Gerard C. Smith was a longtime friend of the Miller Center. In 1987 we published an oral history he gave at the Miller Center. It was part of a series of presentations, writings, and testimony of the leading figures who were engaged in the theory and practice of arms control. The Ambassador was already suffering from ill health, but he joined our modest enterprise with energy, enthusiasm, and his accustomed goodwill.

I thought at the time that his willingness to participate was one more example of dedication to his subject. Not only did he take part in several grueling question-and-answer sessions, but he made an opening statement without notes. He mentioned his father's influence and his injunction *carpe diem* ("make the most of the day"). I imagined I saw the long shadow of his father's example in his life, and in reading his *Memoirs* that image reappears throughout the text. With all the discussions of values in the 1990s, Gerry Smith's values are clearly incarnate in his father.

Since the Miller Center, with a second generous gift from the W. Alton Jones Foundation, had launched a second project on "The Presidency and Arms Control," Ambassador Smith's manuscript came immediately to mind. Beginning as an aide to Atomic Energy Commissioner Thomas E. Murray in the spring of 1950 and continuing in active service through seven administrations and presidents, Smith is uniquely qualified to address the key issues we had in mind in our latest project. We asked who, how, and when particular individuals in successive presidencies were involved in the arms control process. We hoped to learn how seriously presidents and their chief aides were engaged. How willing were they to expend political capital? What was their personal commitment and what skills did they bring to the task? What was the political and international environment in which arms control went on? How are we to chart the rise and fall of support for arms control? What were the most serious obstacles and problems? Who kept the quest alive and who were the enemies of arms control? What accounts for the success and failure of various presidents and leaders? How did the principals, including the president and the secretaries of state and defense, appear to those who were part of the process?

Ambassador Smith confronts many if not all such questions; implicitly, at least, they are the heart of his inquiry. He combines human qualities that are not always found paralleling one another in men of affairs: patience and passion, consistency yet flexibility, realism joined with burning idealism, and an unquenchable conviction that the nuclear problem is the most pressing of our age.

We suffer from many divisions in contemporary society. They create deep cleavages between individuals and groups. As a university man, I am especially conscious of one between theorists and practitioners or men of affairs and those in the academy. Gerry Smith brought the two groups together through his work at the School for Advanced International Studies, through the Trilateral Commission, in his magazine *Interplay*, and above all as exemplified in his personal attitude. Nothing could be more appropriate, then, that a university institute should join hands with a trade publishing house to issue *Disarming Diplomat*.

–Kenneth W. Thompson

Author's Prologue

As I finish this memoir, nuclear-weapons states are decommissioning and destroying nuclear weapons faster than they are building and deploying them. For the past twelve months, the United States, Russia, the United Kingdom, and France have not conducted any nuclear weapons tests, with China setting off a single device. These and other concerned countries are actively discussing a binding international convention banning future nuclear tests. Since the collapse of the Soviet Union in 1991, the risk of nuclear war has diminished. In a powerfully symbolic move, the United States and Russia have announced that they will target their nuclear missiles only at the oceans instead of each other. These extraordinarily positive developments bring into sharp focus a remaining, fundamental problem–the continuing risk of acquisition of nuclear weapons by additional countries. This proliferation problem looms as the most important remaining challenge of the "nuclear era."

As one who grappled with the promises and dangers of nuclear technology during much of the last four decades, I have undertaken this short memoir in hopes of making further, modest contribution to public understanding of the dangers we faced and the risks we continue to confront. It is imperative that we not fall into complacency as a result of the sudden end of the Cold War. A review of past events and the personalities and processes that shaped them may serve as an antidote to smugness. Myth, misconception and plain ignorance have often influenced U.S. policy on nuclear technology and weapons. We have avoided nuclear cataclysm as much through Providence as through wise or well-informed policy.

This review is based upon direct personal involvement through a series of government posts in seven administrations, those of Presidents Truman, Eisenhower, Kennedy, Johnson, Nixon, Ford, and Carter. From 1950 to 1954, I served as an assistant to a commissioner of the Atomic Energy Commission, then a powerful entity with large authority over development of nuclear technology for both civilian and military purposes. In this capacity I first witnessed atmospheric nuclear tests, an experience that many who formulated U.S. policy should have had, but did not. In 1954, I moved to the State Department, where I served as Special Assistant for Atomic Energy to Secretary of State John Foster Dulles in 1954-57, and from 1957 to 1961 as Assistant Secretary of State for Policy Planning. In the Kennedy administration, I served as a State Department consultant on the Berlin Crisis and subsequently as an Ambassador working with our NATO allies on how to limit proliferation of nuclear weapons while ensuring nuclear deterrence against a Soviet attack on Western Europe. This role continued into President Johnson's tenure.

In 1969, President Nixon appointed me director of the Arms Control and Disarmament Agency (ACDA) and chairman of the U.S. Delegation to the first Strategic Arms Limitation Talks (SALT). I have previously recounted the challenges and frustrations of my service (1969-72) under President Nixon in *Doubletalk* (1980). Accordingly, students of these times may want to focus on this previous work in addition to the present memoir that treats these events relatively succinctly. During the Ford administration I was a member of the President's General Advisory Committee on Arms Control. In the Carter administration, I served as the President's Special Representative and Ambassador-at-Large for Nuclear Nonproliferation. During the Reagan and Bush administrations, I remained active in public debate on nuclear issues, as Chairman of the Arms Control Association, by publishing articles and through work with a number of citizens groups, including the Committee to Save the ABM Treaty.

Between government posts, I remained active in international discourse on a wide range of issues, including nuclear non-proliferation. After departing the Johnson administration, I founded and published a magazine entitled *Interplay* devoted to interrelations between the United States and Europe. And upon resigning early in the second Nixon term, I helped David Rockefeller found the Trilateral Commission, serving as its North American Chair until entering the Carter administration. This memoir touches briefly on these involvements, but its central focus is my long and relatively continuous engagement in nuclear policy and diplomacy.

This memoir does not purport to be an autobiography. Indeed, it begins when I was already 36 years of age. Nevertheless, a few words may be in order to describe how I arrived at a career of nuclear diplomacy.

My parents were distant cousins–John Thomas and Mary Agnes Smith. Born in New Haven, Connecticut, both were children of potato famine refugees from County Cavan in Ireland. Before marrying my father, my mother was a school teacher. My father was endowed with prodigious intellect and energy. He graduated first in his class from Creighton University in Omaha, Nebraska, and then graduated from Yale Law School with highest honors. His law school class voted him "Most Likely to Succeed." Succeed he did, becoming the first General Counsel of the General Motors Corporation, a post he held for over 30 years until his retirement in June 1947. Shortly after my father's death in 1947, a colleague told me that he had been the "conscience" of the corporation. His accomplishments were many. He argued several cases before the Supreme Court. He was a gifted linguist–he once taught himself Spanish during a trip to South America to conduct an arbitration proceeding in that language. He was fluent in German and helped GM acquire Opel in the early 1930s. In accord with his extraordinary abilities and his presence at the creation of a huge corporate enterprise, Father received large financial rewards.

I was born in New York City in 1914, the youngest of three children. By my teenage years, my father and mother had cause to worry that the family's growing wealth would tempt me into a life of idleness. Father's oft-repeated advice to me was "be useful and don't become a playboy." This injunction was consistent with his own Latin motto *carpe diem* or "make the most of the day"–a saying that, to my amusement, now appears on tee shirts and coffee mugs.

I recall first being interested in international matters around 1930 when, at Canterbury, a Catholic boarding school in Connecticut, I wrote an article for the school's quarterly magazine on the topic of the Soviet Union's first Five Year Plan. My recollection is that I concluded that the plan would not be fulfilled because Russians were dreamers, not doers. During the long Cold War competition with the Soviet Union, I had many an occasion to recall this initial, juvenile analysis.

After Canterbury I attended Yale College and Yale Law School. As an undergraduate, I majored in history and wrote a thesis on the Battle of Jutland, prefiguring a lifelong interest in naval matters. During these seven years in New Haven, I tried to strike a reasonable balance between the playboy impulse and academic diligence. The result was a first-rate education, but one uncrowned by the academic laurels that my father had earned.

In 1938, I went to work for Father in New York on the General Motors legal staff. Although corporate headquarters had by that time been relocated to Detroit, my father was allowed to keep the legal staff in New York, operating somewhat like an independent law firm in contrast to the fully integrated corporate legal staffs of today. I also was on the boards of several mining companies in which my father had a substantial investment, and actually served as President of the Argonaut Gold Mine in Jackson, California.

With U.S. entry into World War II imminent, in early 1941, I was commissioned as a junior officer in the U.S. Navy. I was posted to Washington, D.C., and spent the war working principally on procurement of electronic systems. While this stint of military service did not prove the epiphany that it did for many who served in harm's way, it nonetheless exposed me to life in Washington, D.C., and to government service. It also led me to the Maryland countryside and to the purchase in 1945 of Ratcliffe Manor on Maryland's Eastern Shore. It is there, nearly 50 years later, that I write this book. In the postwar years, I resumed law practice with my own firm in New York City–briefly in partnership with my father upon his retirement from General Motors, until his sudden death in 1947.

By 1950, I felt the urge to return to public service. My law practice did not hold compelling interest. My father's death left me with a not inconsiderable inheritance, making public service economically feasible. The Korean War emphasized the need for the United States to play a stronger world role, a process in which I wanted to play a part. Accordingly, I did not hesitate to accept an offer to move to Washington to serve as Special Assistant to Thomas E. Murray, a commissioner of the AEC. When accepting this job, I did not realize that I would be wrestling with nuclear issues for most of the balance of my career. Indeed, in doing so, I hope that I have honored my father's urging "to be useful." In my endeavors, I have often reminded myself of a motto first brought to my attention by the Reverend James Keller of the Maryknoll Order, "It is better to light one candle than to curse the darkness."

As readers will discern, I did not arrive in Washington in 1950 as an "arms controller." I shared the conventional perceptions of the times regarding the threat posed by the Soviet Union and the need for the United States to counter this threat–with nuclear weapons if necessary. My early labors were animated by the excitement of being a young man privileged to play in an important game. Only with the passage of years did I fully comprehend the imperatives of tight control of nuclear technology and the reduction of nuclear arsenals. This book describes my long education in nuclear politics and diplomacy. It deserves emphasis that, rarely in the course of this education, did I comprehend its lessons as clearly as I do now with the benefit of hindsight, further study, and long reflection.

This preface would be woefully incomplete without mention of my late and beloved wife, Bernice Latrobe Maguire. She spent her childhood in St. Louis, Missouri, and graduated from Smith College. Before our marriage in August 1941, she worked at *Time* magazine and later headed public relations for the New York department store, Lord & Taylor. As was customary at the time, she abandoned professional pursuits to become my wife and mother to our four children. Her loving care and strong mind were integral parts of my existence during our 46 years of marriage. Although her life would have been easier had I not engaged in public service, she selflessly helped enforce my father's admonition against the easy course. To her, more than anyone else, I am beholden for such results as I may have achieved.

Author's Prologue

In my career I have received indispensable assistance and encouragement from a large number of extremely talented individuals. Most are mentioned in the pages that follow. Special acknowledgement goes to those who have helped me compose this memoir–Henry Owen, Bill McGuirk, Bob Bowie, Ben Huberman, Vice Admiral "Squidge" Lee, John Rhinelander, Phil Farley, Larry Weiler and Bob Schaetzel.

I started this memoir armed with little more than diary notes to stimulate fading memory. Early on I received able research assistance from Jennifer Weeks, but it soon became apparent that considerable professional assistance was in order. I was lucky to enlist the services of Allen Greb of the University of Maryland and Robert Wampler of the National Security Archive, who helped greatly in researching and drafting this memoir. This work has also benefited from the assistance of my son, John Thomas Smith II, who urged its initiation and who contributed significantly to its completion.

Shortly after Hiroshima, Albert Einstein reputedly said, "Now everything has changed except our manner of thinking; thus we are drifting toward catastrophe beyond comparison. We shall require a new manner of thinking if mankind is to survive." Although mankind has survived the first five decades of the nuclear era, I am uncertain that we have yet acquired the new manner of thinking called for by Einstein. There is, admittedly, greater reason to hope than during the Cold War, yet the risks of proliferation of nuclear weapons remain acute. It is imperative that the present generation of political and military leaders and diplomats address this problem with relentless zeal, so that the world may truly acquire a new manner of thinking.

Easton, Maryland
May 1994

Chapter One

The Atomic Energy Commission, 1950–54

Starting an Education

In the spring of 1950, I began my nuclear adventure as a special assistant to one of the five Atomic Energy commissioners, Thomas E. Murray. Murray had been appointed to the Commission on March 20, 1950, following Chairman David Lilienthal's resignation. I was a family friend of the Murrays, and a lawyer with no background in nuclear or atomic energy.

My AEC work, lasting four years through the spring of 1954, provided an education in the technology of terror and promise that atomic energy offered. It also revealed that many policymakers in the U.S. government who dealt with nuclear questions were just as much amateurs as I, and that politics and personalities impinged significantly even on these paramount security issues. It led me to respect the professionalism of a few of our political and military leaders, at the same time that it made me wonder about the wisdom and judgment of others. It also exposed me to the emerging hysteria of McCarthyism, which exacerbated America's multi-decade inability to deal wisely with the Soviet Union. I often reflected on my father's prediction made during the war that I and my generation indeed would have to "deal with the Russians." The AEC experience persuaded me that greater openness and candor and less secrecy could have helped us to reach more sensible decisions on nuclear policy.

By the beginning of 1950, the Cold War between the United States and the Soviet Union was reaching a new level of intensity.

Within months, it escalated further with the outbreak of the Korean War. The atmosphere in Washington was tense. Since 1945 and the failure of the Baruch plan (the U.S. proposal for international control of atomic energy) two key events in the nuclear arena had contributed to the general deterioration in relations between the former wartime allies. Most portentous for U.S. security, Moscow had demonstrated its own nuclear capability, exploding an atomic device in August 1949. Then, the U.S. program itself was compromised. It was learned in February 1950 that British scientist Klaus Fuchs, who worked on both fission and fusion designs at the Los Alamos weapons laboratory, had been a spy for the Soviets. Even before these revelations, President Harry Truman had warned his advisors in July 1949, "I am of the opinion we'll never obtain international control. Since we can't . . . we must be strongest in atomic weapons." So, nuclear weapons became the centerpiece of U.S. defense policy.[1]

The Atomic Energy Commission (AEC), which had taken over U.S. nuclear operations from the Army's Manhattan District in 1946, was considered to be as important as any agency in Washington. Its prestige was high at the White House and in Congress. From the wartime Manhattan Project, the Commission inherited an extensive complex of research laboratories, production plants, and personnel. The complex included the weapon design laboratory at Los Alamos; Sandia Laboratory, responsible for research and engineering on nonnuclear weapon components; and production and assembly plants in a number of states. The Commission employed about 6,000 civilian and military personnel and more than 35,000 contract workers. This vast complex was diffuse and ill-defined. In addition to being geographically dispersed, primarily for security purposes, it was organizationally decentralized, giving local AEC managers a good deal of independence.[2] In 1950, despite having a virtual monopoly over all aspects of the development of nuclear technology for both military and peaceful purposes, the AEC still found itself groping for a particular role in nuclear decision making. In fact, the nation, like Murray, was still unsure of how the new weapons would best support national security needs. Commissioner Murray, with counsel from his assistants, would explore this role over the next four years.

Commissioner Thomas E. Murray

Before his appointment to the AEC, Murray had been an engineer, inventor, and chief executive of an electrical equipment manufacturing company. Born in Albany, New York, in 1891, Murray went to school in New York, and received a degree in mechanical engineering from Yale's Sheffield Scientific School at the age of nineteen. His only public service prior to coming to the Commission had been as a bankruptcy receiver at the Interborough Rapid Transit Company in New York between 1932 and 1940. The Democratic Party in New York City earlier had considered proposing Murray for mayor, and in 1958 he was a serious candidate for the Democratic nomination for governor of New York. Murray served on the board of directors of the Bank of New York and the Chrysler Corporation, the latter with John Foster Dulles, for whom I would later work at the State Department.

As the official historians of the AEC during the 1950s have aptly written, "Murray brought to the Commission a shrewd, analytical mind, the hard-headed practicality of an engineer, and an unswerving determination to keep the United States second to none in nuclear technology."[3] And because of his attention to and emphasis on moral issues, he was at the same time known as the "conscience of the Commission." Murray the engineer and entrepreneur, with over two hundred patents to his credit, was something of a visionary, with much of his energies fueled by strong religious beliefs. He was a serious Catholic and perhaps more religious than any layman I have known. In 1952, he received the Laetare Medal, the highest award that an American Catholic layman can receive.

Murray's highly developed moral judgment constantly guided his decisions as an AEC commissioner and was reflected especially in his views and attitudes toward nuclear weapons. In his memoir, *Nuclear Policy for War and Peace*, he argues that two principles should control nuclear weapons use. The "military principle of necessity of usefulness" had to be constantly balanced against the "higher moral principle of justice in the use of force."[4] Thus, Murray could at the same time favor increasing the number of nuclear fission weapons in the stockpile while attacking the accumulation of very high-yield thermonuclear weapons. He favored a cessation of tests of hydrogen bombs while rejecting, for a time, a complete ban on all nuclear tests. These arguments seem not to be made by an engineer, but by a theologian. Murray indeed had a number of friends as well as several sons in the Jesuit order. Such an outlook was unusual, if not unique, among government officials working on nuclear issues. It tended to make some government officials uncomfortable with Murray.

He was especially influential with the most important man in the national security establishment, President Truman, who once told K.T. Keller, then president of Chrysler Corporation, that Murray was the best AEC commissioner he had appointed.[5] The President also said that Murray was the only commissioner on whom he could completely rely.[6] This special relationship came about as a direct result of Murray's willingness to go straight to the top with what he viewed as important issues. Unlike the other commissioners in those days, he would engage in "end runs," going directly to the President, the secretaries of defense and treasury, and members of Congress to advance his views. In many cases, they were not shared by the other commissioners or by the AEC division heads, who especially resisted Murray's involvement in operational matters. Even though he had not known Murray before he joined the AEC, Truman trusted and appreciated individuals who would speak to him directly on critical questions. In April 1952, I made a diary entry about the public announcement of Murray's nomination for an additional five-year term "to the other Commissioners' dismay."[7]

Other AEC Figures

The chairman of the AEC in 1950 was Gordon Dean, who had been a law partner of Senator Brien McMahon, the sponsor of the legislation establishing the Commission with civilian control of nuclear weapons. Dean struck me as a good bureaucrat who wanted to keep on close terms with the powerful congressional Joint Committee on Atomic Energy (JCAE), whose first chairman was Senator McMahon. Professor Henry DeWolf (Harry) Smyth, who had worked with the Manhattan District, was the only scientist among the five commissioners, although there were many scientists in the AEC's large organization. Smyth had been a professor of physics at Princeton and was the author of the official report issued in 1945 describing the making of the atom bomb. Smyth had no political background. Except in the Oppenheimer case where he was a strong dissenter, he limited most of his interventions to scientific aspects of policy. Sumner Pike had been head of the Securities and Exchange Commission before coming to the AEC. Pike was quite cautious. In 1953, I wrote a memorandum urging that the weapons program be substantially increased, involving much larger production of fissionable material. He covered the document with question marks, which suggested to me that he thought the then-current production rate was about right. T. Keith Glennan, the fifth commissioner, had been president of the Case Institute of Technology. After leaving the AEC, Glennan became a strong advocate of nonproliferation policies.

In Murray's office, I worked closely with his other assistant, William McGuirk, with whom I became close friends. McGuirk, a Naval Academy graduate, was an investment banker who had been working with Murray in New York. After leaving the AEC in early 1952, McGuirk went on to a distinguished career as executive vice president of the Davison Chemical Division of the Grace Company, president of the Mercantile Bank and Trust Company in Baltimore, and chief executive of the *Baltimore Sun*. He was succeeded by Navy Captain James Dunford, an expert on naval nuclear reactors who had worked with Hyman Rickover from the first days of the Naval Reactors Program. Dunford later became Admiral Rickover's deputy.

Robert LeBaron was the chairman of the Military Liaison Committee, the official link between the Pentagon and the AEC. LeBaron had been in the oil business, and had obtained his position as MLC chairman with the help of Admiral Lewis Strauss. Strauss, a self-made Wall Street financier, had served on Secretary of the

Navy James V. Forrestal's staff during the war. He had been one of the original Truman appointees to the Commission in 1946, where he remained for three years.[8] When Strauss rejoined the government in 1953, first as President Eisenhower's special assistant for atomic energy and later as the AEC chairman, LeBaron was not inclined to challenge or disagree with him. In fact, LeBaron was an expert in "double talk," and some of us often were puzzled to know what he was actually trying to say.

My views of the commissioners and the AEC staff were quite mixed. I noted that the commissioners were "children shooting from the hip, instead of [exhibiting] cool, careful planning. Too much for five men–but five men are too many."[9] I was struck with the "ordinariness" of the AEC bureaucrats to whom was left some responsibility for overseeing large industrial operations, the direct management of which was handled by contractors such as General Electric, Westinghouse, and du Pont. The military people involved–Generals J. McCormack and Alfred D. Starbird, directors of the military application division; General Kenneth D. Nichols, who became manager of the AEC in 1953; and General Herbert "Doc" Loper, who was Assistant Secretary of Defense for atomic energy (the top atomic weapons officer at the Pentagon)–were of a higher caliber.

The staff people saw the AEC as a unique organization which served as a central security agency of the U.S. government. Most of them were holdovers from the Manhattan District. They seemed to believe that since they had been in at the beginning, their insights on policy questions should carry the day. The staff particularly disliked the idea of people, such as McGuirk or myself, coming in who were not technicians. Not surprisingly, I did not work well with them. I worked almost exclusively with Murray, who often found himself in disagreement with others in the Commission.

As I saw it, my job was to provide specifics that would inform Murray's intuitive approach to the issues. In this process, I attempted to accumulate as much information as possible within the AEC, as well as to establish appropriate ties with other departments, particularly State and Defense, and with Congress. One part of my job was to write speeches for Murray. I used this opportunity to promote a greater public knowledge and understanding about nuclear questions. At the centennial anniversary of Manhattan College on April 25, 1953, for example, Murray decried the public's "noticeable unconcern" about atomic energy issues, which he attributed to several false beliefs: that the subject was too secret to learn about, too profound to understand, and too ugly to contemplate. On the contrary, Murray, using my draft, argued:

> I am convinced that a broad base of informed and interested civilians is essential to survival in the atomic years ahead. The problems are of such cosmic significance that they cannot be safely "left to the experts." The bald truth is that in this tragic atomic drama there are no experts.[10]

In another speech that I wrote, Murray compared the Soviet-American arms race to the game of "chicken" in which foolish youngsters used to drive their cars at each other to see which would be the first to give way. Murray's speeches used to gripe Lewis Strauss and some of the other commissioners.

Truman's final State of the Union message reflected some of Murray's perspectives on nuclear weapons. The President said that, with the discovery of atomic energy, "war has undergone a technological change which makes it a very different thing from what it used to be." Any conflict might "dig the grave" of both East and West. But not withstanding this change, "atomic power, like any other force of nature, is not evil in itself. Properly used, it is an instrumentality for human betterment." Truman concluded, "We cannot ignore the dangers or the benefits it offers."[11] Despite their suspicions and distrust of Murray, several AEC commissioners congratulated him on this input into Truman's last message.

Pressures for More Nuclear Weapons

Murray and his assistants came to focus on three primary issues: (1) the expansion of uranium supplies and weapons production; (2) thermonuclear weapons development and a second weapons laboratory; and (3) nuclear reactors. Murray worked closely with the military and those members of the congressional Joint Committee on Atomic Energy (JCAE) who wanted to increase the size of the U.S. nuclear arsenal. President Truman had been officially informed about the woeful state of the U.S. stockpile in April 1947. By 1952, both nuclear production and military preparedness had improved dramatically. The improvement was stimulated in large measure by the Strategic Air Command (SAC) and its commander, Lieutenant General Curtis LeMay, who was determined to build up a force capable of fully carrying out SAC's war plan. The arsenal grew from a handful of weapons in 1947 to over two hundred in June 1949.[12] Still, pressure to expand production further came in the aftermath of the Soviet's explosion of an atomic device in the summer of 1949, the Fuchs case, and the outbreak of the Korean War in July 1950. President Truman made a serious gaffe when he later stated his doubt that the Soviets had really developed a nuclear weapon. The AEC commissioners presented the clear evidence to the President. One Congressman said Truman's statement was the most irresponsible he had ever heard.

In 1951, the JCAE and Pentagon led the way in demands for more and larger yield weapons, looking for "every means for maximizing production."[13] Congress and the military wanted to increase both the size and versatility of the U.S. fission stockpile. In 1951-1952, a major study stressed the possible tactical value of small yield atomic weapons, noting especially their potential in western Europe where leaders for years had been urging the development of a nuclear capability to counteract the Soviet conventional (nonnuclear) threat. Tactical nuclear weapons (TNWs) received added impetus from the U.S. Army, which "clearly wanted to have its own tactical nuclear combat support arm."[14] Ironically, many of the experts associated with the 1951-52 study, including Robert Oppenheimer, advocated more and better fission bombs and TNWs at least in part to discourage the development of strategic large yield weapons. As it turned out, proponents of *both* types of weapons systems got their way.

In those days, the JCAE and Chairman McMahon had a monopoly in Congress on oversight of nuclear matters. The JCAE no longer exists and its responsibilities are dispersed among a number of committees. As evidence of Murray's close and informal relations with the JCAE, Senator Bourke Hickenlooper of Iowa once disclosed to Murray that he had offered to toss a coin with Representative Sterling Cole to choose Chairman McMahon's successor, and that he would have offered the chairmanship anyway to Cole if Cole had refused to toss a coin. Cole became the second chairman. Some years later, at Lewis Strauss's strong urging, Cole reluctantly gave up his congressional career to become the first director of the International Atomic Energy Agency in Vienna, which had been set up as a result of Eisenhower's Atoms for Peace proposal of 1953.

My recollection is that members of Congress, even those on the JCAE, had little real understanding of the great issues with which the Atomic Energy commissioners were wrestling, such as whether and how much to expand the fissionable material production complex. They seemed more comfortable with mundane issues such as how much it cost to run the cafeterias, while issues involving billions of dollars needed to support the industrial program generally received less consideration. In January 1952 I noted, "Most of the congressmen had little knowledge about atomic energy"–recalling the poet's conclusion that a little knowledge is a dangerous thing.[15] Six months later, after attending a hearing of the Senate Appropriations Committee, I wrote, "Never did so few know so little about what they have so much control over."[16]

The uniformed military, represented by the Joint Chiefs of Staff (JCS), and the Defense Department strongly supported nuclear expansion. Charged with the effort to establish force requirements, the JCS recommended a 50 percent to 150 percent increase in production over four to six years, costing an estimated $3 billion. But military planners provided no well-defined criteria for the expansion effort. On the question, "How much is enough?" Secretary of Defense Robert Lovett told the NSC in December 1951, "It is my opinion that we must err, if we must, on the side of rather too much rather than too little, within our economic capabilities and the overall defense effort."[17]

Unlike some members of the AEC, such as Glennan and Smyth, who urged caution on the expansion effort, Murray wanted to go full speed ahead. His concerns in this area did not come from any elaborate analysis of stockpile requirements. Being very suspicious of the Soviets, he made gross calculations based on a belief that the United States should always remain ahead in the nuclear weapons race. Others were less convinced of the need for more weapons. Secretary of the Treasury George Humphrey once said, "What difference does it make? We will be ahead at times and they will be at other times." That type of thinking was especially frustrating to Murray.

My thinking in the early 1950s closely paralleled that of my boss. I had read a good deal during the 1930s about Soviet policies. After reading such authors as Schumpeter and Dallin, I became convinced that there was little prospect of harmony between the United States and the Soviet Union. Even during World War II, I was puzzled by the Roosevelt policy that seemed to overlook the innate hostility between the two systems. I believed that it would be a mistake for the United States to expect to have a constructive relationship with Moscow after the war. At times, I even tried to block export of some arms to the Soviet Union. I doubted that the Soviets would cooperate after Yalta. Following the war, I remained anti-Soviet, but not anti-communist in the sense that Senator Joseph McCarthy was. It was perfectly clear that we were in for a long, hard competition.

My sense of the need to increase the nuclear stockpile came from this interpretation of the expansionist tendencies of the Soviet leadership, and was not the product of analytical studies about military requirements. In fact at this time, I knew very little about how much nuclear material was needed to make a weapon; I just had a general sense that we should have more to meet the potential threat. Nuclear weapons information was tightly held. Some policymakers, even those with a presumptive need to know, did not seek such information because of the potential moral and psychological burdens it might impose. As reflected in Secretary Lovett's December 1951 statement to the NSC, whenever we at the AEC asked for advice from the Pentagon about military requirements, the response was, "We'll take as many as you can produce."

Picking a General Manager

My first specific assignment at the AEC was to identify a candidate for general manager to replace Carroll Wilson, who had resigned after stating publicly that he had lost confidence in the Commission. I had never known another case where a subordinate quit because he had lost confidence in his principals! I asked Alfred Sloan, the chairman of the board of General Motors, whether he had a candidate. His reaction was, "Gerard, I trust that we have no lunatics at General Motors." In two or three days, however, Sloan called to say that he had conferred with his friend, Ben Abrams, the head of Standard Oil of New Jersey, and they jointly recommended Marion Boyer, head of the Esso division. I felt that a successful businessman with an energy background (although not nuclear energy) would be a good type of manager. Boyer was recruited and did a fine job.

On Boyer's retirement I recommended as his successor Don Quarles, who was then chief of the Sandia Corporation, a major link in weapons design. Quarles was one of the most impressive men in the weapons business, a hard worker who was always in command of the facts. One commissioner opposed this recommendation, however, and Major General K.D. Nichols got the job. The Air Force then recruited Quarles as an assistant secretary, and he later became Deputy Secretary of Defense, in which capacity he took a lively part in the Eisenhower administration's debates over nuclear issues.

The Search for Uranium

In the early Fifties, the limiting factor in making nuclear weapons was believed to be the availability of uranium ore. The United States, Great Britain, and Canada had formed a uranium supply arrangement called the Combined Development Trust (CDT) in an effort to monopolize the Free World's supply of uranium. It was the general belief that the United States would be fortunate if it could meet its domestic supply needs from the Colorado plateau at the then current rate of production. Having been president of a

California gold mine (the Argonaut, which was the deepest gold mine in the United States) when a price rise in 1933 had stimulated production, I urged that a price increase for uranium would substantially raise production. After I persuaded Murray of this, he became an advocate for higher prices, which pitted him against the opinion of the Raw Materials Division of the AEC and of prominent geologists. After many debates the price was increased and in a few years we had uranium "coming out of our ears."

This was part of Murray's broader effort to increase the U.S. uranium stockpile. Contracting for supplies from abroad took up a good deal of our energies. In addition to Canada and Australia, we looked to Spain and Portugal, which were believed to have developed some reserves. In these two cases the AEC staff had not succeeded in obtaining supply contracts. So Murray, with Truman's approval, personally approached Premier Salazar and Generalissimo Franco and secured contracts for their countries' production. South Africa proved to be a major source of uranium, which prompted me to reflect, "Read some regarding South African racial problems, which now have direct pertinence to AEC affairs." Little did I realize the extent of racial violence that South Africa was to suffer. I participated in the negotiations with South African officials, led by Ampie Roux, to contract for uranium extracted during gold mining operations. Some twenty-five years later, when President Carter asked me to go to South Africa for negotiations in connection with trying to stop the spread of nuclear weapons, I had occasion to again work with Roux. But unfortunately I was not able to persuade his government to sign the 1968 Non-Proliferation Treaty. South Africa has now done so. We have since learned in a remarkable admission from President Frederik W. de Klerk that South Africa indeed had produced a small number of so-called "bombs in the basement." According to de Klerk, in order to conform to the NPT, these weapons are being dismantled and South Africa will no longer pursue a weapons program.

In those days thorium was considered to be a possible raw material to meet our fissile material needs. Brazil and India had large deposits. I do not recall any large contracts being made, but I worked on this matter with Homi J. Bhaba, who later became the head of the Geneva Scientific Conference in 1955.

A Second Weapons Laboratory

In 1951, I helped Murray promote a second nuclear weapons design laboratory at Livermore, California, in the belief that the existing laboratory at Los Alamos, New Mexico, needed some competition. Murray was the commissioner most receptive to this idea. Not coincidentally, he was also a supporter of the physicist Edward Teller, who left Los Alamos in 1951 primarily because of disagreements with Robert Oppenheimer and other Los Alamos scientists and administrators over how to handle the hydrogen bomb program.[18] Murray was an early advocate of the H-bomb development program. But, after observing test explosions in the Pacific, he became a vigorous opponent of thermonuclear testing.

Oppenheimer, who chaired the General Advisory Committee (GAC) to the AEC, was not enthusiastic about a second laboratory. He and the GAC argued that starting a new lab would only dilute the efforts of Los Alamos and that competition would not necessarily improve weapons research. They were only willing to recommend the establishment of a new division at Los Alamos. These arguments appealed to a majority of the commissioners, but not to Murray.[19]

Teller visited Murray occasionally and pressed for both a second weapons laboratory and for the hydrogen bomb program, which he viewed as linked. Noting organizational and leadership problems at Los Alamos, Teller maintained that one lab alone could not handle both fission and thermonuclear development. Teller was a persuasive individual and Murray was ideologically inclined to agree with him. In addition, I told Murray that from a business-competition standpoint, a second laboratory made sense. Although we did not have discussions with him, Ernest O. Lawrence–director of the University of California Radiation Laboratory, inventor of the cyclotron, and promoter of large-scale physics research–worked with Teller to help establish the second laboratory at Livermore, California, in 1952. It is now named the Lawrence Livermore Laboratory.

In light of this laboratory's key role in the 1980s "Star Wars" antiballistic missile efforts urged upon President Reagan by Edward

Teller, I have felt some regret at my minor role in the establishment of the Livermore Laboratory. Teller has been a baleful influence for many years, for example pressing for "clean bombs" and recently fooling President Reagan into believing in the feasibility of a Strategic Defense Initiative to make ballistic missiles "impotent and obsolete." The "Star Wars" cost the taxpayer about $30 billion before being abandoned in 1993 by the Clinton administration. Teller also was a major force in blocking nuclear test ban proposals and trying–though unsuccessfully–to stop Soviet-American strategic arms limitations. In retrospect, I believe that the combination of Teller and the Livermore Laboratory had a pernicious influence on U.S. national security policy.

Nuclear Tests

A formative and crucial part of my education in nuclear matters occurred in 1951 and 1952, when I observed two nuclear tests at Eniwetok in the Marshall Islands–one of the "Greenhouse" series shots in the spring of 1951, and the "Ivy" King shot in November 1952. The former was a tower test with a small yield, and the latter an air drop from a B-36. It had a 500-kiloton yield. I believe it was the largest fission weapon ever detonated.[20] For the first time, watching these explosions gave me a real understanding of the immense destructive energies at mankind's disposal. This had a galvanizing effect on my thinking about the necessity to get such weapons under international control. I read a good deal about international control during this period–and often discussed these issues with Murray. I remember the writings of P.M.S. Blackett and other strategic thinkers. I studied U.S. plans for general and complete disarmament (including the so-called RAC papers on conventional controls). I also remember discussing some of these issues with my colleague Philip Farley, who would join me later in the State Department and who would devote a lifetime to the promotion of arms control.

The 1951 test took place on a Sunday. Accompanied by a few Air Force generals (who all seemed to have Irish names such as Walsh, Sweeny and O'Donnell), we flew to another island to attend

Mass. The priest announced that there would be no sermon that morning because of the event scheduled for the afternoon. That struck me as a good reason to skip a sermon. General "Pete" Quesada, who had been in charge of tactical aviation at the Normandy landings in 1944, was commanding officer of the joint task force that conducted this test. Quesada has been a good friend ever since. Years later he gave me as a souvenir a piece of charred wood that had been close to the explosion and bore the name and date, "Greenhouse '51."

The 1952 test was an air drop. We could see the plane approaching the target, about twelve miles from our observation point. I hoped that the pilot would not get confused and drop the bomb on the observers. The explosion was a hellish exhibition of energetic force, and after the great pillar of smoke and fire started to drift toward us, hard-nosed Senator Henry "Scoop" Jackson, part of a congressional delegation witnessing the test, turned to me and said "Gerry, where is the nearest bar?" Though obviously shaken by the explosion, Jackson did not let this event stand in the way of his hard-line policy against the Soviet Union nor alter his faith in the power of greater and more varied nuclear weapons. Twenty years later, Jackson instigated a "purge" (indulged by the Nixon White House) of the delegation that negotiated SALT I agreements including the ABM Treaty and the interim agreement limiting the numbers of strategic launchers. As chairman of the SALT delegation, I thought this a shameful performance.

I shared Murray's view that observing nuclear tests was essential for decision-makers who influenced nuclear policy.[21] After the "Mike" shot (the first thermonuclear test) he tried unsuccessfully to get Lewis Strauss and the other AEC commissioners to support a Soviet-American moratorium on thermonuclear testing and pressed for greater openness about nuclear weapons policy. It was an uphill battle, and a shocking idea for that time. As I noted earlier, knowledge of the size of the weapons stockpile and other nuclear weapons issues was still tightly controlled. In congressional testimony in 1951, General MacArthur was asked whether he knew the size of the nuclear stockpile. He replied, "I do not. I have no more information on that than the average officer would have."[22]

And yet he favored using tactical nuclear weapons during the Korean War–perhaps because of his ignorance.

Murray observed thermonuclear tests of very large yield. He later wrote that each time he watched a test, "I . . . had a feeling I might be gazing into eternity or into the gates of Hell."[23] That was what I told Secretary of State John Foster Dulles some years later when I was urging him to go to the Pacific and witness a nuclear test. I think he declined lest it affect his political judgment, though much to my surprise this leading Presbyterian told me that he didn't think he believed in Hell!

The Commission voted down a 1953 proposal by Murray to establish a foreign observer program at the "Castle" series of tests in the Pacific. Undaunted, Murray personally urged President Eisenhower that at least a United Nations observer be invited. But Murray's influence at the White House diminished when Truman left office. The reply from Sherman Adams said that the President would not overrule the previous negative majority decision of the Commission, and recommended that Murray not "appeal" his minority position to the President.[24] Murray thought of resigning but did not.[25] I continued to find the idea of an international observer program for nuclear tests attractive. In 1956, after I had become Dulles's principal adviser on nuclear matters, I attempted to revive the notion both as part of a U.N. initiative and as a U.S.-Soviet reciprocal agreement. Again primarily because of internal AEC opposition and concerns about secrecy, nothing came of these observer proposals.[26]

On February 28, 1954, the first shot of the Castle nuclear series, "Bravo" (a 15-megaton thermonuclear test[27]) dropped radioactive fallout on a Japanese fishing boat, the *Lucky Dragon*, ninety miles downwind from the test. When the boat returned to its home port with twenty-seven fishermen suffering from radiation poisoning, the event raised a storm in the Japanese press, which was soon echoed in the U.S. press.[28] The *Lucky Dragon*'s captain knew that ships were advised not to enter the 50,000 square mile zone around Eniwetok, where the test had originally been scheduled, but did not know that the Castle series had been shifted to Bikini.[29] I noted that the Japanese fishermen might be considered the observers that the Atomic Energy Commission refused to have–irony or providence? I think that this event initiated the debate leading to the decision ten years later to agree with the Soviets to stop testing in the atmosphere.

Murray concluded that any wartime employment of large-yield hydrogen bombs would clearly be immoral and should be banned by international agreement. As a first step he proposed a moratorium on testing explosions with a yield of over one megaton. In a letter on March 14, 1954, he urged President Eisenhower to cancel or delay an upcoming test in order to permit an "atomic summit" of Soviet and American leaders. He argued that the American program was so far ahead that the United States could accept a moratorium of one year without jeopardizing our superior position. Murray believed that our weapons arsenal should consist of "thousands and thousands" of kiloton-yield weapons.[30]

Eisenhower consulted about Murray's letter with Dulles and Strauss. Dulles went along with Strauss's flat rejection of the proposal. The President told Murray that his proposal was not acceptable because it relied on cooperation from the Soviets, who thus far had not proved to be dependable.[31] Murray continued to raise the concept of a moratorium, and Dulles and the President began to explore its merits. Eisenhower eventually became an advocate of a test ban if it were adequately verified. The Soviets later agreed to allow some on-site inspections to verify a complete cessation of testing, but both sides could not reach agreement on the number of inspections. After leaving government, Eisenhower was reported as saying that the greatest regret of his presidency was the failure to get a test ban. Now, nearly forty years later, it looks as if nuclear testing may be ended altogether.

I did not share Murray's full enthusiasm for an uninspected moratorium in 1954. I believed that since thermonuclear weapons had already been developed and were available, we should continue to test to improve them. I supported Murray's proposal only if it could be adequately verified, not a likely proposition given Soviet attitudes at this time. I supported the measure, if technical verification were possible, only as a psychological move. A diary entry from 1953 indicates that as early as this date, Murray had agreed to the points I made in a paper on verification and inspection as key elements of any arms control regime. My views were summed up in a diary entry I made on February 2, 1954: "Murray's idea about international control and testing has sharp thorns and promising roses all mixed up." Others, such as State Department Policy Planning Director Robert Bowie, were more positive, hoping that a test ban could be a first step to slow down the arms race and provide Eisenhower with a breakthrough agreement that might overcome the internal bureaucratic logjam within the U.S. government and get the Soviets seriously to nibble at the subject of arms control. I only later came to embrace such larger views, after I moved to the State Department.

Rickover

Alongside of his growing concerns about the development of weapons of unlimited yield, Murray, with my support, continued to be an enthusiast for nuclear electric power. Our efforts in this area brought us into close contact with Admiral Hyman Rickover, one of the most unusual military officers I ever met. He was the driving force in the creation of the American nuclear navy, both submarines and surface vessels. He not only handled all technical propulsion reactor issues, but just as importantly he was responsible for recruiting, training, and inspiring all of the officers of the nuclear navy. For many years, submariners brought up by Rickover contributed a larger quota to the top ranks of the Navy than any other branch of the service.

Rickover was a frequent visitor in Murray's office, and he persuaded Murray to become the chief advocate for nuclear propulsion in the commission. Although Rickover first visited with Murray in order to lobby for this cause, I believe that he came to have a genuine admiration for Murray's foresight and courage. Through this connection, I was able to make some personal contribution to advancing Rickover's career and his goals. I had a small hand in getting Rickover promoted to rear admiral. In July of 1952, then-Captain Rickover was passed over for promotion to rear admiral for the second time in a year, a virtual guarantee that he would have to retire from the Navy. Murray contacted President Truman and told him that this would be a great setback for the U.S.

nuclear reactor program. The promotion file was sent over to our office, and I was instructed to write the precept which directed the Navy selection board to pick one officer with the most experience in nuclear propulsion to be promoted to rear admiral. Some congressmen let it be known that no further promotion of Naval officers would be approved until Rickover was promoted. The Navy soon complied. Rickover ended his career as a four-star admiral with the longest service as an officer in the history of the Navy. A large building at the Naval Academy memorializes his great accomplishments.

I feel one of the most significant, albeit random, events in my career was introducing Rickover to Lord "Solly" Zuckerman, Britain's Chief Defense Scientist. After this, I was told that Solly's first stop on every trip to Washington was for a talk with Rickover. In subsequent years, they were close friends, and Rickover's support for Anglo-American cooperation in nuclear submarine propulsion was a tremendous factor in the success of this joint endeavor.

On November 16, 1953, I visited Arco, Idaho, to observe the Submarine Thermal Reactor (STR), which had been under development since 1950. The STR was the land-based prototype of a reactor to propel the first nuclear-powered submarine, the *Nautilus*, which was being built at Groton, Connecticut, by General Dynamics' Electric Boat division. I went out with Don Quarles, Assistant Secretary of Defense for research and development; Vice Admiral R.F. Good; Rear Admiral Wilson Leggett, Jr., chief of the Bureau of Ships; and Admiral Rickover, who was in charge of the program. According to the official AEC historians, Rickover at this time "carried as much weight [within the AEC] as some division directors and certainly more than any branch chief."[32] In no small measure, this was because of the support and encouragement of Commissioner Murray.

It was an astonishing sight to see a large shaft, which was tended by several enlisted men, turned by no apparent source of energy. After the demonstration, Rickover questioned the enlisted men, who sat across the table from the admirals looking calm and confident. They answered all of Rickover's questions briskly and effectively. It was clear that the other admirals had little knowledge about atomic power. Rickover then turned to them and said,

"Gentlemen, I think this will confirm what I have long thought: that the only difference in the United States Navy between an enlisted man and a commissioned officer is a matter of education." You could have heard a pin drop.

I should add that Rickover was, without doubt, the greatest egotist I ever knew—as well as the hardest worker. He lived in an apartment in Washington which actually included two flats—one for living and one filled with his files and working papers. It was not unusual for him to fly to the Westinghouse Company (the contractor for the first propulsion reactors) at Pittsburgh after his workday in Washington, work several hours there, take the overnight train back to Washington and be the first person in his Navy office the next morning. His egotism can be seen in a chance encounter I witnessed between Rickover and Cardinal Baum, the papal nuncio. Rickover and I were in the garden of the British embassy, waiting to attend a reception following an official dinner for the Queen (neither of us being deemed sufficiently senior to attend the dinner). While waiting, I had occasion to introduce Rickover to Cardinal Baum. Rickover proceeded to tease Baum about some decoration the nuncio had on his chest, and then gave Baum a long lecture on the history of the popes in the fourteenth century, which was not very complimentary. Baum listened patiently, but when he thanked Rickover he added pointedly, "You know my field in the seminary was history."

Rickover's egotism could be leavened with humility. I remember that he once said to me, in regard to developing more and more nuclear weapons, that we were, "Playing God." Though I was sorry to hear that the end of his career was marred by charges of poor judgment in accepting some token gifts from shipyards building submarines, I feel this did not overshadow his long service to his country. I was shocked and ashamed to read his son's public comment that the Admiral then was senile!

The New Administration and Nuclear Electric Power

My first contact with the future Eisenhower administration was on May 16, 1952, when I lunched with Herbert Brownell, who was active in the campaign and became Attorney General. I urged him to push the atomic energy program if Eisenhower was elected, and also offered him some financial aid for the campaign. I noted that Brownell seemed "quiet, tired, shrewd–a good listener." Privately, I was skeptical about Eisenhower but had even less enthusiasm for his Democratic challenger, Adlai Stevenson. In September 1952, I noted, "Ike has gone way down in my estimation; he's old and inflexible but still a symbol of leadership better than Stevenson, who is a 'stand-in' for Truman but talks so independently that the independents will flock to his standard."[33] After the election, I still had my doubts about the new President. Later, while working within his administration for seven years, my respect and admiration for Eisenhower would rise substantially.

Before Eisenhower's inaugural, I undertook without success to get some tickets for the Atomic Energy commissioners to attend the inaugural parade. They were all Truman appointees and had not been invited. I pointed out to Tom Stephens, Eisenhower's appointments secretary, that this was a curious way to win the support of the AEC. I had no luck with officials joining the new administration, but a Democratic senator was able to get the tickets.

When Eisenhower took over in 1953 and later when Lewis Strauss became AEC chairman, the White House looked to Strauss as the primary source of atomic energy information and advice. Murray was rebuffed when he tried to give advice that contradicted Strauss's position. Friction between Strauss and Murray developed almost immediately. At one point in October 1953, Strauss was irritated by Murray's requests to see NSC documents on atomic energy and called an emergency meeting of the Commission to ask whether he (Strauss) was to be Murray's office boy.[34] Bernard Shanley, my brother-in-law and President Eisenhower's legal counsel, expressed concern that I was in the middle of this feud, which had elements of politics as well as personalities. It did not bother me.

As Eisenhower took over, Murray was very concerned about the new administration's expressed interest in cutting back the atomic energy program. He was particularly concerned about the position that Strauss would take. Murray wanted to pin responsibility on Strauss for any cuts. One of the main projects targeted for cancellation was the CVR, a shore-based prototype of a nuclear reactor for propulsion of an aircraft carrier. For several years, Murray, with Admiral Rickover and Senator McMahon, had strongly supported this program. Strauss recommended its cancellation at a March 31, 1953, meeting of the National Security Council.[35] Several weeks later, I wrote, "These are hatchet days for the National Security Council ignoramuses, goaded perhaps by [MLC Chairman] Bob LeBaron to cut out programs they know nothing about, and which they will start up again a year from now."[36] The CVR, however, was canceled and not revived, at least not by that designation.

I worked with James Dunford, assistant to Murray, on an effort to reconstitute the CVR program. Dunford, a graduate of the Naval Academy and MIT, had been among the small group of naval officers assigned to Oak Ridge with Rickover after the war to study nuclear engineering and technology. On April 27, 1953, I prepared a petition for an NSC re-hearing on the CVR cancellation, noting that the "AEC was fixing to pick up the ripe fruit dropped by the Navy."[37] The AEC, finally alert to the fact that it would have no electric power prototype reactor if the CVR was canceled, proposed that the Eisenhower administration convert it into a prototype civilian power reactor. On May 4, Murray promised the President that a civilian CVR would be $50 to $60 million less costly than the military version. On May 5, he persuasively argued his case before the NSC, convincing all except Secretary of Defense Charles Wilson, who commented that the project would "throw good money after bad."

Although the administration approved this AEC plan, it was not clear who would run the project. The administration favored leaving the development of electric power to private corporations. The AEC's idea was to bring in private corporations only as necessary to help the government effort. Murray went further, insisting that Rickover be put in charge of the project. Murray, as I noted at the time, "laid down the law" that the job must go to Rickover, which caused a great deal of heartburn within the AEC.[38] At one point, AEC General Manager Marion Boyer became so exasperated with Murray that he walked out of an executive session. Ultimately, the project was assigned to Rickover, whose experience with reactors outweighed the administration's uneasiness about government involvement in civilian power production.[39] Westinghouse became the primary construction contractor, and Rickover seemed to have no trouble managing both the naval nuclear program and the civilian electric power project.

In October 1953, Murray highlighted the inauguration of the civilian reactor project in a much publicized speech to an electric utility convention in Chicago. The speech made headlines in the *Washington Post.* In it, he stressed that it was just as important in a security sense for the United States to be first in Atoms for Peace as it was to be the first in Atoms for War. As he concluded, "For years the splitting atom, packaged in weapons, had been our main shield against the Barbarians–now . . . it is to become a God-given instrument to do the constructive work of mankind."[40] The reactor was built at Shippingport, Pennsylvania, and started operating in December 1957 under the management of the Duquesne Power and Light Company of Pittsburgh.

In 1954, the administration's policy of favoring private enterprise to develop electric power led it into the so-called Dixon-Yates affair, when the AEC negotiated a contract to have a private syndicate provide nuclear electric power (then being furnished by the Tennessee Valley Authority), to the Memphis area. The plan was basically intended to prevent the TVA from building a large new hydroelectric plant.[41] I wrote a memorandum to Commissioner Eugene Zuckert, who had recently been appointed and who took a particularly keen interest in AEC management questions, urging him not to approve the contract because it called for the AEC to reimburse the private supplier for its federal taxes. That struck me as an indirect and inappropriate government subsidy.

Murray opposed the contract as extraneous to the AEC's responsibilities. He brought it to the attention of the JCAE and ultimately it was canceled.[42] This position earned him Eisenhower's dislike. According to Strauss's biographer, the President told his press secretary, "You tell Lewis [Strauss] to remind me never–and I mean never–to renominate that guy Murray to the Commission when his term expires." In 1957, when Murray's term was coming to an end, a majority of the Congressional JCAE argued for his reappointment. They pointed out Murray's contributions to U.S. security, in particular his promotion of industrial atomic power and his efforts to open up uranium resources. Eisenhower was not impressed. He asked Strauss when Murray's term was over. Strauss answered, "On June 30, and I mark off the days on my calendar."[43] Needless to say, the President did not reappoint Murray.

A Visit to SAC

As part of my continuing effort to learn more about the weapons program, in May 1953 I visited SAC Headquarters at Offutt Air Force Base in Nebraska, with Major General James Walsh, who was head of intelligence for SAC commander General Curtis LeMay. This visit to SAC, the first of three I would make, was at the direct encouragement of General Walsh. A personal friend, Walsh wanted to impress on me the unique capabilities and readiness of our main deterrent force. I kidded him about Offutt's having once been Fort Crook, a remount station for the cavalry during the Indian wars! I had a thorough briefing and was especially impressed by the communications capabilities. At that time SAC bombers were flying all over the world. I was asked to name a place to which I would like to talk. I chose Africa; a button was pushed, and the next minute I was talking to a pilot over North Africa. I was also impressed by the high alert maintained by SAC. There was always a car, with engine running, in front of General LeMay's headquarters. It was quite a sight observing a meeting of all the SAC commanders, who rendezvoused from around the world in their Stratofortress command planes. The high morale of these SAC leaders was obvious. They were a proud lot who obviously felt that the peace of the world was in their hands.

During this visit, I had a rather hasty talk with General LeMay about the question of custody of nuclear weapons and whether he thought the present control arrangements were adequate. I could see that he was not comfortable talking to a junior official about that delicate subject. This was less than a year after the military had been given some custodial responsibility for stocks of nuclear weapons abroad and such numbers in the continental United States as it deemed necessary to assure "operational flexibility and military readiness."[44] I got no indication, however, that SAC could in any way act on its own. Even LeMay did not believe that he had this authority. While my visit was not in any sense a technical voyage of discovery, it was a special event that had the full backing of Murray, who wanted his assistant to learn as much as possible about nuclear weapons and their place in U.S. defense planning.

Incidental to this SAC visit, General Walsh asked me if my wife, a convert to Catholicism, had been confirmed. I said no, and he said that Bishops often visited SAC. My wife and my daughter were soon confirmed and General LeMay gave a reception to honor the event. In later years when some thought I was too much of an arms controller, I was tempted to ask, "How many of your family have been confirmed at SAC headquarters?"

The Oppenheimer Case

In July 1953 Robert Oppenheimer published an article in *Foreign Affairs* in which he compared the United States and the Soviet Union to "Two scorpions in a bottle, each capable of killing the other, but only at the risk of his own life." Like Murray, Oppenheimer urged greater candor about the number, characteristics, and probable effects of U.S. nuclear weapons. He urged that the American public and our close allies be better informed:

> We do not operate well when the important facts, the essential conditions, which limit and determine our choices are unknown. We do not operate well when they are known, in secrecy and fear, only to a few men.[45]

This recommendation for candor and wider dissemination of nuclear knowledge grew out of a report done for the Truman administration by a special panel of consultants on disarmament. Chaired by Oppenheimer, the panel presented its classified report in January 1953. It emphasized the importance of promoting stability through unilateral action; reducing the risks of surprise attack through direct official U.S.-Soviet Union exchanges; and integrating official, public, and alliance views on nuclear weapons. As Oppenheimer noted, the only way to achieve this goal was to have greater openness about nuclear facts. Although I did not have access to the panel report, this specific idea had a profound influence on me. It was at first sympathetically received by the Eisenhower administration. It provided a major inspiration for the President's Atoms for Peace speech in December 1953. Unfortunately, however, Eisenhower ultimately did not fully adopt Oppenheimer's specific recommendations on openness.[46]

To complicate matters, Oppenheimer's patriotic credentials were coming under suspicion at just this time. In May 1953, Senator McCarthy called on FBI Director J. Edgar Hoover to discuss a possible investigation of Oppenheimer. Hoover discouraged such a probe,[47] although at a June 22 hearing of the Senate Appropriations Committee, McCarthy questioned then-AEC Chairman Gordon Dean about Oppenheimer. Strauss also discouraged McCarthy from investigating Oppenheimer. According to Hoover, Strauss felt that such a probe should not be done "prematurely or by a group that did not thoroughly prepare itself for the investigation."[48]

On December 2, 1953, I learned that William Borden, the staff director of the JCAE (with whom I had closely worked for several years), had written a letter to FBI Director Hoover concluding that Oppenheimer was more likely than not an agent of the Soviet Union. Oppenheimer had been the civilian leader of the Manhattan District, which had developed the first atomic bombs, and the nation owed him a great debt. Nevertheless, after a review in the AEC in the spring of 1954, the Commission concluded that it would be prudent to withdraw Oppenheimer's clearance for access to "restricted data"—a craven act by officials fearful of McCarthy.

Murray filed a dissent from the AEC's conclusion. He took an even more severe position than the majority by calling Oppenheimer's allegiance to the United States into question, using the word "disloyal." I felt that it was a theological notion that some friend of Murray's had put to him. Although I had left the AEC by this time, I pleaded with him to omit the disloyal conclusion, for which there was no evidence in the record. He declined, having already made up his mind, and said that his opinion had gone to the printer. At that time Murray apparently was pro-McCarthy, and he might have been looking for some way to advance the anti-communist cause as seen through the McCarthy optic. I felt that the whole Oppenheimer episode was shameful considering that there was no serious evidence. It is puzzling that a man as prescient and humane as Tom Murray could have been so wrong about McCarthy. My relations with Murray were never the same again. I was glad when Oppenheimer later was awarded the Presidential Medal of Freedom, regrettably posthumously.

Oppenheimer's sole defender on the Commission was Henry Smyth, who argued that Oppenheimer's clearance should not be withdrawn. My colleague for years at the State Department, Phil Farley, was a major contributor to Smyth's dissenting opinion. Smyth later recalled that it had not been particularly admirable for him to support Oppenheimer. After all, he could always go back to the secure job of teaching physics at Princeton. What Farley did, however, was in Smyth's opinion courageous. The AEC General Manager pointed out to Farley that his help for Smyth might prejudice his career at the AEC. There was no reason to think that his career in the government would not soon come to an end.[49] Fortunately for the United States, this did not happen, and Farley went on to have a distinguished career in the State Department.

One important consequence of this affair was that after Oppenheimer's clearance was withdrawn in December 1953, Strauss became the government's preeminent voice on nuclear policy. Despite the fact that he had a business background and little scientific training, his counsels, according to a recent history of presidential science advisors, "went essentially unchallenged in the Eisenhower administration when it came to atomic energy."[50] I believe that this development was damaging. The official AEC history states that Strauss had an "almost naive faith in science" and "seemed to believe that with sufficient money and effort almost any technical goal . . . could be attained."[51] This attitude led Strauss to support programs such as the quest for a "clean" bomb, which was said to spare buildings and only kill humans. He viewed radioactive fallout from nuclear tests as merely a public relations problem. He argued for years against a halt or moratorium on nuclear testing. Fortunately, during President Eisenhower's second term, his first science advisor, James Killian, and the President's Science Advisory Committee provided more sensible counsel.

Atoms for Peace

President Eisenhower made his Atoms for Peace address on December 8, 1953. As Oppenheimer had recommended in his *Foreign Affairs* article, the President included some facts about the nuclear arsenal: that the United States had conducted 43 tests since the first Trinity experiment in 1945; that the power of nuclear weapons had increased by more than a factor of twenty-five with hydrogen bombs yielding in the megaton range; that all U.S. armed services had the capacity to employ nuclear weapons; and that the Soviets had developed atomic and thermonuclear weapons. Eisenhower also endorsed international scientific cooperation and commerce in atomic energy for peaceful purposes, and proposed the establishment of what he conceived to be a bank for fissile material from the weapons arsenals of the superpowers. The President called for an International Atomic Energy Agency to receive the fissionable material and coordinate efforts to spread the peaceful uses of atomic energy. Although the fissile material bank was never created, the IAEA has proved a useful agency in safeguarding the use of atomic energy for peaceful purposes and now seems destined to play an important role in the post-Cold War monitoring of declining arsenals of nuclear weapons.

The President's motive was in good part to make people around the world realize that there was more to atomic energy than weaponry. He was hoping not only to give a push to the peaceful uses of atomic energy, but to make a start toward international control of atomic weapons. What President Eisenhower did not realize in making this proposal was that the same facilities needed to generate electricity from nuclear fission could also be the basis for nuclear weapons programs. I think Strauss was in good part responsible for this presidential ignorance.

At the AEC, I was asked to read the President's speech to the commissioners who, except for Strauss, had known nothing about the proposal. Smyth, a leading participant in the Manhattan District and the author of the well-known Smyth Report on the development of the first atomic bomb, described the Atoms for Peace plan as "a thoroughly dishonest proposal." Apparently, he had a clearer idea of the dangers of the plan and its implications for weapons proliferation than the rest of us. Strauss had advised the President on the speech, but had not told the other commissioners about it. Murray actually learned from a newspaper that it was to be delivered. He was outraged.[52] Both Zuckert and Smyth considered resigning from the Commission after being excluded in this way. This was just another example of the negative results of Strauss's having the position of chief nuclear advisor to Eisenhower. By not consulting the other commissioners about Atoms for Peace, Eisenhower did not have the benefit of their input into the plan. When Murray complained to Strauss, he was told, "the speech was none of his business–and anyway you don't show me your speeches" (which was not entirely true).

In later years, Strauss liked to think he was the author of the Atoms for Peace program, but when he first heard Eisenhower's ideas on the subject he said that, while the proposal was novel and "might have value for propaganda purposes," it was not a practical option. Strauss changed his mind and later wrote a paper in favor of Atoms for Peace. He came to agree with his assistant, William Golden, that a small joint effort might be like "getting the first olive out of the bottle." (Incidentally, I used this analogy during the SALT negotiations to limit strategic arms, but it escaped the understanding of the Soviet officials. Apparently, they had no problem getting olives out of their bottles which did not have narrow tops.) It has been reported that a short time before the President's speech Congressman Cole had proposed to Strauss a similar scheme but Strauss had not approved–knowing that the President was about to propose his Atoms for Peace concept.

Leaving the AEC

In 1953, Murray and Strauss had separately sounded me out about becoming an AEC commissioner, to fill a vacancy created by Keith Glennan's retirement. I later wrote of this idea, "Hogwash! With five AEC commissioners from the general New York area and three from New York State, they would not want another New Yorker." I had also declined Congressman Sterling Cole's offer that I replace Borden as the JCAE chief of staff. In early 1954, Bernard Shanley, my brother-in-law, urged me to consider becoming special assistant to Undersecretary of the Navy Thomas Gates, or fiscal Assistant Secretary of the Navy. Shanley was anxious that I "get on the administration team." I also was offered the position of General Counsel of the Maritime Administration as well as a spot in private law practice. I declined them all.

On February 9, 1954, Strauss asked if I would be interested in becoming Special Assistant for Atomic Energy to Secretary of State John Foster Dulles. I think that Strauss felt I was part of the Murray problem, since I had done a good deal of the writing of Murray's speeches, which apparently had not been welcomed by Strauss. After nearly four years, the AEC job was losing some of its luster. The State Department position offered increased opportunity to pursue my strong interest and concern about nuclear weapons and proliferation. I had a high regard for Secretary Dulles, and I had worked on international problems at the AEC.

On March 16, I was interviewed by Under Secretary of State General Bedell Smith. My diary records that "I had to slow him up when he said, 'I guess you had a pretty hard time working for Tom Murray.'"[53] Later he said that the State Department had nothing against Murray. He strongly urged me to take the job, saying that I was a "natural" for it, and spoke of a possible long-term career in the State Department. On March 19, General Smith called. I said if Secretary Dulles wanted my services, I was ready to accept.

Chapter Two

Special Assistant for Atomic Energy Affairs, 1954–57

Introduction to the State Department

From April 1954 until the fall of 1957, when I became Assistant Secretary of State for Policy Planning, I served as John Foster Dulles's Special Assistant for Atomic Energy Affairs (S/AE). In this position, I was involved as a relatively junior official in early policy debates regarding what would be the abiding issues of the nuclear era. My role in these policy debates continued my education in nuclear matters, as I came to appreciate the problems surrounding our efforts to pursue atoms for peace and for war.[1] These included the issues of possible international limitation of nuclear and conventional weapons and forces, the potential impact on weapons proliferation from increasing the peaceful uses of nuclear energy, international safeguards for nuclear materials and technology, the possibility of a moratorium on nuclear testing, the possible legitimization of reconnaissance photography of American and Soviet territory, and the dilemmas created by the integration of nuclear weapons into U.S. and allied defense strategies.

I would also have the opportunity to work with individuals of historical note, including President Dwight D. Eisenhower, Vice President Richard Nixon, John Foster Dulles, Henry Cabot Lodge, Nelson Rockefeller, Curtis LeMay, and the White House Chief of Staff, Sherman Adams. In addition to these well-known persons, I also had the privilege of getting to know the State Department and working with some of its most talented officers: Robert Bowie, Henry Owen, Fred Reinhardt, Chip Bohlen, Tommy Thompson,

Bob Murphy, Ronald Spiers, James Goodby and J. Robert Schaetzel, beginning friendships which would last into subsequent administrations and beyond. State would become my professional home for more than fifteen years, as I found my life increasingly revolving around the central problem of our era–the control of nuclear weapons. One of my first actions was to ask Phil Farley of the AEC to become my deputy. We continued to collaborate for many years. He was and remained one of the wisest officers working on nuclear matters in the government.

Secretary of State John Foster Dulles

When I first joined the Department, I began taking lunch in the Executive Dining Room where I would sit at a table alone, as I did not know any of the others. After two or three days, it was pointed out that I was sitting at the table reserved for the Secretary, where he customarily lunched on cottage cheese and an apple. That was hardly a good way to start things off with my new boss. To bring the story full-circle, I found my inadvertent occupation of Dulles's table something of an omen, for fifteen years later, when I became director of the Arms Control and Disarmament Agency, my office was none other than Dulles's (and Dean Acheson's) former office. It was an immense room with very high ceilings, prompting Acheson to describe it as looking "like the second-class dining saloon on a North German Lloyd liner." I still think that it was the "grandest" office in Washington, and am sure that it made my foreign visitors think that ACDA had much more influence in the U.S. government than was the case.

In my first few months, I was not sure that Dulles even knew my name. But, I had reason to change my impression of the Secretary, and received some reassurance about his impression of me, when, a short time later, I found myself the target of Henry Cabot Lodge's ire. Under Secretary Robert Murphy had directed me to give the British Ambassador a copy of a speech that Lodge, the U.S. representative to the United Nations, was scheduled to deliver before the U.N. General Assembly. I promptly did so. The next day, I was shown a letter from Lodge to Dulles urging that I be fired since it was clear that I had no idea of how to handle diplomatic material, as evidenced by my giving his speech to a foreign government before he had even seen it. A few days later, I was summoned to Dulles's office. Expecting the worst, I somewhat downheartedly went to the fifth floor where my fears were borne out as I saw Lodge there, along with Harold Stassen. To my surprise, Dulles invited me to join them for lunch, saying to Lodge, "You, of course, know Gerry." Lodge graciously said yes, and several days later, I lunched again with Dulles, Lodge, and Strauss, at which time Lodge showed no sign of having wanted me fired some days earlier. That was the end of the matter. On the basis of this firsthand experience of Dulles's diplomatic skills at defusing a touchy situation, my opinion of him soared.

At the start of the Eisenhower administration, Dulles had incurred the dislike of a number of Foreign Service officers by his apparent efforts to ease tensions with Senator Joseph McCarthy, by stating on entering office that he would require "positive loyalty" of all officials, and naming Scott McLeod, a close friend of McCarthy, as the chief security official at State. But gradually Dulles gained the admiration of many officials at Foggy Bottom.

The grim atmosphere created by McCarthy could have a comic element. Shortly after I joined the Department, I was called on by a security officer inquiring about a very high-level State Department official. He claimed that this officer had taken part in a riot at Yale University some years before. I pointed out that in the springtime, many Yale students were inclined to riot, and that it did not seem a serious matter. I was surprised that he would enquire of a relatively junior officer on this subject, but such were the follies of security officers under pressure of McCarthyism in Washington in the early 1950s.

Dulles was careful not to get involved in other agencies' affairs, such as the AEC's authority over nuclear weapons production or the Pentagon's responsibility for military matters. I felt that he was concerned that such trespass would lead others to get involved in State Department business, which he wanted to keep firmly in his hands. However, he held his ground when it came to arguments in the National Security Council. This was even the case when he disagreed with his brother, Allen, who was director of Central

Intelligence. I used to enjoy watching them at NSC meetings when they saw issues in somewhat different lights. Allen would present a case quietly yet forcefully, but in the end would readily accept the political judgment of his brother, who clearly had the responsibility for it. It was a privilege to see these two who knew each other's minds so well working over a subject from different angles. For the most part, though, Allen Dulles kept within the accepted limits of an intelligence officer stating facts while not proposing policy. This, however, did not keep the Secretary of State from referring to Allen and the people at the CIA as "Ivy Leaguers" when he was particularly irate with them.

I used to prepare testimony for Dulles, as when he would appear before the Joint Committee on Atomic Energy. But in other cases, Dulles took great interest in drafting his own statements. He always used a yellow legal pad, which, rumor had it, came from his firm, Sullivan and Cromwell in New York–as had his executive secretary, Phyllis Bernau. He had great confidence in her, as I learned when I took issue with something Dulles quoted Phyllis as saying. To my challenge, Dulles simply replied, "You will soon learn that Phyllis is seldom wrong."

Phyllis later married Dulles's special assistant, Bill Macomber, who went on to a distinguished career as ambassador in several important posts and Assistant Secretary of State for congressional relations. Once when swearing him in to a new position, Dulles said, "He is the finest man who ever worked for me!" After the Democrats took over in 1961, Senator Fulbright told him that his committee would support Macomber for any U.S. Embassy in the world.

Foster Dulles had a strong interest in the integration of Europe–probably in good part owing to his friendship with Jean Monnet, who is generally considered to be the father of the European Community. In the 1950s Clarence Streit published a book, *Union Now*, and tirelessly agitated for a United States of Europe. Dulles told me, "Clarence is right. He is just ahead of his time." Dulles never lost sight of the need for the reunification of Germany if Europe was ever to be united. He would have approved the U.S. role in 1989-90 in godfathering unexpected and rapid German reunification measures.

Dulles's confidence did not indicate a closed mind. I learned that he was anything but the rigid anti-communist ideologue or simpleminded proponent of "massive retaliation" and "brinkmanship," as portrayed in the press and by some scholars. For instance, people who think of Dulles solely as a Cold Warrior because of his "massive retaliation" statements may be surprised to learn that in May 1954, after the *Lucky Dragon* incident, in which Japanese fishermen fell ill from fallout from a U.S. thermonuclear test, Dulles proposed to the President a moratorium on nuclear testing.[2]

In addition, Dulles recommended to the President limiting or ending the production of fissile materials for weapons; withdrawing troops from Europe; and transferring sufficient nuclear weapons to the U.N. Security Council to form an international deterrent force to counter threatening actions by other nations.[3] In 1954 he wrote:

> The increased destructiveness of nuclear weapons and the approach of effective atomic parity are creating a situation in which general war would threaten the destruction of Western civilization and of the Soviet regime and in which national objectives could not be obtained through a general war even if a military victory were won.

He proposed vesting a vetoless United Nations Security Council with control of sufficient atomic weapons and means of delivery to overbalance any atomic or other weapons that might be retained surreptitiously by any other nation. As a step toward this end, he suggested that the United States could seek commitments from nations possessing nuclear capabilities to use their weapons only in accordance with recommendations of the U.N. General Assembly.[4]

Nothing came of these sweeping proposals. Dulles put the idea of a testing moratorium aside, fearing it would be hard to verify that the Soviet Union was honoring it and also that it would slow the U.S. weapons program if Washington should later decide to resume testing. Part of the problem was also rooted in the fact the United States did not have a coherent "disarmament policy" at this time. This hampered our participation in the U.N. London subcommittee negotiations on disarmament. Dulles would return to his idea, though, driven by his own experience, the concerns of allies, and the advice of scientists brought in to advise the

Eisenhower administration. Dulles continued throughout his term to reiterate his nuclear concerns to President Eisenhower, at one point concluding that the only real solution might be abolition of nuclear weapons! Early in June 1954, I noted, "Dulles muses about military defense against communism. Are we right? Is the atom bomb really the deterrent? Is the United States leadership the thing or should we look for other countries to do some leading once in a while?" Those speculations stayed with me as long as the Cold War lasted, and it is interesting to note Dulles's queries about leadership are once again in fashion. Dulles also wondered if smaller-yield tactical nuclear weapons might not be effective in deterring a less than all-out nuclear war. These views anticipated concepts that were considered later, including NATO's "flexible response" doctrine, adopted in 1967.[5]

I recall trying to help Robert Bowie, then director of the Policy Planning staff, to educate Dulles about the defects of the nuclear strategy of "massive retaliation." Bowie (who had been a professor at Harvard and would return there in 1957, and then come back as deputy director of the CIA under Carter) recalls that he drafted a Dulles's 1954 *Foreign Affairs* article with the explicit goal of explaining that the Eisenhower "New Look" was a strategy to bring greater flexibility, giving the United States a capacity to respond to communist threats and aggression at a place, time, and manner of our choice. Bowie recalls that Dulles did not at that time have in mind abandoning massive retaliation in extreme crises. Bowie also used the crisis with Communist China over the shelling of the offshore islands, Quemoy and Matsu, in 1955 to brief Dulles on the horrible casualties which would result from using tactical nuclear weapons on Chinese military targets. As I will describe in the next chapter, after replacing Bowie as head of the Policy Planning staff, I reminded Dulles of these facts. Though Dulles was impressed by demonstrations of SAC's capabilities which he received on visits to Offutt Air Base near Omaha (as was I), apparently Bob's and my efforts would bear some fruit, for during Eisenhower's second term, Dulles would tell the Pentagon that "massive retaliation was a wasting military asset" and that the Pentagon should start developing other plans.

My advice to Dulles about the harsh realities of nuclear warfare continued throughout his time as Secretary of State. I can recall telling Dulles in 1955 that his information on these questions was incorrect. When he retorted, "I don't know where you get your information but it is different from mine," I urged him to get briefed directly by the military.

Both of us would undergo a learning experience in the 1950s as we came to grips with the linked problems of how to promote safely the peaceful uses of atomic energy and how to curb the spread of nuclear weapons. Indeed, it was only when I moved to the State Department and encountered the thinking of people like Bowie, Henry Owen, and Phil Farley that my visceral response to nuclear tests that I had witnessed found political expression in a growing interest in arms control. My education in the political and technical obstacles to this essential goal would begin in these years, as I took an active part in the debates over implementing Eisenhower's Atoms for Peace proposal, the first talks with the Soviets and other nations on safeguarding nuclear materials, the creation of the International Atomic Energy Agency (IAEA), and discussions within the administration on the merits of a nuclear test ban and arms control.

Introduction to Diplomacy: Atoms for Peace and the IAEA

Eisenhower's proposal to harness the power of the atom for peaceful purposes, made to the United Nations in December 1953, was discussed in the previous chapter. As I would soon learn after taking over the S/AE position, the administration was ill-prepared to deal with the political and technical details of framing programs and negotiating an international convention to implement the Atoms for Peace proposals. Like the AEC commissioners, I had not been aware of the proposal before the President's address to the United Nations.

Shortly after I joined the State Department, Dulles told me that he had received a message from Soviet foreign minister V.M. Molotov, reacting to Eisenhower's speech, asking what in the world Americans thought they were doing proposing to spread weapon-grade nuclear materials around the world–the point referred to by AEC Commissioner Henry Smyth. Dulles seemed incredulous and asked, "That's not true, is it?" I had to tell him that Molotov had been better briefed on the technology than American leaders. Dulles asked me to prepare a response to Molotov, which my colleague, Phil Farley, and I drafted. This telegram asserted that "ways can be devised to safeguard against diversion of materials from electric power producing reactors."[6] This prediction would prove to be optimistic, as we are still trying to perfect such safeguards 40 years later, though so far no nation has tried to mount a weapons program solely on a nuclear electric power base.

A number of enthusiasts in the administration saw that the Atoms for Peace program had a major public relations potential. This group was led by Nelson Rockefeller, who was a Special Assistant to the President, and a zealous enthusiast who seemed less than fully concerned with the substance of issues. They proposed that the United States make gifts of research reactors for various unlikely places (including West Berlin), and give assurances to provide enriched uranium for fuel, all with a price tag approaching $15 billion. These proposals quickly met opposition from State and AEC, as we tried to cool off these publicity seekers. Generally, we argued that no one knew enough about the technology to implement this scheme. Trying to conduct policy in such a difficult area could be frustrating because of the interventions and conflicts between strong-minded officials. As I noted later in 1955, "Geneva–where Nelson Rockefeller becomes Assistant President for exchanges of atomic data and Stassen pushes for dramatic small steps and the professionals at home sit on their hands and wring them at the same time." I believed (and Lewis Strauss agreed) that it was unwise to get so far ahead of the technical possibilities of atomic energy just to secure some short-term public relations advantages. Specifically, we pointed out that giving away research reactors could in the long run prejudice sales of such reactors, and that it would be necessary to train foreign scientists and technicians before most recipient countries could make good use of these complex machines.[7]

Such comments, which Dulles sent on at our suggestion, did not improve S/AE's standing at the White House, where some of Rockefeller's enthusiasm was obviously shared. I recall a discussion in November 1954 with President Eisenhower and his assistant, Sherman Adams. They were enthusiastic about nuclear power but had little knowledge of the problems involved. Eisenhower talked about the grain combines that were used in Kansas when he was a boy, and compared them to modern equipment, to make the point that we should use nuclear power right away and not wait for "the last word." But he did sound a note of caution against being optimistic about nuclear power reactors for some years, and then Eisenhower proceeded to digress on the need to do something for Mexico, speaking in almost nineteenth-century terms about America's responsibility to its southern neighbor. I am sure that this President would have been a strong advocate of NAFTA.

Throughout 1954, I worked on planning for the proposed International Atomic Energy Agency (IAEA) to supervise the "Atoms for Peace" enterprise (having no inkling that some twenty-five years later, I would be the U.S. representative on the IAEA's Board of Governors under President Carter). Much of this planning would be upset when the Soviets made an abrupt about-face from their originally negative attitude. At first they were critical of the idea and would not agree to take any part in the agency. Then, after the United States had begun discussions with many other countries and Dulles was preparing to address the United Nations on the moves the United States was planning to make to carry out the Atoms for Peace proposal, the Soviets ended a long silence on the proposals and indicated they were ready to join in the talks. This forced us to rethink our plans and assess the Kremlin's motives. As I summed up the basic questions at the time, "Do we want the Russians in the Agency? and if so, do we want them in the Agency planning now?" I realized it was impossible to establish the agency on American terms first and then accept Soviet membership at a later date, yet there was the clear risk that bringing them into the talks could destroy the progress made so far.[8]

As we grappled with these issues, I took part in interagency meetings with officials from the Pentagon, CIA, the AEC, the White House, and members of Congress, as well as with foreign diplomats, to discuss such questions as what relationship the new agency would have to the United Nations, and whether it would be worth supporting if the Soviets refused to cooperate. Also considered were ways to implement other aspects of the Atoms for Peace plan, such as preparing to declassify some reactor information. My role in these discussions with foreign diplomats–including in time with Soviets–introduced me to multilateral diplomacy, especially through the work of the Preparatory Commission of the IAEA, which prepared the ground for a conference at the United Nations on a charter for the IAEA.

Eisenhower had appointed an industrialist, Morehead Patterson, as the chief delegate to these negotiations on the IAEA. One difficulty was that Lewis Strauss opposed Patterson. I believe that Strauss thought Patterson had a possible conflict of interest as he was the head of a company that had a potential interest in building nuclear reactors. After some grumbling over a few weeks, the matter was resolved. Later, Patterson was succeeded by Jerry Wadsworth in January 1956. Jerry was Cabot Lodge's deputy at the United Nations. When he entertained foreign diplomats, he would often break out his guitar and sing. I thought that was much more sensible than the usual staid receptions that were the staff of life for U.N. delegations. I was touched when, in April 1956, Jerry wrote to Dulles:

> It is a foregone conclusion that we could never have completed this job if it had not been for the persistent negotiating and advising work done by Gerard Smith and his deputy, Philip Farley. I have rarely come across a pair of men who were so eminently qualified to advise and to lead in matters like this recent negotiation. On several occasions, notably during the discussion on the Article having to do with safeguards, I asked Gerry Smith to take the Chair and handle the entire U.S. position, which he did far better than I could have done.[9]

On a later occasion, Jerry flattered me further by referring to me as a "tower of strength" during the negotiations. "He has been an indefatigable and loyal worker," Jerry wrote to Dulles, "and to him must go a large measure of whatever credit is due for the development of the [IAEA] Statute."[10]

The work of the IAEA Preparatory Commission was one of the earliest sustained negotiations involving the Soviet Union and one of its satellites, Czechoslovakia. Here, I worked with that impressive statesmen, Sir Percy Spender of Australia, and had the good fortune to work with Father Theodore Hesburgh, the President of Notre Dame University who represented the Vatican. He was a fine priest with a well-developed sense of humor. Years later, I was at a table with him at a meeting of the Trilateral Commission in Paris. A leading French politician spoke at great length, and Father Hesburgh passed around a note which said, "If I had a pistol I'd shoot him!" He was a much more reasonable colleague than Krishna Menon of India who, with the French and Soviet representatives, worked hard and not unsuccessfully to water down the safeguards provisions which we had proposed. Some fifteen years later, I found that negotiating with the Soviets in the 1950s had not been a bad preparation for the SALT negotiations.

This experience also afforded some insight into the workings of the Soviet system. For example, as the Preparatory Commission was finishing its work, I gave a luncheon for the Soviet delegate, Ambassador Georgi N. Zaroubin. I asked him how the Soviet Union went about staffing international organizations such as the IAEA that we were hoping to establish. He said that various Soviet agencies were advised that the Soviet Union needed a representative for an international organization, the agencies designated prospective candidates, and the government picked the best person. The top scientist on the Soviet delegation to the conference was a metallurgist named Vasily Emelyanov. Zaroubin said that Emelyanov would be the most qualified person to represent the Soviet Union at the IAEA, but he was anxious to get back to his laboratory. Of course, Zaroubin stressed, the Soviet Union would not think of pressing him to take a job he did not want. I was not surprised to hear several months later that Emelyanov would be the Soviet representative. He served at the IAEA for many years. While there, he was assigned as his deputy Molotov, who had lost favor with the Moscow leadership and had been banished to Mongolia as ambassador before being sent to the IAEA. Emelyanov was reported to have said, "What a great nation the Soviet Union is! He, a simple metallurgist, had as his deputy the illustrious former foreign minister, V. Molotov!"

After lengthy negotiations, the IAEA statute was hammered out, and the agency inaugurated in October 1956. By this time, new arrangements for sharing technology for the peaceful uses of nuclear energy had arisen to compete with the IAEA. One was EURATOM, a European agency which Eisenhower and Dulles had pressed for as a means to promote European integration. This idea had not been fully shared by Lewis Strauss, whose lukewarm support worried me and others because it denied the United States a united voice in its efforts to take a leadership role in European policy. Strauss was concerned lest the IAEA slip away from American control. To forestall this, he persuaded a reluctant Congressman Cole to agree to be its first director. The United States did make an effort to give the IAEA a strong start, when Strauss announced at its inauguration that America would make available to the new agency 5,000 kilograms of U-235, provided the United States and the IAEA could reach agreement on terms. I noticed at the time that the other nations gave a tepid reception to this announcement, and concluded they preferred to make bilateral deals with the United States rather than work through this new international agency.[11]

Starting in 1954, preparations went forward for an international scientific conference on the peaceful uses of atomic energy, which Lewis Strauss announced in April 1954. This conference took place in Geneva in the summer of 1955. I was the chief American political advisor. I was also involved with the talks on nuclear safeguards which were held in Geneva immediately following the scientific conference. The first conference would leave us somewhat hopeful for the future of U.S.-Soviet scientific cooperation, but the second would only accent the serious problems surrounding the safeguarding of nuclear materials against diversion to military uses, and the links between this issue and parallel efforts to prevent the spread of nuclear weapons.

As did the IAEA, the two Geneva conferences had their roots in the Atoms for Peace speech to the United Nations in 1953. Isidor Rabi, who had replaced Oppenheimer as head of the AEC General Advisory Committee, agreed with Strauss that an international scientific conference might have propaganda value in winning worldwide support for Eisenhower's plan among scientists. Strauss and I arranged for Rabi's appointment as head of a planning group. I offered State's full cooperation in arranging the conference, but a number of unanswered questions about Russia's role, what information the United States would be willing to release, particularly regarding reactors, and where and under whose auspices the conference should be held, delayed planning. State began leaning toward holding it under U.N. auspices to avoid the political problems raised by questions about Chinese and East German participation.[12]

We worked with British and Canadian officials on the agenda for the conference, and were helped by John A. Hall, who was director of the AEC's office of international affairs. Hall was a Harvard Ph.D. in government who had worked at State between the end of World War II and 1948, when he came to AEC to work as liaison with State. Together, with technical experts, we grappled with such contentious issues as what data the United States, Britain, and Canada could release on such key subjects as power reactor technology, production of fissionable material, and heavy water. Rabi was named the U.S. member of a U.N. advisory committee making formal arrangements for the conference, and he secured the appointment of Walt Whitman of the GAC as its Secretary General. This made Strauss and other U.S. officials happy, as they had been leery of having any communists as conference officials.[13]

Strauss was much less pleased over State's acquiescence to Britain's nomination of Homi J. Bhabha (a well-known Indian physicist who had taught at Cambridge) as President of the conference. Under Secretary of State Hoover shared Strauss's concerns about Bhabha. I thought it was a tempest in a teapot. To ease Hoover's mind, I advised that the main U.S. interest was to appoint M.I.T. professor Walt Whitman as Secretary-General of the conference, a much more influential office, and that it would probably be necessary to accept Bhabha as President to get Whitman agreed on.[14] Bhabha and Whitman were eventually appointed. In his opening address, Bhabha skipped lightly over the potential for generating electric power from fissionable material and spoke of the greater possibilities of fusion reactors. More than thirty-five years have passed since his predictions, and nuclear power from fission reactors is widespread while fusion is still not in sight. Some years later, I was sorry to learn that Bhabha had been killed in an airplane that hit Mont Blanc on its way to Geneva. One of the key facilities in the Indian nuclear program, the Bhabha Atomic Research Center at Trombay, is named after him. I believe a good deal of work on India's weaponry is done there.

The Geneva Scientific Conference agenda included presentations on reactor technology, biological and ecological effects of radiation, industrial uses of isotopes, and applications of atomic energy in the fields of biology, agriculture, and medicine.[15] Its content was a matter of some delicacy because of concern that the Soviets would learn about nuclear technology from the U.S. papers. As it turned out, we learned that the Soviets were quite far advanced in nuclear technology. This pervasive worry over revealing nuclear secrets to the Soviets prompted me to ask Wally Barbour, the Deputy Assistant Secretary of State for European Affairs, if there was any danger in my going to Geneva with my head full of nuclear weapons secrets. His advice was, "Just stay off the back streets at night."

Dr. Willard Libby, an Atomic Energy commissioner, was vice chairman of the U.S. delegation and acted in Lewis Strauss's absence as chairman. Libby had developed the carbon dating process, which has been extremely valuable in establishing dates of materials going back deep into antiquity. Libby came to me before the conference to point out that a meeting of the ongoing series of talks in Geneva between the United States and the Chinese communist government (on unrelated issues such as the dispute over Taiwan's status) could lead to some difficulty. He felt that the Chinese would make a major offer in the bilateral negotiations and spoil the public relations impact of the Atoms for Peace scientific conference. To prevent this, he insisted that I immediately get in touch with Ambassador Alexis Johnson, the head of the U.S. delegation to the talks with the Chinese, and have him postpone his next meeting, which was to take place the day before the scientific conference opened. I thought this was a pretty wild calculation and refused to do so. Libby then insisted that I contact Dulles and have him instruct Johnson to postpone the talks with the Chinese. Again

I refused, pointing out that this was not something about which we should trouble the Secretary of State. Years later, Libby told me how sorry he was for getting so upset about this very unlikely contingency.

During the conference, it was great to see Soviet and American scientists affably exchanging views on the peaceful uses of nuclear energy. This was the first time that they were allowed to talk to each other. The atmosphere was quite electric. I was amazed to see that even the Soviets seemed caught up in the enthusiasm. I watched the drama of Soviet scientists explaining their reactor technology to U.S. scientists, an openness which I attributed to a Kremlin decision to exploit the wave of world interest in the peaceful uses of atomic energy, not to any conversion to cooperation through a "Spirit of Geneva." It was clear there were limits on what the Soviet scientist could discuss. When Wally Zinn, the director of the Argonne National Laboratory, asked a Soviet representative about the composition of the fuel elements in their reactor, he was told, "The factory doesn't want me to say what's in it." Despite these limits, I felt then that if only our scientists and their Soviet counterparts could have exchanges about controlling nuclear weapons, the chances would be better than if it were left to politicians, bureaucrats and military officers. However, it did not work out that way. Now, the end of the Cold War has opened the way to many exchanges, including those between members of the U.S. National Academy of Sciences and Russian scientists. As it was, I believed the Geneva scientific conference helped to confirm U.S. leadership in the peaceful uses of atomic energy. It also served to refute Soviet charges that America was focusing exclusively on military uses for this technology.[16]

I was less sanguine about the results of the talks on safeguards which followed the scientific conference. We then believed that the main safeguard problem relating to peaceful use of atomic energy was how to guard against the risk of diversion of materials from peacetime reactors to military purposes. Here, as with the IAEA in general, the decision of the Soviets to participate compelled us to take the question of safeguards more seriously. The Soviets, while resisting some of the specific safeguards that we suggested, had continually stressed safeguards as a principal problem to be addressed in any program to promote international cooperation in peaceful uses.

Once they had agreed to meet with a panel of experts for the purpose of discussing technical issues regarding safeguards, the job fell to me and Hall of AEC once again to draft an agenda. I was the political advisor to the experts who talked with the Russians. Our chief representative was Dr. Isidor Rabi. His Soviet counterpart was Professor Dmitrii Skobelitsyn.

The only agreement reached was on procedural matters. These talks revealed the range of difficult technical and political issues the administration would have to face before it could reach consensus even within its own ranks on acceptable safeguards, much less reach agreement with the Soviets. Consensus within the U.S. delegation on an American position on safeguards would be frustrated by Howard Zinn's criticisms of the proposed system of inspection and detection. Faced with Zinn's arguments, we were forced to come up with a fallback scheme for tagging fissionable materials so they could be traced through the fabrication and reprocessing cycles.[17] It later became obvious that this procedure was not realistic.

The evening before the talks were to start, it was pointed out that since these meetings constituted a negotiation on Swiss soil, we had to get permission from the Swiss government. I put in a hurried call to Francis Willis, the American ambassador, and described our dilemma. She was a first-rate professional and obtained the necessary permission overnight, but when she called early the next morning to pass on the approval, she added, "Don't you ever do that to me again"! It would turn out that we could have spared Ambassador Willis the trouble, for the discussions were marked by Soviet criticisms of U.S. proposals, including the tagging proposal. Wally Zinn did some back-of-the-envelope calculations suggesting that there were ways to denature fissionable material by diluting enriched uranium with uranium-232, but they were not persuasive to the Soviets. Since the approach was never followed up, I can only assume they were not persuasive to American experts, either.[18] It soon became clear that there was little common ground between the two delegations. The only agreement that was reached was when Rabi passed Skobelitsyn a piece of paper outlining what the next steps in the discussions should be, on which Skobelitsyn wrote, "I agree."

After the Geneva safeguards conference, I had to admit that the United States had only a limited grasp of the safeguards issue. As the official AEC historians conclude, both the United States and Soviet Union had come to these talks unprepared for serious technical discussions. Rabi argued (and I agreed) that the United States faced a number of difficult technical problems and had to solve them before it could reconcile full U.S. participation in the International Atomic Energy Agency. Rabi recommended to Strauss that the AEC carry out technical studies to develop the U.S. control plan in greater detail, while parallel political studies were made on the feasibility of controlling diversion of nuclear materials.

Rabi still believed the United States would have a secure position in the proposed agency given its advantages in the supply of enriched materials and its ability to give technical aid, but he warned that the United States had to establish firm controls at the start, or the situation would soon get out of hand. In particular, the United States needed to face the major security dilemma: the spread of nuclear power technology would also give nations the ability to become weapons producers.[19] The proliferation risks persist, but diversion from peaceful to military purposes seems less dangerous. Nations going for nuclear weapons build plants specifically for that purpose.

Rabi believed the United States and the Soviet Union shared a community of interest in solving this problem, a belief which I shared. After the safeguards conference, it was clear that the earlier Soviet insistence on linking peaceful uses and arms control was valid. As I saw it, the essential difference was that safeguarding arms control required broader control over atomic energy programs, while detecting diversion from peaceful uses required relatively less comprehensive measures. Still, the similarities were undeniably compelling, as I was learning during these years.[20]

Chapter Two

Arms Control

During my years at S/AE, the Eisenhower administration, and Dulles in particular, gave increasingly serious attention to the question of arms control, especially a nuclear test ban, prompted by the growing public concern over fallout from nuclear tests, alliance pressures for the United States to get serious about disarmament negotiations with the Soviets, and the growing realization that, while general disarmament was likely a chimera, a test ban treaty might serve to halt what Dulles would call the "pernicious" spread of nuclear weapons. My work on these issues, combined with the influence of people such as Bob Bowie and Henry Owen, would instill a deep conviction that a way must be found to halt the proliferation (a word which Dulles coined for nuclear spread) of weapons of mass destruction. I used what talents, experience, and influence I had to help Dulles grasp this nettle.

My work as Special Assistant for Atomic Energy matters quickly brought me into contact with the issues of radiation fallout from nuclear testing. During my first year, I briefed Under Secretary Bedell Smith on the *Lucky Dragon* incident, which underscored the medical and political perils of nuclear testing. Part of my responsibilities was to report to Under Secretary Smith whenever the United States detected a Soviet nuclear test. We constantly had planes flying over the Pacific Ocean to pick up radioactivity in the atmosphere, a clear signature of a nuclear test. A meeting would be called in a CIA office including representatives from the Pentagon, the AEC, the FBI, and myself representing State. After sifting through the available information, I would report on the Soviet tests to General Smith or his successor, Herbert Hoover, Jr.

Bedell Smith, who had been Eisenhower's chief of staff during World War II and then head of the CIA, was a hard-boiled non-West Pointer. When he resigned from State, we gave him a dinner. I was pleasantly surprised to hear him say in his toast, "I served in the U.S. Army for almost forty years and in the State Department for some months. I have made more friends in State than in all my years in the Army." Smith himself admitted, "That's a hell of a thing to say."

The following story used to be told about the general. During the First World War, he enlisted in the Army by overstating his age. After a battlefield promotion, he rose to become a lieutenant general. But somewhere along the way, his deception was discovered and he got a nasty letter from a personnel officer stating that was "conduct unbecoming" and reducing his number on the promotion list. When he was director of the Combined Chiefs of Staff in Washington, he remembered this letter and called the Army personnel office to ask for his file. The general on the line said that could not be done. Smith asked if that officer liked his job and, receiving an affirmative reply, Smith ordered his file to be delivered to him pronto. He leafed through it and tore out the offending letter.

Concern over the public reaction to fallout intensified in the fall of 1954, as the administration debated the release of a report on the effects of thermonuclear testing, based on the results of the recent "Bravo" shot (which had poisoned the Japanese fishermen). By this time, Willard F. Libby had replaced Smyth as the principal AEC scientist, and he became the chief AEC spokesman on fallout. Being a strong proponent of nuclear testing, Libby was inclined to downplay the health risks involved. He was quoted as saying that a person wearing a luminous dial watch would be exposed to more radiation than was produced in the atmosphere from nuclear testing. At about the same time Lewis Strauss was reported as observing that mutations caused by antibiotics could have more dangerous results than radiation from nuclear testing. We at State were much more concerned, and after the AEC gave a briefing on October 13 on the fallout from "Bravo," a number of my associates were concerned over the anticipated negative impact publication of this fallout information would have on U.S. public support for the AEC program. After listening to their arguments against the immediate release of a public statement, I informed AEC on October 21 that State's informal consensus was that publication should be put off for some months.[21]

In fact, it was not possible to keep this information under wraps, and the public debate soon spread and grew heated. I sought to insure that the eventual AEC statement on fallout would be in accordance with a planned UK statement, due on February 15,

1955, which would also provide information on fallout. Finally, it was the imminence of this British statement which forced the United States to release its statement on "The Effects of High-Yield Nuclear Detonations." Eisenhower approved its release on February 3, 1955.[22]

Pressure on the administration to do something about nuclear testing continued to grow, and as a result Eisenhower and Dulles would move from just considering U.S. arms control proposals as primarily public relations moves to taking them more seriously. At the same time arguments for a test ban shifted from emphasis on reducing fallout to curbing proliferation and checking the Soviet-American arms race, since it was believed that other countries would have to test before building any weapons. The difficulty in pursuing such proposals successfully lay in the deep suspicions with which the United States and the Soviet Union viewed each other. This was demonstrated on the Soviet side during the Geneva summit conference in 1955, when Eisenhower unveiled his "Open Skies" proposal to legitimize airborne reconnaissance photography over U.S. and Soviet territory. The goal was to reduce the risk of surprise attacks. I remember noting at the time that Oppenheimer, who had described the superpowers as "two scorpions in a bottle," now would have to view them with Brownie cameras. Open Skies received a good response from the press and the American public, but the Soviets, who saw the proposal as a fig-leaf for espionage, did not accept it. The Soviets clearly had been caught off guard by Eisenhower's proposal at Geneva. Livingston Merchant, then Under Secretary of State, told me that his Soviet counterpart at the summit had reacted by asking, "Where in the world did you come up with that gimmick?"[23]

On the U.S. side, there were repeated warnings that a test ban, if not verifiable, could leave the United States in a dangerous position should the Soviets decide to cheat. I still had some slight reservations about ending nuclear tests. If these weapons were too dangerous even to test, how long would they be an effective deterrent to war? I soon swallowed this scruple.

I felt that interest at high levels of the U.S. government in banning tests would be increased if the President and the Secretary of State actually had firsthand exposure to nuclear tests as I had in

1951 and 1952. I tried without success to get President Eisenhower to observe a nuclear test. Word came back that the President probably had declined because he thought that viewing a test would prejudice his image as a man of peace.[24] Later, in February 1955, Eisenhower at least considered witnessing a test, calling AEC Chairman Strauss and telling his military advisor General Andrew Goodpaster that he was thinking about "taking a look." The President did not follow up on this, however.[25] By way of contrast, during the SALT negotiations, when I asked Vladimir Semenov, the head of the Soviet delegation, if his leadership had observed nuclear testing, he assured me that all members of the Politburo had.

As discussed in the previous chapter, I also asked Dulles to join me in observing a nuclear test, but he declined. Again, I think he felt that it would upset his political judgment if he actually came close to a nuclear explosion. Though I failed in this regard, I now feel (and new evidence strongly suggests) that Dulles did undergo a shift in his thinking about the question of a nuclear test ban, and arms control in general, during these years. As I noted earlier, in 1954 he had briefly considered the idea of a moratorium on nuclear testing, perhaps in reaction to political pressures after the *Lucky Dragon* incident. After this, for a time Dulles appears to have considered proposals for a test ban, which were usually advanced as a means to deal with the fallout problem, as propaganda ploys not to be taken too seriously. However, by 1957, as the result of the influence of James Killian and the President's Science Advisory Committee, and perhaps because of my influence, Dulles had come to take test ban proposals more seriously. A test ban might be a first step towards arms control, serve to curb the proliferation of nuclear weapons, and in the process lock in the U.S. nuclear superiority for a time.[26]

The difficulties surrounding a test ban meant that Dulles and the administration could not rush to embrace this solution. The military were strongly opposed. The efforts of Thomas Murray, my boss at the AEC, to persuade Dulles and Eisenhower of the wisdom of a test ban on multimegaton weapons, illustrated these obstacles. My relations with Commissioner Murray had turned cool when I became a State Department official. He felt that I was not pushing his ideas forcefully enough. In addition, he had not liked my effort to change his opinion in the Oppenheimer case. I arranged an appointment for Murray with Dulles who had agreed, subject to Strauss being informed. Murray blew up at this condition, but later apologized to me. He used the meeting to recommend to Dulles that the United States should agree to a moratorium on thermonuclear (but not atomic) tests, telling Dulles that it was possible to distinguish atomic from thermonuclear explosions and that such a moratorium could be independently verified.[27] Dulles later said of Murray, "He's an old friend, we served on the Chrysler board together, but I don't think his judgment is good in this field." I pointed out that Murray had been uncannily right in a number of instances.

Murray continued to push for limits on the development and testing of large thermonuclear weapons. I continued my efforts with Dulles, even screwing up my courage to the point once where I bluntly told the Secretary that his mind was too dogmatic when it came to disarmament. Though Dulles was moving towards favoring an end to testing, the situation was difficult for him because he was very conscious that nuclear testing was a prime responsibility of the AEC and that he had to deal with the head of the Commission, and he could not afford to run around Lewis Strauss and entertain the unorthodox views of one of the other commissioners.

However, within the next year as more people became concerned about radiation fallout, ending tests became a matter of great interest to President Eisenhower. In March 1955, Murray appealed directly to the President to consider a moratorium of a year or more on testing large thermonuclear weapons. Murray argued that the United States was far ahead of the Soviet Union in developing such weapons, and that it would be to our interest to delay future tests.[28] At a meeting in late March 1955 concerning Murray's letter with National Security Advisor Robert Cutler and other Pentagon, CIA, and NSC officials, I said that while Murray's letter had first met negative responses in State, now many people there were inclined to find his arguments persuasive. In retrospect, I now regret also saying that I personally found them less than persuasive, though I admitted this was not a clear-cut matter. I did note in a paper for Dulles that if Murray's assumptions were technically valid, a moratorium could be useful from a psychological point of view. Subsequent discussion soon revealed that, whatever the technical merits of Murray's argument, there were serious misgivings about the impact of a test moratorium on America's ability to maintain its nuclear stockpile. In the end, it seemed clear Murray's proposals would be rejected, and ironically I was asked to draft a letter to Murray setting out the reasons.[29]

In 1956 I attempted to revive this idea both as part of a U.N. initiative and as part of a Soviet-American bilateral agreement. Again primarily because of AEC opposition and concerns about secrecy, nothing came of the matter.

Murray would eventually go public with his campaign for limits on testing in a November 1955 speech and open Congressional testimony in April 1956.[30] Shortly after this hearing, Adlai Stevenson, the Democratic presidential candidate, began to make a major issue of ending nuclear testing. It proved a popular subject, since concern was rising over the possibility of cancer caused by fallout radiation, and because many people thought that limiting testing would be a good way to start on the road to nuclear disarmament. The Eisenhower administration was quite defensive about the proposal, although I believe that Eisenhower favored a mutually agreed verifiable Soviet-American test ban. Indeed, after he left office, he said that his greatest regret was failing to negotiate such a ban. Strauss suspected that Murray (a Democrat) had inspired Stevenson's endorsement of testing limits, and directed the Atomic Energy Commission to recall all of Murray's classified papers on this issue.[31]

At this time, I remained somewhat ambivalent about a test ban. I wrote in my journal that I had "very mixed feelings" about the prospect of a moratorium. One thing I was sure about, however. I did not think that it was a good idea to mix politics with national security concerns. As I wrote, it was "tragic to have a test moratorium tossed around in a partisan politics storm; the Russians must be impressed with this display of internal U.S. strain produced by nuclear weapons policy."[32]

It was in connection with the administration's efforts to deal with the test ban issue during the 1956 campaign that I had a run-in with Sherman Adams, the White House Chief of Staff. Adams called a meeting to consider what the administration's public position should be, and Dulles asked me to represent him. When Adams saw me at the White House, he perhaps recalled that I had served in the Truman administration. He told me bluntly to "get out." I pointed out that Secretary of State Dulles had asked me to represent him at the meeting. He merely repeated, "Get out. If you're needed, we'll call you." I waited outside of his office for several hours. When the meeting was over, Lewis Strauss, who had overheard our exchange, came up to me and said, "Gerry, keep cool." When I returned to the State Department and told Dulles about the episode, he said, "Sherman talks to me that way—but not often." When Adams later was forced to resign because of an indiscretion involving accepting a vicuna coat from a government contractor, I joined Dulles in watching Adams make his farewell statement on television. I thought I saw something of a smile on Dulles's face.

A test ban did not prove to be a decisive issue in the election. I recall standing next to the President when Stevenson conceded. Turning to an aide, he said, "You take his surrender."

Around the world, though, fallout anxieties were rising. At the March 1957 summit between President Eisenhower and British Prime Minister Harold Macmillan in Bermuda, I persuaded Eisenhower and Macmillan to note in their communiqué the need to exercise restraint in nuclear testing. They stated that although a test ban could not be enforced or verified in the absence of broader arms control agreements, nuclear powers nevertheless should exercise restraint in their testing programs. The United States pledged to conduct tests in a manner to keep radiation levels well below the levels believed to be hazardous; to continue advance announcements of test series; and to permit limited international observation of U.S. tests if the Soviets would do the same.[33] Macmillan was reported as commenting that this was the most significant part of the communiqué.

By this time, Dulles, having recovered from his first bout with the cancer which would eventually claim him, was moving to seize the high ground in disarmament, both abroad and at home. In the summer of 1957 he made a speech that put forward a three-point program to slow the spread of atomic weapons. This plan included ending all production of fissionable materials for weapons;

transferring some of the existing stocks of weapons materials to peaceful uses (possibly under the IAEA's control); and proposing a testing moratorium of about ten months.[34] This proposal was a direct effort to solve the proliferation problem.

Dulles now moved to take control of U.S. disarmament policy away from Harold Stassen–dubbed the "Secretary of Peace" by the press–following a major diplomatic blunder by Stassen. Governor Stassen had been placed over a White House Special Staff with the responsibility for disarmament policy. To everyone's surprise, the 1957 London negotiations turned into the first serious arms talks of the postwar period, in part due to Stassen's efforts to get agreement on the outline of a first-stage plan, starting with a test ban, and with promises of a second stage. Unfortunately, at the London talks in May 1957, Stassen exceeded his authority by giving a paper outlining a new allied position to Valerian Zorin, the chief Soviet delegate, before it had been seen by the allies.[35] The new position was substantially more flexible than earlier offers–for example, it stated allied willingness to discuss Soviet proposals for force reductions and to make a commitment not to be the first to use nuclear weapons.[36] The U.K., French, and West German governments were furious that this had been done without prior allied consultations on the document's proposals. Germany's Chancellor Adenauer was especially upset, as Stassen's proposals suggested the United States would proceed to the second stage of reductions without demanding progress on German reunification. Stassen argued that his paper was unofficial–just a "talking paper"–and that the allies knew all about its substance (and they had been shown the paper by Lawrence Weiler, a State Department officer who later became a leading arms control official and Counselor at the Arms Control and Disarmament Agency, at the same time that Robert Matteson of Stassen's staff was showing it to Zorin). Stassen subsequently talked to Zorin and explained that the paper had no official standing. Zorin agreed to treat it as "nonexistent."[37]

But Stassen's fate was set, for now Eisenhower was angry. He described Stassen's action as "idiotic," and both he and Dulles dressed down Stassen severely. I think that Dulles not only was upset that an agent of the United States government got out ahead of the administration, but also felt that this was a potential entrenchment upon his relationship with the President. Dulles's unique access to Eisenhower was his first priority, and he had already had a whiff of this kind of infringement in the case of Nelson Rockefeller. As Dulles put it, they had to bring Stassen "to heel."

Several months later the President sent Dulles to London. Dulles made a point of saying that "no particular incident" had moved Eisenhower to send him there, merely a recognition of "the fact that there were so many points to be buttoned up at the same time that it could be done more effectively" with him in London. It seems clear that lack of confidence in Stassen led to the President's decision that Dulles should now head up the London delegation. This is confirmed by a telegram from Eisenhower to Prime Minister Macmillan on July 26 stating, "In order to renew our contacts with our delegation in London and to make certain that in the highest echelons our thinking along disarmament is well coordinated," the President had decided to send Dulles to London.[38] Dulles asked me to join him there.

By this time, the President was getting alarmed over the large number of tests set for the "Hardtack" series in the spring and summer of 1958. He was concerned over the public perception of inconsistency in the United States conducting such tests while claiming a readiness to suspend testing as part of a disarmament program. This concern would join with Dulles's realization, by late summer of 1957, when it was clear the U.N. disarmament subcommittee talks were going nowhere and the Soviets were offering a two-year moratorium on testing, that the United States had to revise its disarmament position by tightening the link between a test moratorium and inspections. So, in a meeting on August 9, Eisenhower, Dulles, Robert Cutler, and I hammered out a new position. In brief, it offered a test moratorium for two years, during which the nuclear powers would seek to solve the problems surrounding inspections for testing, stockpiling and producing weapons-grade nuclear material. If no solutions to these problems were found, the United States would be free to resume testing, or the moratorium could be extended for another two years by mutual agreement.[39]

This new U.S. position was rejected by the Soviets, who saw in Stassen's fall from grace the final signal for seeking a new forum, preferably bilateral, for disarmament talks. Testing would continue, as the United States, Soviet Union, and Britain continued to test in 1957. Shortly thereafter, the two superpowers did agree on a moratorium which several years later ended when the Soviets tested a large-yield device. Although it was fashionable to claim that the Soviets had broken the agreement, it was generally forgotten that the President had previously stated publicly that the United States felt free to resume testing. While the final meetings of the U.N. disarmament subcommittee in London were disappointing, they did mark a new departure for my career at State. I had already gotten the sense that my stock had risen in Dulles's eyes after I turned down Lewis Strauss's latest offer to become an AEC commissioner. Then, I had been summoned to London by Dulles (who was in Canada at the time), to assist him in the presentation of the new U.S. position. I had already been helping Bowie brief Dulles on disarmament questions and proliferation problems. Dulles later expressed his satisfaction that I had been able to steer him carefully through the shoals of disarmament, which even in those days was a complicated subject with which he did not feel entirely confident. Dulles told me that even though I was far outranked on the London delegation by an Army major general and a career ambassador, I had been more useful than they.

Another sign that I was rising in Dulles's estimation came during this time in London. While he was strolling with Harold Macmillan, Dulles asked me to join them. The conversation was not about affairs of state; I remember Macmillan saying, "Foster, how times have changed. When I was a lad, I came here [to Lancaster House] to dancing class." I didn't think of it at the time, but several of my friends said that Dulles's invitation to join him and Macmillan was a subtle sign that he would soon offer me some higher office. On the plane returning to Washington he told me that he had greater things in mind for me (he had said something similar in July, during another trip to London). I felt that after this London mission Dulles's confidence in me had increased. Confirmation came on August 23, when he offered me the position of Assistant Secretary of State for Policy Planning, replacing Bowie, who was returning to Harvard. (I later learned that I was not the first choice. General "Abe" Lincoln was first considered but Senator Fulbright objected, fearing that would tend to militarize foreign policy.)

I replied that this offer was a tall order. Dulles rehearsed the arguments in my favor–an orderly but imaginative mind, no desire for the limelight (perhaps because of my decision about the AEC position), and my "masterly handling of disarmament," at which point I said, "Whoa!" I then suggested that Bowie's judgment would be useful, as he knew both the job and me. I later learned that Bowie reportedly told Dulles it would just be a matter of "robbing Peter to pay Paul," as I was already so involved in advising Dulles on nuclear issues. So the matter was decided, and on October 10, I took up new responsibilities as Assistant Secretary of State for Policy Planning. Following in the footsteps of George Kennan, Paul Nitze and Bob Bowie, I knew I had large shoes to try to fill.

Chapter Three

The Policy Planning Staff, 1957–60

The Policy Planning Staff–New Responsibilities and New Colleagues

I was nominated to be Assistant Secretary of State and director of the Policy Planning staff to succeed Bob Bowie on August 28, 1957. I unofficially took up my duties in October, and the Senate confirmed my nomination in January 1958. The Policy Planning staff, or S/P, was a post-World War II creation. The three previous directors, George Kennan, Paul Nitze, and Bob Bowie, were all more experienced in international relations than I. The S/P staff, which numbered about ten, did not engage in "master planning" of foreign policy. We merely tried to take a longer-range view than was possible for other State Department officials working on day-to-day problems.

The staff was essentially an instrument of the Secretary, providing reports on issues and questions he asked about or that we thought he ought to have. We often acted as a gadfly and promoter of policy changes. While special efforts were made to keep the staff detached from daily operations, much of our useful work came from personal contacts between members of the staff and of the geographical bureaus rather than from drafting formal papers. Members of the staff with appropriate expertise would sit in on meetings of the geographical bureaus to try to sow Policy Planning's perspectives, and at times these ideas would mature into new policies. Finally, the Policy Planning staff served as a conduit for ideas from outside the State Department. We consulted many such outside experts, such as Paul Nitze, Jerome Wiesner, Dean Rusk, Ernest Lawrence, Arnold Toynbee, Admiral Rickover, and Albert Wolhstetter. Interaction with outside research groups also was encouraged, including the staff of the Council on Foreign Relations in New York.[1]

My concerns about my qualifications for taking over new and broader responsibilities were offset by the prospect of having a number of well-qualified professional Foreign Service officers on the staff. For example, my first deputy was Albert Matthews, who had long experiences in the Middle East. He was succeeded by George Morgan, who had served as minister in Tokyo. One of the keenest officials with whom I worked in the State Department was J. Robert Schaetzel, who went on to become the United States ambassador to the European communities. He has continued to be a major factor in the work to get the United States government seriously interested in the problem of stopping the proliferation of nuclear weapons.

Last but emphatically not least, Henry Owen was an outstanding member of the staff whose output was probably twice that of any other officer. He went on to be director of Policy Planning, as well as a close friend. In addition to his service in connection with issues of nuclear weapons and arms control, I should mention his key role in laying the groundwork late in the Eisenhower administration for the "Alliance for Progress," inaugurated under Kennedy. At Owen's suggestion, I proposed the idea of a substantial grant to the Latin American republics for economic development. The sum we proposed was five hundred million dollars. Secretary Christian Herter (who had succeeded Dulles as Secretary of State) liked the idea, and, at the next NSC meeting, he made the proposal. Eisenhower said this was exactly what he had been looking for to give a new direction to U.S. policy in Latin America. I noticed that the director of the Bureau of the Budget did not share the President's enthusiasm for the idea, and was scowling, as he had not been consulted on the matter. The funds were appropriated, laying the basis for the larger program Kennedy proposed in 1961. Owen's interest in economic matters would continue to grow, and his last government duty was as a "sherpa" preparing for summit meetings of the Heads of Government of the major industrialized countries, the so-called G-7 meetings. Henry has also served as director of foreign policy studies at the Brookings Institution and was a leader in setting up the Bretton Woods Committee (a group working for increased funding for the World Bank and the IMF).

As Policy Planning staff director, I attended National Security Council meetings with Dulles from 1957 until his death in 1959, and subsequently with his successor, Christian Herter, until 1961. My responsibilities included briefing the Secretary on the NSC agendas. This role gave me specially good standing in the State Department and the Pentagon. Each week after the NSC meeting I would discuss the current issues with General Earl Wheeler and two other officers, General Ollie Pitcher (U.S.A.F.) and Admiral "Count" Austin. Wheeler was director of the Joint Staff of the JCS–in some respects my opposite number at the Pentagon. He would later become chairman of the Joint Chiefs of Staff. Wheeler himself did not attend NSC meetings and found these informal talks helpful. Apparently, the Joint Staff did not feel sufficiently debriefed by the chairman of the JCS (General Nathan Twining during my time at Policy Planning) who regularly attended NSC meetings. The benefits were mutual, as the military learned what the President and the Secretary of State were thinking about, and I gained insights into military thinking. There was never any publicity about these meetings, which encouraged frank discussions. Such close State-JCS relations have not always been the norm. During Richard Nixon's presidency, when Kissinger was National Security Advisor, the JCS actually resorted to a spy, who regularly rifled through Henry Kissinger's briefcase, to get this sort of information. The Secretary of Defense also arranged to intercept Kissinger's back channel cable traffic. For his help in this respect, one high-ranking officer reputedly received an extra star.

I also served as the State Department's representative on the NSC Planning Board, which prepared papers for consideration by the NSC. James Reston of the *New York Times* once described this group in a 1958 article entitled "The Anonymous Advisors" as part of "that largely anonymous but immensely powerful staff that serves the President in the White House" and was "a mystery to even the most observant members of the Washington community."[2] I recall that Robert Cutler, who was chairman of the Planning Board at this time, complained shortly after I joined that the quality of the discussion had fallen greatly since Bowie had resigned. I was not sure whether this was a reference to me or to the general level of the proceedings. Despite this ambiguous remark, Cutler continued to be a friend until he left the administration.

The third part of my work was to serve as a sort of general utility advisor to the Secretary of State. These duties involved preparing drafts of speeches, testimony, and policy statements, and accompanying Dulles (and then Herter) to conferences abroad, such as NATO ministerial meetings between 1957 and 1961, as well as SEATO and CENTO sessions. I also served on the U.S. delegations to the Four-Power Foreign Ministers Conference on Berlin in Geneva in the spring and summer of 1959, accompanying Secretary Herter, who succeeded Dulles in 1959 after illness led to the latter's resignation and death. I also served at times as State's representative on interagency groups, e.g., the Interagency Working Group which prepared a report on issues for the Geneva Surprise Attack conference in the fall of 1958.[3]

Travels with Dulles were interesting. In 1958 I accompanied him to a meeting of SEATO–the Southeast Asia Treaty Organization–in Manila, including stops in Honolulu, Wake, and Guam. The meeting lacked the excitement that surrounded meetings of NATO ministers. Dulles's speech to the meeting included a suggestion of mine, a quotation from Clausewitz that "the conqueror is always peace-loving, he would just as soon march peacefully." On leaving for Okinawa and Japan, Dulles's plane had to wait until Admiral Stump's plane had taken off, he being the Commander in Chief, Pacific. While a good deal of time went into "ruffles and drums," I heard Dulles say, "What a lot of nonsense." He did not like to wait for anybody except the President, who occasionally would come out to the airport when Dulles was taking off for some ministerial meeting.

Another trip that comes to mind was a visit to Taiwan with Dulles in 1958, where Dulles passed on a Policy Planning staff paper, largely drafted by George Morgan, on a new "spiritual" role for Taiwan in Asia. Dulles was pleased with this paper, but so far Taiwan has not taken on such a role. Here, I met the Nationalist Chinese leader Chiang Kai Shek and his wife, Madame Chiang. They were an interesting duo, the Generalissimo repeatedly going

"Ha, ha, ha," while I talked with his wife about her honorary degree from the University of Michigan. Chiang showed a flicker of interest when he learned about my atomic energy background, and during a diplomatic reception we had a fairly long exchange regarding Taiwan and atomic energy, at the end of which I suggested that Chiang invite Lewis Strauss to Taiwan.

John Foster Dulles–An Appreciation

These new duties brought me into a much closer working relationship with Dulles, a vantage point from which I could observe the play of his mind and personality. His was a complex personality, linked with an equally complex and formidable intellect. Historians have recently begun to write about an "unexpected" Dulles, a development which was touched upon in chapter 2.[4] I would now like to give a broader picture of Dulles than in chapter 2, the man at work and at more relaxed times, as I was privileged to observe him during my time at Policy Planning.

Dulles undeniably was and liked to be a public figure, and he liked publicity though basically he was quite shy. He knew he was no ordinary man whom luck had shot up to the top. He had outthought, outworked, outbluffed, and outdared all comers and had great inner self-confidence. The common observation that he carried the State Department in his hat was nonsense to all who worked with him. He soaked up others' ideas, polished them, worried them, worked them over, and then acted on them. His stamina was extraordinary, and his mind seldom at rest. Once one foreign policy problem had been dealt with, he was impatient to move on to the next. To watch Dulles grapple with a problem was like watching a bird dog at work sniffing for its prey. He got a little excited as he worked over a solution, breathed a little faster, and obviously enjoyed the thinking process. After an overnight Atlantic trip, he was always ready for long hours of work in London, Paris, or Bonn. While I would feel quite bushed about midnight the following night, Dulles showed little sign of any strain. Yet he was not a merciless taskmaster, and could view with patient humor those who could not match his pace. I discovered this once when, as I climbed out of an airplane berth after nearly ten hours of sleep, Dulles, who had already been at work for six hours, announced, "Here comes the indispensable member of the delegation."

I never saw Dulles relax with a book or magazine. If time permitted, he worked, organizing his thoughts and writing on one of the ubiquitous yellow pads. He constantly whittled at his pencils and chewed them and sometimes put their erasers in his ears and constantly doodled as he listened to arguments he knew by heart. He had a particular passion for redrafting speeches, often preparing ten or twelve drafts of a speech in search of just the right wording. He was fond of the English language and would complain jokingly when his staff urged him not to use rhetorical flourishes in his speeches. He could bristle with impatience when advisors said "Don't say that in a speech, you already said it." He believed that repetition was a virtue in the ideological struggle with the Soviet Union. On several occasions, my speech-writing triggered debates over language. Dulles once sternly advised me that the word "crisis," which I used occasionally, should be reserved for the most extreme circumstances. On a less serious note, he once pointed out, to my chagrin, that I had struck a phrase from a speech which was a direct quotation from the Declaration of Independence.

Dulles believed that the course of history depended a good deal on him. I don't think that either Christian Herter or Dean Rusk, Dulles's immediate successors, had that feeling. I remember him saying, "You know, the Soviets respect me because I'll fight." His use of the first person singular, which some people took as arrogance, really was just his feeling that the role he projected was essential. Dulles's at times unconscious egotism (well justified in my opinion) showed up in July of 1957 when he persuaded Adenauer to agree to a proposed Western disarmament plan calling for Soviet overflights of Germany. Tired and sick, he asked me to join him for a drink as we were flying back to Washington. He calmly told me, "I am the only man in the world who could have persuaded Adenauer to accept that." This strong self-confidence could also flash brightly negative at times. "Not as long as I am Secretary of State" was his reply to one of my suggestions for a settlement about the Offshore Islands in 1958.

In his approach to diplomacy, Dulles brought a unique mixture of moralism and pragmatism, of devotion to detail combined with an inclination to conceptualize and place problems in their larger context, all harnessed to an instinct for the essential and a flair for the dramatic. Undeniably, he saw a fundamental difference with the Communists in that they did not believe in God. Yet, the moralist could also be quite pragmatic, and in fact a great and resourceful infighter who knew all the tricks of bureaucracy. This meshing of the moralistic and pragmatic could be seen in his frequent comparison of the East-West struggle to a chess game–he was not so much concerned about lost pawns as he was about a checkmate leading to the gradual isolation of the United States. Dulles's attention to detail is shown by his insistence on recording all important and even not so important conversations in memoranda, based on his conviction that precise records set down soon after the fact would always beat general recollections. As his files at the Eisenhower Library attest, this determination to keep a factual record of his talks produced a voluminous mass of records, which is a gold mine for historians.

Still, this was no mindless obsession with detail, for Dulles had an unerring instinct for sensing the essential facts which underlay both danger and opportunity for the United States. Far from being the stolid, unexciting statesmen of some accounts ("Dull, Duller, Dulles," as some wags put it), he had a talent for homing in on what was newsworthy and something of a flair for the dramatic. He worked at the news, paying close attention to the headlines overseas and staying in close touch with James Hagerty, Eisenhower's press secretary, who also sometimes handled the Secretary's press relations. Dulles would pore over the transcripts of his press conferences, which often were the peak of his already exacting days as, like a fencer, he would parry, jab and feint with the assembled press, while addressing them with a frankness often missing in his successors. His ability to deal with the press is all the more remarkable given his confession to a colleague that he was "almost scared to death" during press conferences, and that "his knees knocked together when he walked downstairs to meet the press." His dramatic side also surfaced at NSC meetings, where Dulles often played a key role in dramatizing the events and issues confronting the administration, all the while seeking to put them in the perspective of past events and prospective developments.

Not surprisingly, such a forceful mind had strong opinions about the men with whom he worked abroad and at home. He and West German Chancellor Konrad Adenauer obviously enjoyed a mutual attraction and admiration, both of them being politicians and moralists who knew and liked the fact that they had strong religious convictions and shared a deep hatred for the authoritarian and atheistic aspects of Marxism. Still, Dulles could find his patience tasked by the recurring need to counter the Chancellor's inbred suspicion and to salve "Der Alte's" constant need for reassurance by the Americans. Dulles and General Charles de Gaulle were equally determined to leave their stamp on history, which they both clearly did. De Gaulle also shared Dulles's devotion to detail. I recall one session with de Gaulle at Rambouillet, when Eisenhower introduced me to the French leader. I was struck when de Gaulle came into a room and noticed a briefcase unattended by a French officer, a detail which de Gaulle quickly corrected. Dulles, perhaps fortunately, would die before the French General became the cause of serious divisions in the Western alliance, testing the abilities of Dulles's successors.

Within the administration, Dulles's personal dealings were guided by one central principle: to do or permit nothing to undermine his standing with Eisenhower, for he knew that his continued strength and authority rested on an indubitably firm axis with the President. His sensitivity to this connection meant that Dulles at times would temper his own views, especially regarding military matters, if he knew they ran counter to Ike's own strongly held convictions. For example, I believe that Dulles would have allocated more spending for national security, but he did not press this point, not wanting to buck Eisenhower, who was bent on reining in the budget. This was not a cynical maneuver on Dulles's part, for he shared Ike's concern over the dangers of allowing the United States to become a garrison state, and as a conservative, the Secretary was opposed to government intrusion into private affairs. He also took a hardheaded approach to new commitments of U.S. aid in support of our security efforts. As he once remarked to me, just as in war we do not deploy forces according to sentiment, so it is in the Cold War with calls on America's economic resources.

As I observed Dulles at NSC meetings, I saw that he would usually defer to the military judgment of Eisenhower first, and the JCS second. I feel he was guided in this by his concern not to jeopardize his standing as a diplomatic expert with Eisenhower, as well as to avoid giving the military any excuse to meddle on his turf. Dulles had a healthy respect for the military, though I believe he knew he was the intellectual superior of many if not all of the military officers in the government, and he knew they knew it. I think Dulles respected Lewis Strauss as one of the cleverest men in government. I got the feeling he was somewhat bemused that Charles Wilson of General Motors was Secretary of Defense, and he entertained higher hopes for Wilson's successor, Neil McElroy. McElroy, however, proved not to be a dynamic leader of the Pentagon, and posed obstacles to revising the strategy of massive retaliation.

To work closely with Dulles as he grappled with many of the key decisions of the Cold War was exhilarating. My staff and I found ourselves dealing with a wide range of problems, including the promotion of Latin American development and better U.S. relations with its southern neighbors, planning for a new regime for the Panama Canal, the fostering of closer mutual defense ties in the Middle East and Southeast Asia, and the search for a new role for Taiwan in the future of China. But I would find that my personal attention and deepest concerns continued to focus upon nuclear weapons and the Soviet Union. Between 1957 and 1961, I would be caught up in a series of developments, beginning with the successful launch of the Soviet satellite Sputnik and continuing to include fundamental reassessments of and new directions in U.S. nuclear weapons policy and strategy, a series of crises ranging from Lebanon to China to Berlin, and new moves toward arms control with the Soviet Union. The Berlin Crisis would lead to new hopes for reaching agreement with the Kremlin not only on that crisis but also on arms control. These hopes would be dashed, however, by the aborted summit meeting in Paris in 1960. These events and issues continued my education in the dilemmas of trying to control nuclear weapons, either in the pursuit of deterrence, or in the effort to stem the arms race between the United States and Russia.

Sputnik and the Gaither Report

On October 4, 1957, barely a week after I informally took over policy planning, the Soviets launched the first earth-circling satellite, the 184-pound Sputnik I. A major psychological shock to the U.S. leadership and body politic, Sputnik and its much heavier successors, Sputnik II (1,120 pounds–with a dog on board!) and Sputnik III (2,926 pounds), had direct implications for national security. Moscow now had the bomb *and* the technological capability to deliver it with intercontinental missiles. This potential to strike the United States directly with nuclear weapons within thirty minutes drove home the notion of vulnerability to surprise attack.

I remember thinking that this was a particularly bad time to be taking over my new responsibilities within the State Department. To my mind, the Sputnik launches represented the most significant triumph achieved by the Soviets since the seizure of power by the Bolsheviks in 1917. With American technological leadership seemingly shaken to its roots, I knew that there would be rocky times ahead for our foreign policy and diplomacy. I could not recall that I had ever felt so glum about the prospects for U.S. prestige and leadership in the international area.

Very soon after Sputnik I, the gloomy mood in Washington was punctuated by more ominous news. In November 1957, the so-called Gaither Committee presented its highly classified report to the President and the NSC. This committee was chaired by Rowan Gaither, until he had to cut back his participation owing to illness and was replaced by Robert Sprague. (Sprague was the only man I knew who took a briefing on nuclear weapons effects to heart. He was ill for several days.) Among its other major participants were Paul Nitze, John McCloy, Robert Lovett, Herbert York, Jerome Wiesner and William Foster. Its report, formally titled *Deterrence and Survival in the Nuclear Age*, made the case that the strategic balance was tipping toward the Soviet Union and that the United States–and in particular SAC, the backbone of our strategic deterrent–was becoming dangerously vulnerable to nuclear attack. In the words of one of its principal drafters, Paul Nitze, the report painted a bleak picture of the Soviet threat and the need to meet it militarily. The Gaither report was "a stark, broad-brushed portrait of the Soviet threat, dauntingly unequivocal in nature and magnitude."[5] It recommended across-the-board increases in strategic forces, active (antimissile) and passive (fallout shelter) defenses, and an increase in conventional forces. These conclusions had the endorsement of a large and diverse group of nuclear specialists, including over one hundred scientists, weapons experts, academics, defense intellectuals, and former officials–a veritable who's who of the nuclear establishment.

President Eisenhower was fully aware that the U.S. missile and military space programs had been moving steadily forward since at least 1955, albeit in extreme secrecy as "black programs." He reacted coolly to both Sputnik and the Gaither report. Ike was determined to head off this latest attack upon his principles of budgetary probity, and refused to join the chorus of Cassandras. He pointedly made clear his disagreement with the conclusions of the Gaither Committee. At a November 7, 1957, NSC discussion of these issues, the President emphasized that "it was essential that we neither become panicked nor allow ourselves to be complacent." He added that the government had before it a "big job of molding public opinion" and "avoiding extremes."[6] He was especially concerned that implementation of the Gaither Committee recommendations would lead to just such extremes. Too much spending might ruin the United States and undermine democratic principles, turning the country into a virtual "garrison state."[7] Eisenhower did move to implement one of the report's recommendations, ordering that a third of SAC's bombers must either be in the air constantly or able to be launched within 15 minutes, thus reducing any vulnerability to surprise Soviet attack.[8]

Secretary Dulles shared with Eisenhower the belief that Sputnik did not mark such a fundamental change in the strategic balance of power as to warrant the tremendous new national defense expenditures ($45 billion over five years) called for by the Gaither report. He agreed with Eisenhower that when it came to military capabilities, "enough is enough."[9] Led by Don Quarles of Defense, a doctrine of sufficiency in lieu of superiority began to gain ground. Indeed, by this time Dulles was beginning to realize that the strategic balance was relatively stable, and that we would need to develop a military strategy of another type if we wanted to use U.S. power for anything except to deter a massive Soviet attack.

But Dulles was concerned about the psychological effect of Sputnik on America's world position. Immediately after the launch, as part of our preparations for the upcoming NATO Heads of Government Conference, he communicated with a number of knowledgeable people outside government as to whether Washington should change its foreign policy and if so, how? One response to this query stands out in my recollection above all others. Paul Nitze, who had been so instrumental in the final Gaither report and was subsequently disappointed that Eisenhower and Dulles did not take all its advice to heart, answered Dulles by letter, concluding with the blunt and insensitive suggestion, "Why don't you resign?" Dulles showed me Nitze's letter and his reply to it, which in effect graciously said that Paul's "advice" did not annoy him.

Although Sputnik had a more profound personal effect on me as I took over the reins of Policy Planning, I also thought, as did the President and Dulles, that the Gaither report was too alarmist. The one area in which I was in some agreement with the committee's findings was civil defense. The United States did not seem serious about the threat of nuclear war because we never had a major fall-out shelter program. Congress had not been willing to appropriate the large sums that would be required for such a program, over and above the funding for offensive strategic forces and active defenses. Dulles also regarded civil defense as a low priority, and he repeatedly tried to persuade me to give up this idea. He used to argue, "The American people will just not burrow underground." In retrospect, he undoubtedly was right. In addition, he liked to point out that a vast shelter program to protect Americans alone would place a heavy strain on relations with our allies. At the time, however, I took civil defense much more seriously, perhaps because I had been with the nuclear weapons program for a long time and had seen what nuclear explosions could actually do.[10]

Ultimately, despite the effort to keep Sputnik in some perspective, the rapid technological advances it portended in the development of weapons of mass destruction and the means to deliver them across vast distances at previously incomprehensible speeds meant that the calculus of power might be shifting. This would have critical consequences for U.S. strategy, America's relations with its allies, and its efforts to deter the Soviet Union.

Nuclear Strategy and the Dilemmas of Massive Retaliation

In an ironical way, an error I made in drafting a speech for Dulles served to underscore this growing ambiguity about the nature of power in the nuclear era. Following one NATO conference, while flying back home, Dulles asked me to draft his report to the American people on the meeting. I included the following passage from St. Luke: "When a strong man fully armed guards his own palace his goods are in peace." After I handed Dulles the manuscript, he called me to the back of the plane and asked where I had gotten the quotation. I told him, and he asked for a Bible, which fortunately I was able to find. He read and reread the passage and the next day called me in and asked–knowing that I was a Catholic–"What do your theologians say is the meaning of this passage?" I said it meant that security lies in strength. Not satisfied, he asked me to check with a Scripture scholar. I asked a friend learned in the New Testament, who said the passage referred to Satan, pointing out that the next line referred to Christ: "But when one stronger than he assails him and overcomes him he takes away his armor in which he trusted and divides his spoil."[11]

Shamefaced, I reported this to Dulles who got a great kick out of it. "Just think what my Presbyterian friends would have said if they heard me citing this passage to the country at large." Dulles once said he knew more about the Bible than anyone else in the State Department. I never again quoted Scripture in a draft for him. Dulles would remember this episode to his final days and continue to find humor in it. A few years later when Dulles was ill and was staying at Douglas Dillon's house in Hobe Sound, Florida, President Eisenhower addressed a NATO meeting in Washington and included the same passage from St. Luke. I immediately wired Dulles that I had nothing to do with it. One of his aides later told me that Dulles laughed at this report; if not his last laugh, it was at least one of them.

This humorous denouement notwithstanding, even Dulles's own remarks in the month after the launch of Sputnik reflected the double-edged nature of power in this new age. On the one hand, he observed that the United States had "in terms of actual military power and potential military power, for some years to come, a very marked superiority . . . particularly in terms of heavy bombers which are now [1957] and for some years to come, will be the preferred and most effective means" for the delivery of nuclear weapons. On the other hand, about three weeks later he was also heard to say that, in light of Russia's proven technological skills and power to mobilize them, there was little chance of restoring the "preponderance of power" which the West, and especially the United States, had enjoyed over the past decade.

Underlying this Dulles remark was the looming reality of what was termed at the time "nuclear plenty" for both the United States and the Soviets–what has since come to be better known as nuclear parity between the two superpowers. This approaching new era, and its implications for growing U.S. vulnerability, served to raise complex and potentially divisive questions about U.S. nuclear strategy and the idea of massive retaliation, as well as about the future viability of NATO strategy and the effectiveness of our so-called "nuclear umbrella" over our European allies. These issues exercised the minds of experts within and outside government, as seen in a Council on Foreign Relations meeting I attended in 1958 where I joined Robert Sprague, Tom Finletter, Klaus Knorr, Hamilton Fish Armstrong, Walter Millis, and Hanson Baldwin in listening to a fascinating talk on strategic deterrence and foreign bases by Albert Wohlstetter.

In response to these new strategic realities, the United States, and Dulles personally, would move on several fronts to search for some means to resolve the dilemmas posed by nuclear plenty. Reassessments of U.S. nuclear strategy and important decisions regarding NATO nuclear weapons policies would move forward in the late 1950s, as the United States sought new ways to bolster the political and military utility of nuclear weapons. On another front, Dulles and the administration would make significant changes in their approach to arms control with the Soviets, motivated in part by the difficulties highlighted by the effort to rethink nuclear strategy and policies and the dangers emphasized by a series of crises in which nuclear weapons played a role.

Given the complexity of these issues, it is not surprising that the Eisenhower administration did not speak with one voice, which made Dulles's efforts to explain U.S. policy to our allies more difficult. From my vantage point, I was able to watch him as he sought to reconcile a number of views, within the government and the NATO alliance, all the while taking care that he did not disturb his essential constituency of one–the President. Though, as I will discuss later, Eisenhower in some ways by this time might be considered almost a nuclear abolitionist, his pragmatic evaluation was that until real, verifiable arms control was possible, the United States would have to rely upon the threat of massive retaliation for its security in the event of a general war crisis with the Soviets. His personal commitment to fiscal probity also served to deepen the emphasis upon nuclear weapons in U.S. strategy and planning. As he saw it, providing the strategic nuclear deterrent and its protection (a costly responsibility) was America's primary role within the Western alliance, while our allies should provide more of the essential local military forces needed for their defense as well as to provide flexibility in dealing with local threats. To the degree that the United States still had to keep ground forces in Europe, Eisenhower pressed the Pentagon to "streamline" these divisions through the introduction of tactical nuclear weapons. His views would also serve to complicate Dulles's diplomacy in NATO.

As might be expected, there was ample support for Eisenhower's views in the military services. General Thomas Powers, who had succeeded Curtis LeMay as SAC commander, was fully committed to the principle that America's nuclear retaliatory capability was the best guarantee of peace. General Nathan Twining, who had replaced Radford as JCS chairman, was a strong supporter of nuclear air power. On the civilian side in the Pentagon, however, there were signs that some were becoming concerned over the future prospects for a strategy of massive retaliation, or at least its consequences if carried out in an era of nuclear plenty. For example, I recall Don Quarles, the bright former director of the Sandia weapons design program, speaking while Secretary of the Air Force, about a "balance of terror" in 1957. Then, in late 1958, I noted that Quarles was arguing that a "respectable posture" of defense and "superiority" meant the same thing, implying that a strategy of minimum deterrence or sufficiency might be adequate. Still, Quarles had some doubts about the efficacy of deterrence should a war threat come, as seen in his doubts in 1959 when he was Deputy Secretary of Defense that "any atomic power would accept defeat while withholding its nuclear weapons," a belief Eisenhower also shared. (This is exactly what the United States did in Vietnam and the Soviet Union in Afghanistan, though it is possible that Quarles's observation might have been limited to direct super-power war, as I believe Eisenhower's was.) Such concerns were only intensified by the anticipated arrival of ballistic missile technology, with all the consequences for surprise attack and U.S. vulnerability that this would entail.

One general consequence of deepening concern over massive retaliation was a search for new options, for greater flexibility that would give the United States and the West choices between surrender and Armageddon. Bowie told me that Dulles was shocked by a briefing he received at SAC headquarters in Omaha which indicated SAC had a capability if not an intention to engage in what could be termed nuclear carpet bombing of the Soviet Union. Despite the desire for new options, by the end of the Eisenhower administrations, strategic nuclear planning had come to be embodied in a general war plan known as the Single Integrated Operational Plan (SIOP) which in essence called for launching all our nuclear weapons in one massive strike.

I had come to believe that the United States needed to bolster its conventional force capabilities to secure flexibility and diminish a dangerous over-reliance upon nuclear weapons, a position which I reached in part as the result of long discussions with Bob Bowie. First Bowie, and then I, tried to educate Dulles about the deficiencies of massive retaliation and the need for greater flexibility. In these efforts, I believe we had some success. Dulles, however, at first turned to tactical nuclear weapons as a possible solution to the nuclear rigidity and political dilemmas created by massive retaliation, particularly with respect to U.S. relations with its allies, as seen in his *Foreign Affairs* article of 1957. Interestingly, my former boss in the AEC, Thomas Murray, also pushed for tactical nuclear weapons during this period. The new "strategic imperative," he argued, was "a balanced stockpile, with emphasis henceforth on the manufacture of atomic weapons which lend themselves to discriminating use. Our need is for tens of thousands of such weapons." For him, there was a real moral distinction between multimegaton weapons (the "big cheap bomb") and small weapons for battlefield use.[12] I was opposed to taking this route, believing that more conventional weapons, not tactical nuclear weapons, was the key to flexibility and political acceptance of the use of force against limited threats. In the second Quemoy-Matsu crisis in 1958, which I will discuss later, I showed Dulles the danger of too-casual use of tactical nuclear weapons. Dulles was also motivated by his felt need to give our allies a sense that they had a greater say in the use of nuclear weapons for their own defense, and to get the United States out of the position of "holding the bag" for Europe's security.

In his final years, Dulles moved away from his earlier support for the doctrine of massive retaliation. A series of meetings involving Dulles and other senior administration officials in 1958 clearly demonstrated this fundamental shift in his thinking. I attended a meeting convened on April 7, 1958, by Secretary of Defense Neil McElroy that included Dulles, Lewis Strauss, Assistant Secretary of Defense Donald Quarles, Presidential National Security Advisor Robert Cutler, Chief of Naval Operations Admiral Arleigh Burke, Army Chief of Staff Maxwell Taylor, and a number of other top military officials. Here, Dulles announced that evolving world conditions, especially increasing Soviet nuclear strength, were limiting the effectiveness of the massive retaliation concept, and that unless the United States developed new doctrines he did not think that we could hold the Western alliance together for more than a year. He argued that although we were producing many tactical nuclear weapons, we lacked a doctrine for using them, and that it was crucial that the problem be addressed at the highest level. There was agreement among some of the others present, including Burke, Taylor, and McElroy, that we had not developed nuclear weapons options below the massive retaliation level.[13]

Another meeting on June 17, centering on discussion of a recent study on limited war, gave further evidence that Dulles was moving away from reliance on massive retaliation. In addition to Dulles and myself, Undersecretary of State Christian Herter, McElroy, the service secretaries, and the Joint Chiefs also were present. Dulles in his remarks noted the growing doubts among our European allies that the United States would be willing to defend Europe as American vulnerability to Soviet nuclear weapons increased. Pointing to the French push for their own nuclear weapons, Dulles asked the group what he should say when he met with de Gaulle in a month. Dulles argued that if we did not find some new strategic concept that the allies would accept, with provision of tactical nuclear weapons to the allies for area defense, they would make costly efforts to acquire their own nuclear forces, and then would move toward neutrality. To keep them from doing so, he called for exploring a wider internationalization of nuclear capabilities within NATO.[14]

Most of the others present agreed with Dulles. The main exception was General Maxwell Taylor, who wanted to go even further and faster. He was pushing for greater development of low-yield nuclear weapons as part of a broad move away from massive retaliation and toward a strategy of preparing to fight a limited war with or without nuclear weapons. This position created quite a split within the Pentagon, where the Air Force in particular held that current policy was the right approach. Taylor made a strong pitch for his position in an NSC meeting in 1958, calling for a revision of the Basic National Security Policy guidance to reflect the reality of mutual deterrence. He thought he had the State Department on his side, but Dulles was still thinking the issue through, and as Taylor later wrote, "to my disappointment Secretary Dulles and his advisors did not provide the strong support for a new strategy which I had hoped for."[15] I was the sole advisor sitting behind Dulles, and I agreed with Taylor, but hardly thought it would be prudent to speak up and disagree with the Secretary. The decision was postponed until the Kennedy administration. Throughout the Eisenhower administration, when appropriate opportunities occurred, I argued the case for building stronger conventional forces, thereby reducing reliance on tactical and strategic nuclear weapons.

Finally, on November 7, 1958, I accompanied Dulles to a meeting at the Pentagon at which he said very soberly that massive retaliation, which he acknowledged that he had fathered, was outmoded and that we would have to develop a doctrine–and forces to support it–to meet less than all-out threats. I had never seen him so solemn: he talked for at least half an hour, without any interruption, about why he thought a change in U.S. military policy was necessary. It was agreed that my office and someone at Defense would start working out a new policy. That study continued under Secretary of State Herter, giving me the chance to continue efforts, now aimed at Herter, to move the government away from massive retaliation as well as any optimism about the use of tactical nuclear weapons. I wrote to Secretary Herter in October 1959, commenting on the Pentagon's arguments for continued reliance on massive retaliation and reductions in conventional forces:

> The drift of Secretary McElroy's thinking seems to be that it is in the U.S. security interest to more and more depend on the total war nuclear deterrent. . . . This can only mean that he favors a modification in the direction of the "trip-wire" concept which requires fewer conventional forces and places a heavier deterrent burden on the general war strategic bombing capability. . . . I believe that any move which will increase our dependence on the strategic bombing deterrent would be contrary to the new emphasis on maintaining balanced forces which the President approved only a few months ago. . . . There is no comfort in Secretary McElroy's stated belief that in a limited war situation the "use of tactical nuclear weapons would not necessarily start a general nuclear war." If there is even a 50–50 chance that their use would start a general nuclear war, I would think that they would be completely ruled out as limited war options by the dictates of common sense.[16]

I tried to persuade McElroy of the merits of this analysis, but to no avail. I recall a conversation with him at the Geneva Berlin Conference in 1959. I was arguing for strengthening our nonnuclear military forces because I was convinced that in any hostilities short of a major Soviet attack, we would not resort to nuclear weapons. McElroy merely said, "If you are right, our planning is all wrong." He did not elaborate, but some years later, after both the United States and the Soviet Union had failed to win wars while not using nuclear weapons, I recalled this conversation, but McElroy had passed away in 1972, so we could not renew our debate.

There was serious resistance to such views. For example, Admiral Radford, during a brief return to duty in Twining's absence, took advantage of the opportunity to complain to Eisenhower in 1959 about the "State Department's idea" that the United States could have a conventional force of large size and fight a sizeable war with this force without having to use nuclear weapons. Radford felt all the "whipped-up concern" over the use of nuclear weapons was groundless, and that the real worry was that the United States would not use these weapons if the situation called for it. Radford singled me out in particular as the culprit trying to push through a change in U.S. policy, even though Herter had sought to disabuse the Admiral of this suspicion. It was reported that Eisenhower did not disagree with Radford. Such opposing views within the administration, combined with other political and technological problems, would prevent us from resolving this problem during the Eisenhower administration. I believe it was only fully addressed in the first Kennedy budget message, when the language we had been reaching for since 1957 was finally put into national policy. Despite this ultimate failure, I still believe that the most important thing I did as director of Policy Planning was to help begin the process and move Dulles away from the massive retaliation strategy.

Nuclear Weapons and the Atlantic Alliance

One critical and pressing concern recurring in Dulles's rethinking was the impact of nuclear plenty on NATO. He recognized the potential strains which could emerge in the alliance if the United States was the major if not the sole holder of weapons upon which the European allies' fate depended in the event of war.

Dulles also grasped that the logic of NATO strategy, authorizing SACEUR to plan on the assumption that nuclear weapons would be available for his use, would lead the allies to demand a greater say in the life-and-death decisions regarding the use of nuclear weapons to defend Europe. Dulles realized that belief in the U.S. commitment to NATO was the central pillar of the alliance. It was for this reason that he strongly opposed President Eisenhower's inclination to reduce U.S. troop levels in Europe, for he knew these troops had taken on vital importance as a symbol of the U.S. commitment. On a number of occasions I heard the President tell the NSC that he wanted to bring some Seventh Army troops back from Europe, only to ruefully add, "But Foster Dulles won't let us do that." Sometimes the President would recall that it was his understanding, dating back to his time at SHAPE, that after the Europeans had built up their conventional forces, we had planned to withdraw some of our troops. Then he would add teasingly, "But Andy (Goodpaster, his military advisor) tells me that I'm wrong."

Eisenhower's views were one factor Dulles had to deal with as he sought some solution to NATO's nuclear dilemmas. To the degree that the President's desire to scale back the U.S. ground forces in Europe became known to Europeans, it only exacerbated their worries about a reversion to U.S. isolationism. Also, the President's desire to streamline U.S. divisions through the introduction of tactical nuclear weapons, combined with the growing integration of nuclear weapons into NATO strategy and plans, fed the allied desire to take part in the alliance's nuclear defenses, both as a matter of national pride and as a means of insurance against possible U.S. refusal to use its nuclear weapons in the event of a Soviet attack on Europe. Dulles was quite sensitive to these allied concerns and, as I noted earlier, first looked to tactical nuclear weapons as a possible means of taking them into account. As he argued in his 1957 *Foreign Affairs* article:

> So long as collective security depends almost wholly upon the deterrent of retaliatory power and the ability to wreak great destruction upon an aggressor nation, there has to be almost sole dependence upon the United States. . . . However, as nuclear weapons become more tactical in character and thus more adaptable

> to area defense, there will inevitably be a desire on the part of those allies which are technically qualified to participate more directly in this defense and to have a greater assurance that this defensive power will in fact be used. Such factors are already leading to study of a so-called "atomic weapons stockpile" which could be established by the United States in the European NATO area, and, as becomes appropriate, made available to NATO.[17]

This atomic weapons stockpile idea had in fact been pushed since 1956 by NATO SACEUR General Lauris Norstad as the means to address both the political problems arising out of NATO's nuclear strategy as well as to meet the military need to insure the quick provision of nuclear warheads to his forces in an emergency.[18] Limited at first to the stockpiling of warheads for nuclear-capable artillery and NATO air defenses, this stockpile would also in time be tied to a NATO intermediate range ballistic missile (IRBM) force. Norstad would also begin speaking of the possibility and even desirability of making NATO into a nuclear power. Similar ideas and concerns would eventually lead to the concept of a NATO multilateral nuclear force, or MLF, which will be considered in the next chapter.

Dulles came to favor developing some new structure to spread responsibility for nuclear weapons among the NATO powers, involving a greater predelegation of nuclear authority to SACEUR. As he considered such ideas, I think Dulles was sensitive to the fact that the Germans especially had to be given a more responsible role within the alliance and not kept permanently inferior to Britain, whose nuclear weapons program the United States was assisting, and France, which was planning to have its own nuclear program. Such principles of nuclear sharing and equality within NATO would uneasily coexist with British and French national nuclear aspirations, and persistent fears aroused by the prospect of German forces equipped with nuclear weapons. I was in favor of nuclear cooperation within the NATO framework. As to bilateral nuclear cooperation, while I was in favor of the steps taken towards closer cooperation with our wartime nuclear ally the British, I was opposed to helping the French program (France was not a good partner in NATO), and uneasy (as were most Germans) about any German involvement with a national nuclear weapons capacity, even within a NATO framework.

Since Dulles looked to the Policy Planning staff for work on NATO policy, I was drawn into discussions in the State Department and the administration on devising a new concept and framework for U.S. nuclear weapons policy in NATO. A major initiative in this direction occurred at the NATO Heads of Government meeting in Paris on December 16–19, 1957, where the United States agreed to place nuclear warheads and intermediate range ballistic missiles (IRBMs) in Europe at the disposal of SACEUR.[19] In a background paper for this conference which drew heavily on Dulles's thinking, the Policy Planning staff made the following arguments for this plan. First, sharing knowledge about nuclear weapons and war plans with NATO would increase mutual confidence within the alliance. Second, for European NATO countries to have full confidence in the U.S. nuclear security guarantee, it was necessary that the weapons be close at hand and that the Europeans have some control over their use. Third, greater cooperation in nuclear planning would decrease allied fears that nuclear weapons would be used irresponsibly. Fourth, only collective policies would make NATO countries truly secure, especially with the development of long-range ballistic missiles and in the absence of comprehensive arms control agreements–and if NATO countries were part of such collective arrangements, they were more likely to forego developing their own nuclear weapons.[20]

On the eve of this NATO conference, I proposed a new concept to incorporate and advance these principles, fearing as I did that the NATO atomic stockpile idea was a facade for continued U.S. control of alliance nuclear weapons which would not last long. As I noted on December 8, 1957, I conceived the idea of a North Atlantic Community Nuclear Authority, or NACNA.[21] This was an ambitious project, under which the North Atlantic nations would manufacture nuclear weapons on a joint basis, hold them in joint custody, and jointly operate the alliance's nuclear systems. Dulles agreed with this concept, but it failed to generate much interest. As I will detail in the next chapter, NACNA would evolve under Dulles's successor, Herter, into a proposal, first elaborated by Bob

Bowie and then made in December 1960 to the North Atlantic Council, which led to the Multilateral Force concept, or MLF.

The British

A distinctive feature of U.S. policy during this period was the revival of closer Anglo-American nuclear relations following the Suez debacle in 1956. Eisenhower was determined to restore the spirit of cooperation that he felt should mark U.S./British relations, and he found an eager partner in this endeavor in Harold Macmillan, his old wartime friend who became Prime Minister on Anthony Eden's resignation in January 1957.

Helping the British program was made easier by the fact of Anglo-American nuclear cooperation during World War II. The possibility for continuation of this cooperation was cut off by the U.S. Congress, which was ignorant of the wartime joint effort. Anglo-American nuclear cooperation had fallen upon hard times following the series of spy scandals in the late 1940s, and despite amendment of the McMahon Act which authorized the sharing of nuclear weapons information with other governments in 1954, the relationship had not reached the intimacy desired by the British and many on the U.S. side (although not Eisenhower's atomic energy advisor Lewis Strauss). The Joint Committee on Atomic Energy in Congress was a formidable obstacle to any renewal of close cooperation with the British. I can still recall an incident when a British official inadvertently had access to our hydrogen bomb design. Senator Anderson of the JCAE made a point of telling me that we should take a hard line in making clear our unhappiness with the British over this, urging the administration to "rub the cob in hard." Unable to obtain the assistance they desired from the United States, the British had pressed on with their own nuclear weapons program, and by 1957 were planning their first thermonuclear test. There was now a desire in the United States to benefit from any advances and insights the British might have gained in their program, *e.g.*, in the area of instruments for collecting data on nuclear tests[22], which gave new motivation for seeking closer cooperation. Eisenhower believed strongly that the United States should not be stingy with its allies regarding the sharing of information about weapons, and in particular felt the British should be helped, as they had contributed their nuclear technology and radar to defeating the Nazis in World War II.

Dulles agreed. The new course of cooperation was charted when Eisenhower and Macmillan met in Bermuda in March 1957 to survey the wide range of common problems facing the two countries. Agreements were reached in principle for the United States to provide Britain with first-generation IRBMs. In time, the United Kingdom would be free to arm these missiles with their own warheads, but until then they could use U.S. warheads, which would be stored in Britain and released through what became known as a dual-key procedure, under which both governments had to agree before their employment. This meeting was followed by another in October 1957, at which the two sides worked out the details of the IRBM agreement as well as of other agreements to share nuclear weapons technology. My deputy, Phil Farley, and I negotiated this nuclear sharing agreement with Lord Plowden, the head of the U.K. Atomic Energy Authority. Macmillan said the sharing agreement was the most momentous development in Anglo-American relations since the war. Lewis Strauss opposed sharing nuclear weapons information with the British, and at first called for giving London only information that the Soviets already had. I pointed out to Dulles that this would make such an agreement meaningless, and Strauss was overridden by the President.[23]

In July 1958, the United States and Britain signed the new agreements on nuclear weapons cooperation and placement of IRBMs in Britain. Closer nuclear cooperation between the United States and Britain was renewed, including weapons data, special nuclear materials, and nonnuclear components of atomic weapons. To facilitate this closer relation-ship, the McMahon Act was further amended in 1958, with language specifically crafted to meet the needs of the renewed U.S.-British nuclear partnership. I considered this deal so important that I passed up a meeting with the President on other issues to attend the signing. I did not then anticipate that a few years later, these agreements would give rise to new arrangements under President Kennedy which would complicate efforts which I was supporting to promote the MLF in Europe.

The French

Not long after the signing of the new U.S.-British nuclear agreements, de Gaulle, who had returned to power in 1958, visited Washington. France already was well on the way to producing nuclear weapons and wanted equal status with Britain and the United States. There was an intense debate within the U.S. government on the merits of helping the French. Although a few French scientists had participated in the wartime development of atomic weapons, there had not been any Franco-American arrangements such as existed with Britain. There were some, such as Donald Quarles, who thought that French nuclear weapons would be of some benefit to the United States. Dulles was reaching for some arrangement that would convince the French that they did not need to have nuclear weapons. I am not sure that Dulles was clear as to what such a Franco-American arrangement would be, but I believe that he was thinking in terms of some kind of automaticity–a pledge that if France were attacked, its access to U.S. weapons stationed on French soil would not be subject to an American veto.[24] There also was some thought in the administration that we could transfer technology and material for weapons to France, as we had to Britain, if doing so would ease French objections to Britain joining the European Economic Community.

I had objected to helping the French program since that would have made the policy of stopping nuclear proliferation, or spread as we called it then, all the more difficult. Evidence that France contributed to the start-up of the Israeli nuclear weapons program would bear out such fears. As it was, de Gaulle would not accept allowing any other country to have influence over French defense decisions, even if cooperation with the United States would have been rewarded with nuclear assistance as was the case with Britain. De Gaulle flatly told Dulles that he would not allow U.S. weapons to be deployed on French territory. I remember Dulles saying that he felt de Gaulle had not fully appreciated the significance of Dulles's hinting that a sharing arrangement could be made. As John Newhouse observes, de Gaulle saw ideas like interdependence and integration as mere fig leaves for U.S. domination.[25]

About this time the Dutch government showed interest in the United States helping it to develop nuclear-powered submarines. One night when I was cruising in an American submarine I was told the captain had a message for me from Admiral Rickover. As the captain began his report, I interrupted him and said Rickover wanted the captain to tell me not to help the Dutch submarine aspirations. To the captain's surprise that I could surmise Rickover's message, I pointed out that years of working with Rickover led me to know how his mind worked. Several such nuclear submarine cruises (including one from which a 1500-mile missile was test-fired) led me to appreciate what a formidable deterrent the submarine missile fleet was!

The Germans

The existing British nuclear program and the prospective French one underscored the difficulties facing any effort to implement a NATO nuclear authority, if the hope was to avoid the proliferation of new national nuclear weapons systems. The British and French examples also served as warnings for those, including me, who worried about what the future could hold for West Germany and nuclear weapons, if we did not treat Germany on the basis of equality with others. Though West Germany had forsworn the manufacture of nuclear weapons on its territory in the 1954 agreements that paved the way for its admission to NATO, these were no bar, as Dulles once told the British, to Germany obtaining the weapons from another country. For me, the only safe way to address Germany's desire to be treated as an equal with Britain and France would be through participation in some kind of NATO-integrated nuclear force, which would create serious obstacles to Bonn ever using these weapons unilaterally. My concern would have been greater if I had known, as has been revealed by the release of long-classified documents, that Chancellor Adenauer was determined to keep the nuclear option open for Germany.

Moscow viewed these developments with growing alarm. It is no coincidence that the NATO decisions of December 1957 on setting up a NATO atomic stockpile and the provision of the U.S. IRBMs to NATO was quickly followed by the Polish Rapacki Plan, which proposed the creation of a nuclear-free zone in Central Europe. When the United States and its NATO allies refused to be diverted from the decisions they had made, the Soviet leadership, now under Nikita Khrushchev, embarked upon a great gamble in an effort to bring the West to the bargaining table over Germany's fate. Khrushchev's gamble would ride on what he felt was his ace in the hole–the unique and precarious status of West Berlin. In fact the Berlin Crisis of 1958-59 was the last of three crises while I was at Policy Planning which highlighted the dilemmas and dangers of attempting to utilize nuclear weapons in the pursuit of diplomatic objectives.

Nuclear Weapons and Crisis Diplomacy–Lebanon, Quemoy-Matsu, and Berlin

There is a saying: When the only tool you have is a hammer, everything begins to look like a nail. In a similar vein, the progressive integration of nuclear weapons into U.S. strategy and forces created a situation in which political and military crises, be they large or small, came inevitably to involve a nuclear component and so could be viewed as nuclear crises to one degree or another. In the late 1950s, three such crises involved political disorder in Lebanon and the Middle East; renewed tensions with Beijing over the offshore islands Quemoy and Matsu; and finally, Nikita Khrushchev's threat to allied rights in West Berlin. The Berlin Crisis would finally bring Eisenhower and Khrushchev to a personal meeting and a planned summit in 1960, only to have the hopes for an easing of world tensions run aground on yet another combination of technological advances and nuclear fears, as Khrushchev's protests over the U-2 reconnaissance program to monitor Soviet progress in nuclear weapons wrecked the Paris summit.

Lebanon

The spring of 1958 was a particularly troubled time in the Middle East, even for this uniquely troubled region, and events there were causing growing alarm within the Eisenhower White

House. Egyptian leader Gamal Abdel Nasser was continuing to press his campaign of radical Arab nationalism, announcing in January of that year that Egypt and Syria were going to unite to form a new nation, the United Arab Republic. The UAR, under Nasser's leadership, embarked upon a renewed effort to fan the flames of pan-Arab feelings throughout the Middle East against the conservative feudal monarchies of the region, such as Jordan, Iraq, and Saudi Arabia. Added to this political instability was the fact that an arms race was under way in the area, as the United States provided Saudi Arabia, Iraq, and Jordan with military equipment, the Russians took care of Egypt and Syria, while Israel looked to France for much of its needs.[26]

The crisis which would lead to U.S. intervention came in Lebanon and was set off in April 1958 by the decision of the Christian and pro-Western Lebanese President Camille Chamoun to violate political tradition and the constitution by seeking to serve a second term as president. This action provoked Muslim rioting, and soon Christian and Muslim militias were engaged in a de facto civil war in Beirut. A year earlier, Chamoun had asked the United States for military assistance in standing up to an earlier pan-Arab threat to his government, and Eisenhower had taken steps to position Navy and Marine forces to intervene. U.S. intervention had not proved necessary then, but this second time it looked as if the United States might have to go in, and soon. Throughout May and June, the administration debated the risks of military intervention. Eisenhower seemed inclined to accept the necessity of acting, while some in his administration counseled caution in light of the many unknowns and the risk of adverse Arab and Soviet reactions.[27]

Matters finally came to a head in July 1958, when pro-Nasser leftist rebels took over the government of Iraq and assassinated the royal Hashemite family. It was an especially bloody coup with a number of Europeans killed. Despite the lack of clear evidence, Nasser's hand was seen behind the Iraqi coup, as well as behind anti-Western and in particular anti-American outbursts that accompanied the coup. Assistant Secretary of State, Bill Rountree, was sent on a mission to Baghdad to make contact with the new Iraqi government. When he arrived at Cairo en route to Iraq, there were a number of signs at the airport, "Kill Rountree." It was during this turmoil that Chamoun again asked for U.S. aid, as did the Saudi leadership, which warned that if the United States did not act firmly, Saudi Arabia might have to reach an understanding with Nasser.

I was at the White House with the President when the decision was made to intervene. It was the most somber session I had ever attended. The first issue to be settled was the risk of Soviet retaliation. Dulles said this would turn on the Kremlin's assessment of the world power balance. With JCS Chairman Nathan Twining's support, Dulles argued that the United States would be better off acting then than in the future. With his great sensitivity to Eisenhower's views, Dulles still ticked off the likely international critics of U.S. action, but then made the case that the dangers of not acting outweighed any possible risks from acting. After this discussion, Eisenhower, who usually would say nothing to prejudge the outcome of a decision, announced, "We have to make good on our outstanding check." He then added, "Well, I had made up my mind before you fellows started talking." As the President saw it, either the United States had to act or pull out of the Middle East, and this was unthinkable, given the region's immense strategic and economic importance.[28]

With Eisenhower's decision clear, the discussion turned to how to carry it out. Some congressional opposition was encountered, in particular from William Fulbright. Eisenhower took the position that he was informing the congressional leadership of his decision, not soliciting their advice, on the assumption Congress would not openly oppose the President on a matter of such magnitude. In this he was proved correct, and the very next day, July 15, U.S. Marines began landing in Beirut. It was at this point that an unanticipated nuclear complication entered the picture. I learned that the first wave of U.S. forces to land in Beirut had Honest John missiles with nuclear warheads. The Marines had these weapons in their transports. Such artillery was part of the normal support for the new Army "Pentomic" battle groups, and so would also be accompanying the Army airborne units dispatched from Europe to take part in the operation. I thought that putting nuclear weapons into the Middle East was foolish and quite dangerous. In those days the services felt rather naked unless they had nuclear weapons–although the notion that they would be needed to fight revolutionaries in the Middle East seemed silly.

I urged Dulles to talk to the President about removing those weapons. As a result, the nuclear warheads were ordered removed. New instructions went out telling the U.S. commander in Lebanon not to land Honest John launchers en route from Europe to Beirut. It now appears that the JCS had anticipated some questioning about the presence of nuclear weapons in the U.S. landing forces. The Joint Chiefs planned to take the line in response to any questions that these weapons were a normal part of the Pentomic force structure and stress that the Honest Johns were dual-capable (able to deliver both nuclear and high-explosive warheads). The U.S. commanders were to follow established policy in neither confirming nor denying that nuclear warheads actually were with the U.S. forces, and saying that the United States could not foresee any circumstances requiring the use of nuclear weapons in the Lebanese situation. Newly declassified records also reveal that there were actually only eleven experimental high-explosive (nonnuclear) warheads available for the Honest Johns. These were being held by the U.S. Army in Europe, and moreover, General Lauris Norstad, the NATO SACEUR, had first call upon them for a special NATO requirement "of major political importance." Norstad was strongly opposed to releasing them unless there was an overriding political consideration, which he did not see in the Lebanon situation.[29]

When the decision was made to intervene I noted, "No happiness here over this evil choice apparently forced on us as an alternative to quitting the Middle East. Like a funeral." During the crisis, I wrote optimistically in my diary, "We will be in and out of Lebanon in thirty days," and that was about how it worked out. I thought it was a great success that the troops were out so quietly and quickly, and without casualties. Much of this success can be attributed to the deft diplomacy of the U.S. ambassador on the scene, Robert McClintock. Despite his practice of driving around Beirut in his official car with his dog, flouting a strong Arab dislike for canines, he served as an able mediator between the arriving U.S. forces and the local Lebanese military, arranging for a safe landing and transport of the troops into Beirut. Despite the avoidance of local hostilities during the landing, I had never felt so much tension about possible war with the Soviets. After the troops had gone in, I told Dulles that I was glad that week was over. Somewhat to my surprise, he replied, "Don't think I wasn't scared." That was the only time that I heard him use that word. Dulles believed that the Soviet Union was also "scared to death" regarding the Middle East dilemma. They knew they were facing general war or loss of position in the Middle East. This crisis abated after a constructive and conciliatory speech by the President to the United Nations. The Policy Planning staff had a hand in initiating and drafting this important address.

Quemoy and Matsu

Just as the Lebanon crisis was winding down, on August 23 the Chinese Communists resumed bombarding the islands Quemoy and Matsu, replaying their 1955 pressures on Taiwan's Chinese nationalist government which controlled the islands. Dulles announced that the President had full authority to use force to defend the islands, and the U.S. assembled forces in the Formosa Straits, including air and naval units equipped with nuclear weapons.[30] Dulles, apparently as the result of some lobbying by a Pentagon group pressing for more decisive action, expressed interest in the possibility of using tactical nuclear weapons against Communist artillery batteries located near the city of Amoy which were shelling Matsu. My reaction was that the Secretary (and other U.S. political officials) had no real idea of what a tactical nuclear weapon could do: some had yields much larger than the Hiroshima bomb, but the word "tactical" made them sound tolerable and usable.

Bowie later told me that Dulles had entertained similar thoughts during the first Quemoy-Matsu crisis in 1954-55. At this time, Bowie had arranged a briefing for Dulles underlining the high civilian casualties expected from any use of tactical nuclear weapons on Communist Chinese military positions. Hoping to bring these same points home to the Secretary, I asked Dulles if he would sit through a briefing by nuclear weapons experts before any decisions were made. He agreed. After the nuclear weapons experts went through the plans to take out with tactical nuclear weapons the

Communist batteries, I asked for their civilian casualty estimates. Their answer was around "one hundred and eighty-six thousand Chinese." I don't recall Dulles mentioning using tactical nuclear weapons again.

The Second Berlin Crisis

Hard on the heels of the second Quemoy-Matsu crisis came the opening of the second Berlin Crisis. The divided city of Berlin, the former capital of Germany, had been jointly occupied by the United States, Britain, France, and the Soviet Union since the end of World War II. Deep in the heart of occupied East Germany, Berlin was destined to be a flashpoint in the Cold War, both for its unique geographic and diplomatic status as well as a symbol of the great unresolved issue of the war–the problem of Germany's future. In 1948-49, Joseph Stalin had tried to use West Berlin's vulnerability to put pressure on the West to abandon its plans to merge the three Western occupation zones into a new West German state, but had been forced to relent in the face of the West's determined response to his blockade of this democratic oasis within the Soviet zone. Still, this anomaly in the heart of the Kremlin's main East European satellite remained a bone in the throat of the Soviet leadership. It was also one of the persistent dilemmas for the Western alliance, especially after 1954 and NATO's adoption of an avowed strategy of nuclear defense–how, with such a strategy, could and should the West respond to a renewed Soviet assault upon Western rights in West Berlin? Were these rights so crucial as to warrant risking nuclear war to protect them?

These questions moved from the realm of speculation to urgent reality when, on November 27, 1958, Khrushchev issued an ultimatum to the West demanding a treaty within six months that would redefine the status of West Berlin (that is, for the NATO allies to agree to East Germany taking over West Berlin), and threatening that if such a treaty were not signed, the Soviet Union would make its own arrangements with East Germany in six months. There has been much historical speculation about Khrushchev's motives, but only recently have formerly classified records shed light on this question as well as on the Western allies' response.[31] McGeorge Bundy's recent analysis of Khrushchev's motivations is compelling–that the Soviet leader, having decided that neither side in the Cold War wanted a nuclear war, was convinced there must be some political advantage to be secured through brandishing the threat of such a war. As Bundy and others, such as Robert Bowie, have argued, Khrushchev found in the Berlin Crisis a situation allowing him to ratchet up and down tensions in an effort to secure Western recognition of the East German regime. Also persuasive is the argument, advanced most forcefully by Marc Trachtenberg, that Khrushchev was driven as well by Soviet concern that the recent U.S. moves within NATO to share nuclear weapons would inevitably lead to the West German Bundeswehr being armed with nuclear weapons.[32]

I thought at the time that we might go to war should Khrushchev carry out his ultimatum. Some of my colleagues at State seemed ready for this step–Bob Murphy, for example, said we should send a division up the Autobahn and see what the Soviets thought about that. Eisenhower was determined to stand firm upon allied rights in Berlin, and was on the record as saying he was prepared to go to war if need be to safeguard them, but he was equally determined to make sure matters did not come to that point. Dulles's response to Khrushchev was that the West would not negotiate under threat, and at the December 1958 NATO ministerial meeting he persuaded the allies to endorse that theme without any ambiguity and with complete confidence. He accomplished this in great part by assuring the NATO ministers that the United States still had undeniable nuclear superiority over the Soviets should war come. Dulles was emphatic about the need for Western unity in response to this threat. He believed this would have a strong psychological impact on the Soviets, who were equally determined to provoke hesitancy and division within the Western ranks. Both he and Eisenhower were agreed on the need especially to protect the U.S. investment in West Germany, which was seen as pivotal to overall U.S. and Western plans and hopes for Western Europe.

Dulles's marshalling of the alliance's ranks at the end of 1958 was a courageous performance, not only because of the threat to the

West, but also because Dulles's health was bad. He looked ashen and was shaky; he had to sleep on a board and was not getting much rest. Still, he continued on schedule, travelling in late January 1959 to Paris, Bonn, and London to shore up the allies' resolve.[33] In February, he was diagnosed as having a recurrence of the abdominal cancer which had struck him during the Suez Crisis of 1956. He was given only a few months to live.

These last months would prove to be particularly depressing for Dulles, for his successes at the NATO meeting in December 1958 were a high point of sorts for allied unity, to be followed by the emergence of strains and divisions between the United States, Britain, France and West Germany on the proper policies to pursue in response to Khrushchev's threat. As he neared the end of his days, Dulles grew increasingly despondent over the fate of the alliance, fearing that only the United States had the will to make a strong stand against Soviet threats to Western rights in Berlin. Toward the end as I visited him at Walter Reed Hospital, Dulles was worried about the Berlin situation and preoccupied with how successor statesmen would respond to Soviet challenges. He hoped that they would be as "stout" as his generation, but his fear they would not was obvious. He was particularly worried about the future of British-American relations, given the widespread perception that Macmillan's government was inclined to pursue appeasement of the Soviets. During my visit with Dulles at Walter Reed (where, by tragic coincidence, General George Marshall also lay dying in a nearby room), he observed that "the last time the Soviets had to pay a price to have a summit meeting; this time we have to pay a price." This statement foreshadowed Eisenhower's invitation to Khrushchev later that year to visit the United States and meet at Camp David.

His powers waning as he waged his final battle, Dulles finally resigned in April 1959, and Under Secretary Christian Herter, who had been serving as Acting Secretary for several months, became Secretary. I was part of the U.S. delegation to the Geneva conference on Berlin with Britain, France and the Soviet Union. It was in the middle of this conference that Dulles died on May 24. He was buried on May 27, ironically the date of the expiration of Khrushchev's six-month ultimatum. A number of us flew back from

Geneva for the funeral. Herter invited Soviet Foreign Minister Gromyko to ride in his plane, which I took as a sign that relations between the two superpowers were not as bad as some thought. The funeral jammed Washington's National Cathedral. When the front of the cortege entered Arlington Cemetery, it was reported that some cars had not yet left the Cathedral grounds. After the service, Senator Wiley was quoted as saying of Dulles, "He's off on another great adventure!" A year later, the Senate of Berlin decided to honor Dulles by naming a Berlin street "John Foster Dulles Allee." While riding with Dulles's sister, Eleanor, to the dedication, I asked her what the masses of people lining the street were chanting. She said, "Where but for you [Dulles] would we be?" Eleanor Dulles's own expertise was considerable on problems involving Berlin, and her range of personal intelligence contacts within Germany was large. Dulles himself used to tease her by saying that she had even penetrated the Berlin Senate.

The pressing problems of diplomacy could not stop for long even for the passing of such an important world figure as John Foster Dulles, and I was soon thrown back into the complicated diplomacy of the Berlin Crisis. The Policy Planning staff had been involved in the administration's policy debates from the very start of the crisis in late 1958. My participation took on a variety of roles. For example, I would be involved in joint State-JCS meetings on the crisis to coordinate policy between Foggy Bottom and the Pentagon. I was also involved in numerous meetings devoted to contingency planning, in which a wide range of scenarios for possible Western responses if Khrushchev carried through on his ultimatum were designed and debated.[34]

Looking back through the available records dealing with the Berlin Crisis, I see that an early concern was that the United States was assuming a peculiar posture, given the unfortunate congruence of this crisis and the pressures for budget cuts in our defense spending on nonnuclear forces. My diary reveals my worry that Dulles's ill health was removing a much-needed strong voice of authority from the table as the NSC debated national security policy. I tried to impress upon Herter the need to avoid any cuts in our limited war forces. Still, I was forced to note during an NSC meeting in early December that it was "sad the United States can't afford enough for a real army."[35]

Another concern of mine was the need for the United States to make sure the public understood what was at stake in the dispute with the Soviet Union. I feared that the stakes in this crisis might appear ambiguous to the public, in contrast to the dramatic situation in 1948 when Stalin imposed a blockade on Western access to West Berlin. I argued that the United States and its allies had to make their case clearly to the public, and at one point stressed the desirability of having television coverage of any Western effort to exercise allied rights in Berlin should the Soviets and East Germany take steps prejudicing these rights.[36]

My desire to assure strong public support for the West's position was joined by an equally strong wish to bring some flexibility into the West's negotiating position in order to avoid a dangerous deadlock, together with worries over the impact the crisis was having on the cohesion of the Atlantic alliance, a crucial component of the West's diplomacy that Dulles had struggled so hard to sustain. To bring such flexibility into the negotiations, I endorsed the idea of proposing a "guaranteed city" status for Berlin. Eisenhower himself at one point considered a variant of this idea, involving a U.N. guarantee of the city's status. The idea which I developed in Policy Planning would have "involved the substitution of [a] Four Power guarantee of Western civil and military access [to Berlin] for the Allies' juridical status [derived from the situation at war's end], with the West Berlin government free to invite the Allies to maintain garrisons up to some agreed levels." Apparently this idea was viewed with a certain degree of skepticism by our allies, particularly the British, as they felt that the Soviets would never accept any arrangement which permitted the United States and its allies to maintain military forces in Berlin.[37]

I laid out my apprehensions over the general European situation during the Berlin Crisis in a memorandum for Secretary Herter in June 1959. I sought to underline the "portentous events" occurring in the Western alliance as the Geneva conference on Berlin was taking place: West Germany was in the throes of its worst postwar political upheaval, putting at risk the future of Adenauer, who himself remained deeply suspicious of allied firmness in the face of

Khrushchev's threat; France under de Gaulle was "brazenly" moving away from NATO; and Macmillan's government in London was taking a position inconsistent with that of the United States in regard to the most pressing political issue of the day–the potential risks and benefits of a summit meeting with the Soviets to address the Berlin Crisis and other important East-West issues. I found that, like Dulles in his final days, I was becoming increasingly worried about the future of the so-called "special relationship" with Britain should these policy differences persist and deepen. I suggested to Herter that, from the Soviet viewpoint, the cumulative impact of these developments might be much more important than the present Geneva talks. The risk existed, I argued, that the Berlin crisis might later be remembered not for the specific dispute over the status of the city, but because it changed Anglo-American relations for the worse, led the United States to begin a military withdrawal from France, and marked the beginning of the end for Moscow's most determined foe in Europe, Adenauer. Recommending that Herter and Eisenhower have some heart-to-heart talks with allied leaders in London, Paris and Bonn, I concluded by stating, "It seems to me that we are at a crossroads in American postwar policy towards Europe."[38]

The Geneva Foreign Ministers meetings took place between May 11 and June 20, then resumed on July 13 and lasted until August 5. The importance of this conference was reflected in the composition of the U.S. delegation: Secretary Herter; Bob Murphy, the Undersecretary; Fred Rinehart, the Counselor; Loftus Becker, the Legal Advisor; Fran Wilcox, the Assistant Secretary for U.N. affairs; Jack Irwin, the Assistant Secretary of Defense for International Security Affairs; Bill Bundy from CIA; and myself, as well as a full quota of German and Berlin experts. Henry Owen accompanied me and wrote many of Herter's statements. Henry's enthusiasm and morale kept many of us cheerful during the very bleak days of that conference. With Herter heading up the delegation, the U.S. office in Geneva became something of a mini-State Department, as we had to deal with a range of other urgent foreign policy matters in addition to the Berlin situation. The change of pace from Dulles to Herter was marked. Delegation luncheons were easygoing, and Bill Bundy opened the daily intelligence briefings by reporting baseball scores, making sure always to report on the results of Boston Red Sox games (Herter having been governor of Massachusetts).

In trying to reconstruct my feelings on the chances for success in these talks, I have come across an entry in David Bruce's diaries that indicates I was less than sanguine about the prospects. According to Bruce, in May 1959, I agreed with Livingston Merchant and Fred Reinhart, two State Department colleagues, that the West could not get a standstill agreement from Khrushchev on Berlin as the price for a summit conference, for if the United States asked for this, the Soviets would immediately bring up the issue of reciprocal U.S. undertakings to stop high altitude intelligence flights over the Soviet Union, to postpone arming the Bundeswehr with nuclear weapons, etc. As Bruce saw it, we believed the United States could only hope to maintain the status quo in Berlin without any formal engagement from Khrushchev, with the expectation it would not be upset while negotiations were in progress. For his part, Bruce could not agree with this minimalist approach.[39]

As it was, the Geneva talks failed to resolve the stalemate over Berlin, but in August a new U.S. initiative produced hopes of breaking this logjam. Eisenhower announced that he and Khrushchev had agreed to visit each other's countries, a move that took the steam out of Khrushchev's threats and brought a welcome reduction in the level of tension.

This new U.S. initiative led to the meetings between Eisenhower and Khrushchev at Camp David and preparations for a formal summit meeting in 1960. The hopes engendered by these moves towards negotiation would be dashed, however, not by a resurgence of tensions over Berlin, but because of a new crisis which erupted from our efforts to keep track of Soviet nuclear weapons advances. By a strange twist of fate, what would later prove to be a key means of monitoring arms control agreements–verification by overflights (although in space)–would undermine the hopes, which I shared, that the summit might provide the occasion for important advances in arms control.

Arms Control

During my tenure in Policy Planning, my responsibilities with regard to arms control continued and were shared with my friend, Phil Farley, who succeeded me in the Special Assistant, Atomic Energy (S/AE) job. Previously, as Special Assistant or Atomic Energy (S/AE), I had worked extensively on disarmament and arms control issues, devoting as much as ninety percent of my time to that important subject by mid-1957. I undertook with Dulles to develop U.S. positions for the London Disarmament conference on a full range of nuclear and conventional questions. In fact, many of the State Department's most innovative ideas, and a large portion of its accomplishments in the atomic field, can be attributed to Farley. Phil, however, was and continues to be one of the most modest men I have ever met, and he never wanted (and seldom received) adequate credit for his contributions to U.S. security.

In general during Eisenhower's second term, the administration became more serious about arms control as opposed to earlier vague and broad notions about general and complete disarmament. In large part, because of the President's active interest and involvement, arms control for the first time became an actual component of national security decision making, and the nuclear test ban became the first real litmus test of whether Washington could negotiate seriously with the Soviets. During this critical time, Farley and I continued the education of Dulles and of ourselves on these matters, and the Secretary continued his evolution, in the words of the historians Richard Hewlett and Jack Holl, toward being Eisenhower's "most dependable disarmament champion."[40]

Inside the government, the Pentagon and AEC continued to flatly oppose a test ban and remained highly skeptical about *any* arms control. Dulles had a healthy respect for both Strauss and the uniformed military, although he knew he was the intellectual superior of any military man in government (and they knew this as well). He did not like to step on toes or go outside the purview of his own department, but–with our help from below and Eisenhower's from above–he challenged both Strauss and the JCS on this matter. The new President's Science Advisory Committee

(PSAC), created in the immediate aftermath of Sputnik, would also have an influence on Dulles's evolving thinking on arms control.

Dulles never gave up the belief that armaments themselves did not cause tension, but governments and people did. He continued to be extremely cautious about the Soviets. I remember that he was fond of repeating Lenin's statement that "promises are like pie crusts–made to be broken."[41] He used this phrase as an example of how untrustworthy communist leaders could be, even after Ambassador Charles "Chip" Bohlen pointed out to him that Lenin in fact had been referring to agreements between party factions. The only way for the West to deal with such a regime was from a position of unshakable determination and commitment to defend its rights and principles. As I mentioned earlier, Dulles would worry until the day of his death that the next generation of Western statesmen would not be as "stout" as he had been in dealing with the Soviets, whom he believed had respected him because they knew he *was* willing to fight *in extremis*.

To be strong was one thing. But prodded by his staff, Dulles also came to see the merit of pursuing areas of possible agreement with the Kremlin, fearing the consequences if the United States should become increasingly isolated on this issue. Ultimately, he rested his support for arms control in general and a test ban in particular on that basis. In an April 1958 meeting with his newly appointed disarmament advisors–General Walter Bedell Smith, General Alfred Gruenther, Robert Lovett and John J. McCloy–that both Farley and I attended, Dulles asked what for him was the critical question: "Do we want further refinement of nuclear weapons at the cost of moral isolation of the United States?"[42]

Ironically, Sputnik had an indirect but nonetheless key salutary effect upon this evolution in Dulles's thinking. We could provide Dulles with the necessary political and strategic background on arms control issues, but to support a specific measure such as the test ban, the Secretary required the type of technical expertise that only scientists could provide. Because of Sputnik, this expertise was brought into the policy arena in the form of the President's Science Advisory Committee (PSAC) and the new Special Assistant for Science and Technology. Unlike Strauss and the government scientists at the weapons labs, this prestigious group included many who had begun to think less about technological solutions to the security dilemma and more about arms control. As MIT President James R. Killian, named by Eisenhower as the first Special Assistant, later recalled, "PSAC felt strongly about the futility of trying to achieve additional security by the unlimited pursuit of weapons technology."[43] When asked to examine the test ban problem, Killian and PSAC concluded that a test cessation would be in the U.S. national interest and that it could be monitored. It was on the strength of PSAC's advice that Dulles could confidently state that the time was right to take the risk of a test ban as an "opening wedge" in the disarmament field.[44]

I, too, began to see the issue of arms control in a broader context during the period 1957-60. Taking my cue first from Bowie, then later from Farley, Owen, and other arms controllers within the administration, I moved beyond thinking about the question simply from a psychological or public relations point of view. I do not specifically remember having major concerns about the dangers from fallout, nor do I remember the growing worldwide concern about this danger as a motivation for my interest in a test ban. Of the various dimensions of arms control–quantity, quality, use, and spread–I came to the conclusion that the number of weapons was less important than their nature, and that the most important need of all was to control the number of possessing nations.

On nuclear testing in particular, I started to believe that getting a headlock on that problem would be a significant first step in regulating the East-West confrontation and in helping to stop the spread of nuclear weapons. I thought then–and still do–that you cannot have a serious nonproliferation policy and at the same time continue to test weapons. Self-control is in fact the essence of nonproliferation. It has been extremely difficult to get that point across, however. In the 1950s, the administration could never seem to make up its mind about a test ban or nuclear sharing with our allies. We vacillated with France, for example. As mentioned earlier, I objected to helping the French program, but others in the government, such as Under Secretary of State for Economic Affairs Douglas Dillon, a former ambassador to France, did not. Even Secretary Dulles took a somewhat selective approach to the problem, talking not about nonproliferation generally but about the need to prevent the "promiscuous" spread of nuclear weapons to "irresponsible" nations.[45] Later, the United States would adopt a clear double standard with regard to Israel, sharing technology and maintaining a conspiracy of silence about the Israeli program. Today, some continue to argue for a policy aimed at "irresponsible" proliferators only. I continue to believe that trying to "manage" nuclear spread in this way is a misguided and counterproductive idea.[46]

In addition to the test ban, I became involved in two other specific issues during 1958 that related to U.S. policy on the control of armaments. In February, I consulted with James Killian, Eisenhower's science advisor, about organizing U.S. space efforts, and in the summer, I took part in the deliberations of an Interagency Working Group on the surprise attack problem. Killian and the PSAC produced a set of recommendations on the U.S. space program that Eisenhower incorporated in a public report, *Introduction to Outer Space*, released on March 26. This report, in my opinion one of the key documents of the space age, has withstood the test of time remarkably well. It stressed the civilian exploration of space. One of its central points was that space should not become a "future theater of war," and that military uses should be restricted to communications, reconnaissance, and meteorology.[47]

In July 1958, Secretary Dulles asked Killian and PSAC to examine the scientific and technical aspects of the surprise attack problem. At the same time, I became involved with the Interagency Working Group on Surprise Attack, chaired by George Kistiakowsky of PSAC (who the next year would succeed Killian as White House science advisor). The Working Group and the State Department subsequently became involved in a clash over the terms of reference for the upcoming talks with the Soviets at the Surprise Attack Conference. Led by Farley, Owen, and Lawrence Weiler, another arms control veteran, State took the position that to be meaningful the discussions should be broad-ranging. The U.S. delegation should have authority to talk about not only techniques of inspection but also actual limits or controls on readiness and forces as a way to lessen the chances for surprise attack. The JCS dissented, saying that the meetings should be restricted to methods of inspection and surveillance. Ultimately, the JCS view prevailed, and the conference, which met for only six weeks in late 1958, produced no substantive results.[48] The arrival of U.S. Air Force commanders in their huge Stratofortresses at the air field in Geneva was likely only seen by the Soviets as a blatant show of American power, As I commented later, the conference was something of a "circus" and had been undermined by the interest of both sides in obtaining a propaganda advantage.[49]

Secretary Herter and Summit Diplomacy: Camp David and Paris

In 1959-60, the Policy Planning staff took a leading role in helping to prepare the President for a summit conference with his Soviet counterpart, Khrushchev. Policy Planning had already been thinking about summit preparations for some time. There was general interest in the possibility of a summit, as seen in the Cosmos Club seminar on the topic which I attended in February 1958. Here, I spoke on possible disarmament agreements that might emerge from a summit, in a way which I noted seemed not to impress Dean Acheson. The other participants ran the gamut: Hubert Humphrey was windy; Dean Rusk was very sound; Nitze was very brief; Senator John Sherman Cooper was quite sage.

Finally, after the intrusion of the crises in Lebanon, Taiwan and Berlin, the summit process got back on track in late 1959, as I have related. By this time, Chris Herter was firmly in place as Secretary of State after Dulles's death. Herter was a great contrast to Dulles. Dulles was admired, but not liked by many people. Herter was a charming man–human, sincere, and self-deprecating. Despite these personal attributes and the fact that he did acquit himself well as Secretary, some felt he was out of his depth. I remember even Dulles once saying to me, "Did you ever notice that every time we send Chris over to the Pentagon to get something done, we lose." This was an extraordinary disclosure to make to an assistant. Still, when Dulles was dying, I heard he told Eisenhower that Herter would never understand it if he was bypassed for the Secretary's job, and so the President after some delay appointed him. One of my colleagues later told me that Herter felt deeply wounded by the delay in his appointment.

When Herter took over I offered my resignation, but the new Secretary refused, saying that the best thinking in the State Department was coming out of the Policy Planning staff. Herter was inclined to be more liberal than Dulles on most issues, although he did not initiate any major policy changes. This was especially true in the arms control and disarmament field. Herter summarized his personal thoughts on disarmament in a memo to Eisenhower shortly after he became Secretary in July 1959. "[I]n my judgment," he wrote, "the implications of the arms race are so grave as to give both sides powerful inducement to stop it." Even "slow progress could spell the difference between doom and survival."[50] By September, he even thought that the Pentagon would accept some form of nuclear disarmament. I noted in my diary, "I doubt it!"[51]

In laying the groundwork for the 1959 Eisenhower-Khrushchev meeting at Camp David and the ill-fated 1960 Four Power summit at Paris, it was easier to work with Herter than it would have been with Dulles. Although his views on arms control evolved greatly, as I have tried to emphasize, Dulles never liked summit diplomacy as a method of carrying out business with the communists. He believed summit conferences should only follow long and careful preparations and negotiations at lower levels. Both privately and publicly, he repeatedly cautioned that the "spectacle" of a summit could produce unexpected and unwarranted results, and could be used by the Soviets for propaganda purposes and to divide us from our allies. In fact, I think Dulles felt a little lonely in his last two years, as most of us in State gradually adopted a more flexible attitude regarding the value and utility of summit meetings.[52]

The Policy Planning staff tried to stress the opportunities rather than the problems presented by Khrushchev's visit to the United States in September 1959. No one thought that major breakthroughs could be made on the most contentious political issues, such as Germany and Berlin. We did believe, however, that there had been a steady evolution in the Soviet leadership's outlook on war and peace issues. We tried to convey the message to Eisenhower that while the Soviets had not suddenly changed from devils to angels, they nonetheless had apparently learned the nuclear facts of life. Like U.S. officials, they also seemed worried about the devastation of nuclear war, the economic burdens of the arms race, and, perhaps most important, the spread of nuclear weapons around their borders. Thus, a few days before Khrushchev and his entourage arrived, I proposed that our basic objective should be to impress upon the Soviet leader "the urgent reality of the danger of nuclear devastation and the need for placing certain limits upon our competition."[53] And while the Camp David conversations centered primarily on Berlin, the two leaders did agree that arms limitation was the "most important problem" facing the international community.[54]

As newspapers hailed the "spirit of Camp David," the Policy Planning staff found itself in early 1960 preparing for another summit. We again believed that little could be accomplished with regard to Berlin at such a meeting, but we had higher expectations about getting down to specifics on arms control, in particular moving the test ban negotiations forward. On February 18, 1960, Secretary Herter gave a major address on "National Security with Arms Limitation" before Washington's National Press Club. Prepared by the Planning staff, Herter's speech summarized what we hoped to achieve with arms control. The speech first argued that arms limitation was an integral aspect of national security planning, and in fact complemented "national security programs." It emphasized two "new dangers" of the arms race: (1) the U.S.-Soviet "spiraling competition" and (2) the consequent proliferating production of nuclear weapons. Finally, moving from the general to the specific, it concluded that a test ban, with proper international controls, "would be a useful step toward the goal of halting the proliferation of national nuclear weapons stockpiles."[55] Whatever hopes we had, however, were dashed in May by the Soviet shoot down of the U-2 spy plane and capture of its pilot, Gary Powers.

In late April 1960, I left Washington with Herter for meetings in London, Tehran, Istanbul, and Athens. My private jotting at the time reflect a more relaxed atmosphere, likely born both of the hopes engendered by the upcoming summit and Herter's more easygoing style. As I noted regarding our visit to Athens in May, "So much more easygoing than in Dulles's days—working dinners become bridge games—unpleasant decisions are put under the rug—life isn't as serious, and the future is looked at less—words are mouthed instead of thoughts . . . the cutting edge is duller, though the charm much thicker."[56]

These placid reflections were interrupted while we were in Istanbul, when word came that the Soviets had shot down the U-2. We had known that this would happen someday. But I also knew that the reconnaissance pictures we had been studying for several years had been extremely useful and worth the risk. We returned to Athens, where we stayed overnight. The next morning, Herter reported that he had finally gotten to bed at about 2:00 a.m. He then had received a call from the Queen of Greece offering advice on how to handle the U-2 matter! On the plane back to the United States, Herter ordered me to coordinate a position for the inevitable congressional investigation of the affair. Livingston Merchant and I spent the entire trip to Washington trying to develop a persuasive case for the U-2 flights.

The summit meeting was still scheduled to take place on May 16. Flying to Paris in the backwash of the U-2 shoot down, we had little hope of finding a negotiating atmosphere. This was particularly frustrating. After months of pinpoint planning, we felt we were exactly where we had started the autumn before, especially on arms control issues. On May 15, with delegations from the United States, Soviet Union, France, and Britain assembled in Paris, Khrushchev issued a six-page ultimatum demanding that Washington apologize for its past provocations, punish the responsible officials, and pledge not to commit such acts in the future. In addition, he demanded that all the parties present pledge not to violate each other's sovereignty. If these conditions were not met, Khrushchev threatened to break off the summit.[57] That night I had dinner with Chip Bohlen and Llewellyn "Tommy" Thompson, two of our veteran Kremlin experts. They read Khrushchev's ultimatum and were trying to decide on advice for Eisenhower—whether to attend the meeting at all or break it off before Khrushchev did. I tried to duck the question, saying that they were the Soviet experts, but when they pressed me, I voted (as they did) for Eisenhower to go through with the planned meeting. He had little choice.

The opening day of the conference left no doubt that we would get nowhere. Khrushchev blasted the President for the U-2 flights. Eisenhower seemed to take his tongue-lashing fairly coolly. I waited in the garden of the Elysee Palace until the session broke up, and then hurried back to the U.S. Embassy on the Place de Jena. I was standing at the bar when the bartender said, "If you don't want to get run over, you'd better move." Eisenhower was bearing down with his mind set on a gin and tonic. His first words were, "You might have thought we'd done a Hungary!" (A reference to the brutal Soviet action in Hungary in 1956.)

When we returned to Washington after the abortive summit meeting, Herter, Undersecretary of State Dillon, and Chip Bohlen testified on the U-2 incident and the summit before the Senate Foreign Relations Committee. Herter gave a good account of himself and the department. The hearing in fact was surprisingly bland, with Republicans and Democrats reluctant to attack the U-2 program. Chairman J.W. Fulbright offered some relatively minor criticism based on Eisenhower assuming responsibility for an act of espionage. But Fulbright also said that he had been humiliated by the U-2 revelations.[58] Contrary to this view, I urged Herter to stress the great national security success of the U-2 flights, which had enabled us to keep close track on the buildup of Soviet ballistic missiles. This he did. "The U-2 program was an important and efficient intelligence effort," he told the committee. "[W]e considered that the great benefit derived [in intelligence information] justified the risks involved."[59] Still, the shoot down had to be considered a disaster from the point of view of diplomacy.

After the Paris summit, I prepared a press report to the nation on the meeting and "flesh[ed] out the problem in the face of expected Soviet moves in the U.N. Security Council." I suggested a study be given to the idea that the United States submit to a U.N.-mandated outer space regime, even if the Soviets refused to participate. As far as I know, this idea did not receive study, but Eisenhower apparently approved it, for it resurfaced in Eisenhower's address (which I drafted, drawing in many instances upon ideas of Henry Owen) to the opening session of the U.N. General Assembly on September 22. In this speech, Eisenhower offered American cooperation in demilitarizing space efforts. As

Eisenhower stated, the U.N. members should agree that "'subject to appropriate verification . . . no nation will put into orbit or station in outer space weapons of mass destruction'; and that 'all launchings of spacecraft should be verified in advance by the United Nations.'"[60] The speech was a success, but unfortunately the U.N. meeting was marred by the spectacle of Khrushchev's splenetic harangue to the General Assembly, which I happily missed due to a doctor's appointment.

Last Days with the Eisenhower Administration

During 1960, at the urging of Henry Owen, I made one other proposal in the arms control field that today would be considered in the realm of so-called confidence-building measures. This was the hotline, a direct communications link between Washington and Moscow which we thought would be useful in times of crisis to reduce the possibility of miscalculation by either side. I was told that Ambassador Merchant objected (I never heard on what grounds), and the idea was dropped. During the Kennedy administration, however, Owen revived the idea, working with Walt Rostow, one of my successors as head of Policy Planning. On July 30, 1963, Kennedy wrote to me:

> I want you to know how pleased I am over the conclusion on June 30th, 1963 of the communications link agreement with the U.S.S.R. Such a practical step toward reducing the causes of nuclear war is bound to serve our national interests as well as those of all mankind. You should be gratified by this happy result of the idea that you first proposed five years ago and which you and your other colleagues in the Policy Planning Council of the State Department have persistently advanced, on appropriate occasions, since that time. I congratulate you on making the original contribution and on the part you played in bringing your concept to successful fruition.

The hotline proved useful especially during the Arab-Israeli war in 1973, and more recently was modernized by the addition of satellite communications circuits and high-speed facsimile capabilities.[61]

Some years later, the publisher of *Parade* magazine called in great heat after reading about my alleged claim to authorship of the hotline concept, which he claimed to have first proposed in his magazine. I pointed out that there was enough credit for us both, and that the matter had been floated in official circles at the same time or before he had published it. When he said he had received a letter of commendation from President Kennedy, I referred to my similar missive, and the call ended on a more relaxed note.

As is usually the case, foreign policy became caught up in politics in 1960 as the presidential campaign moved into high gear, and John Kennedy made the administration's foreign policy record a key element in his bid for the presidency. I had some tangential connection with the Republican campaign, drafting two speeches for Nixon, one of which dealt with the space accomplishments of the U.S. program under Eisenhower. After Nixon lost the election to Kennedy in 1960, I submitted my resignation to President Eisenhower. Late in 1960, I wrote a foreign policy report to accompany Herter's resignation. I met with Eisenhower on November 17 in Augusta, Georgia. He was wearing the golf club's green jacket, and he referred to Kennedy as that "arrogant, self-confident young man." We also dined with the Nixons at Herter's house, where I heard Pat Nixon say that her husband had been defeated by the blacks and Jews and Catholics. I was tempted to expostulate, but I kept my mouth shut. Hers was not an easy life. May she rest in peace.

That same evening, one of the other dinner guests was Gordon Grayson. I told a favorite story of Lewis Strauss about an official returning from World War I who, getting off the train at a station in Virginia, was met by an old family retainer. On the way to his plantation, the following conversation occurred: "George, I've been away a long time." "Yes sir." "I have worked with President Wilson and Poincaré and Lloyd George and a number of other great statesmen." "Yes sir." "What do the people down here say when they hear about all these great things I've been doing." "Oh, they just laugh." On hearing this story, Grayson quietly said, "Yes, that was my father."

When the 1950s began, I was a neophyte in the arcane affairs of nuclear weapons and diplomacy. The subsequent decade had brought me into ever closer involvement with these issues, experiences which had served to strengthen my developing views and convictions on the relationship between nuclear weapons and national security. During my years at Policy Planning, the United States was in many ways on the defensive in the face of Sputnik, Berlin, China, and pressures to end nuclear testing. At points, we seemed on the brink of disaster. As I noted in my diary at the end of 1958, "We looked down the gun barrel several times . . ." during that year. While few really thought that we were nearing the end, a realization that nuclear warfare might be the terminal point for mankind began to spread. Dulles himself pointed out once that nuclear war might end all life in the northern hemisphere, an observation Eisenhower also made. Throughout the turmoil, I believe that we managed some significant accomplishments. Most important, the Policy Planning staff led the way to a major reconsideration of strategic nuclear policy, moving away from massive retaliation and toward greater reliance on conventional forces. In so doing, we helped establish a foundation in arms control that would produce significant agreements in later years.

These years had taken their toll on me. I find that as early 1958, I was confiding to my diary that I was increasingly frustrated by my disagreements with official policy, and wondering if it was possible to change policy without the impetus provided by a crisis. Much of the excitement and attraction of attending foreign conferences had also diminished. On a more personal note, I knew that my wife Bernice was somewhat bored with government life and the way in which the demands of my career ruled my schedule and tied us down. So, in 1961 at the end of the second Eisenhower administration, I could look back at the previous decade with a sense of accomplishment mixed with the desire to move on to new challenges. When I left the Policy Planning staff in January 1961, on a cold winter's day, I faced, for the first time in over a decade, the unusual prospect of a future life outside the government. This hiatus was to prove remarkably short.

Chapter Four

Alliance Diplomacy and the NATO Multilateral Force

Academic Interlude

On January 19, 1961, I departed the State Department for what I thought was the last time. As I walked home through the snow, I wondered what to do next. Including more than four years in the Navy, I had served some fourteen years in government. While I was quite sure that these years had been more productive than practicing law in New York, my interest in more government service was no longer keen.

As an interim move, I accepted an offer from Francis Wilcox, former Assistant Secretary of State for International Organizations, to establish a new base in Washington. He was the Dean of the School for Advanced International Studies of Johns Hopkins University (SAIS). Fran had been with us on the Geneva delegation for the Berlin negotiations in 1959. He was the most idealistic–in the best sense of the word–officer with whom I had ever worked. Also at SAIS was Herter, who with Paul Nitze had helped found SAIS. Having such a *pied-à-terre* in one of Washington's major policy institutions would allow me to pursue a continuing interest in foreign policy, in a more relaxed manner than my days at the State Department, and to continue my education, especially by engaging in discussions with some preeminent scholars in the field. After some months of working in this academic atmosphere and attending meetings of the Research Center, I decided to have an office of my own and invited Chris Herter to join me. We had a happy relationship for several years. I continued my interest in SAIS for many years, later serving on its Advisory Council.

When Kennedy was elected, it was obvious that he wanted quickly to put his brand upon policy. I was clearly linked to the foreign policy of Dulles and Herter, which Kennedy had sharply criticized in the election campaign, and so I had no expectation of working for the new administration. I did note, however, that Kennedy's foreign policy speeches bore a similarity to views which the Policy Planning staff had promoted without much success. I had good friends who remained in government, such as Henry Owen and Phil Farley, with whom I kept in touch. Contrary to my expectations, I was soon asked to serve as a consultant to the new administration, making my "retirement" from government service rather short-lived. These new duties would thrust me back into the familiar tangle of issues and problems surrounding U.S. nuclear weapons policy. The bulk of my time would be spent in the trenches fighting for a new NATO nuclear force to solve the alliance's strategic and diplomatic dilemmas. My return to the State Department would be initially spurred, however, by the revival of the Berlin Crisis, which had preoccupied many of my working hours under Dulles and Herter.

Recalled to Government Service: The Berlin Crisis and European Security 1961-1962

As discussed in chapter 3, Khrushchev's threat to turn access to West Berlin over to the East German government had created a crisis in 1958-59, as the Allied powers sought a way to protect their rights in West Berlin, a symbol of the West's commitment to freedom and security in Europe. This phase of the crisis was smothered, as Eisenhower and Khrushchev met at Camp David and made plans for a major Four-Power summit to be held in Paris in the spring of 1960. But the U-2 incident brought all hopes for this summit crashing down, leaving U.S.-Soviet relations as uncertain as ever, with the Berlin issue merely quiescent for the time being.

Berlin tensions then moved back toward crisis levels following the confrontational meeting between President Kennedy and Soviet

Premier Khrushchev in Vienna in June 1961. Here the young president made it clear to Khrushchev that he was prepared to stand firmly behind the West's position on its rights in Berlin. With neither side ready or willing to back down, the prospects were for a very cold winter, as Kennedy is reported to have commented at the end of the talks. Returning to the United States feeling that the Soviet leader had tried to bully him, and determined to back up his strong words in Vienna with action, Kennedy moved quickly to mobilize America's conventional forces to prepare for a possible showdown over Berlin, and set in train diplomatic and military planning to deal with such an eventuality. This planning took on added urgency with the erection of the Berlin Wall in August 1961.[1]

Presumably because of my connection with the Eisenhower administration's planning for the earlier phase of the Berlin Crisis, and probably at the suggestion of my colleagues in the State Department, I was asked to take part in these planning operations as a consultant. A number of Berlin Task Forces were established to focus on various aspects of contingency planning for U.S. policy and actions. I was asked to chair a task force on European security and surprise attack dangers. Besides myself, John T. McNaughton, who was Secretary of Defense Robert McNamara's General Counsel, served on this task force, which also included representatives from the Joint Chiefs and government experts on NATO and the Soviet Union. We were also to back up discussions on this subject with Britain, France, and the Federal Republic of Germany, as well as to keep NATO informed through the U.S. ambassador to the North Atlantic Council, Thomas Finletter, a former Secretary of the Air Force.

Our work included an analysis of U.S. policy goals regarding a possible European security agreement, should the Berlin Crisis serve to open up avenues to pursue such an agreement with the Soviets. As had been the case during the Eisenhower years, this question was inextricably tied to the problems of arms control. Eventually, arms control came to have a higher priority, and in November 1961 the task force was rechristened the Arms Control and Berlin Negotiating Study Group.[2]

Though my responsibility on the Berlin Task Force centered upon European security and arms control issues, I had given thought to the pressing question of how the United States and its allies should respond if Khrushchev followed through this time with his threat to cut off West Berlin. I had pulled my musings together in a paper entitled "Minos," which I wrote while out of government and which I sent around to a number of people in the new administration. It also reflected my growing concern with finding a new strategic concept which would release the United States and its allies from the dilemmas created by overdependence upon nuclear weapons, largely held by the United States, as the basis for our national and collective security. The confrontation with Khrushchev over Berlin served to underscore these dilemmas and the pressures they placed upon NATO cohesion in a crisis.

Perhaps not surprisingly for a former naval officer, I came to focus upon sea power as a possible means of resolving these dilemmas. I had first become interested in the potential of a maritime strategy as the result of contingency planning carried out during the Berlin Crisis in 1959. At that time, Policy Planning had drawn up a memorandum entitled "Berlin Contingency Planning: Pacific Counter-Blockade," which laid out the advantages the United States and the West could exploit in mounting a seaborne response to any Soviet tightening of the screws on Berlin.[3] The United States and its NATO allies had a strategic advantage over the Soviets which was a gift of geography–our vastly superior access to the seas. I felt that we could exploit this gift to build up sea pressure against the Communist world, in the process creating a more effective deterrent against aggression with less risk of war than that of the then-existing strategy. As I adapted this idea in the subsequent "Minos" paper, "The important thing is to capitalize on any Berlin adversity that may be coming our way by creating a power and an international political structure to assure that never again will freedom have to bend to Communist pressure." I proposed to establish this new structure on the seas, noting, "Orbiting astronauts may be the first humans fully to appreciate the profound relationship between oceanic control and political influence on planet earth." I noted that "in devoting the great technological effort and psychological commitment to space, Soviet leaders may consciously or unconsciously be striving to break out of the geographical encirclement by the seas."

A number of points gave weight to this analysis. First, though the expanding Soviet submarine fleet, which "reflects their awareness of this handicap, can produce great shipping destruction, it cannot change the sea access problem plaguing the Soviet Union. . . . The Russians know in their historical bones that their earth-domination desires could be frustrated if the free maritime nations wake up to the implications of their latent sea power in a time of nuclear standoff." Second, I argued that Communist use of the sea was "at sufferance." Our foreign bases were nourished on the "legal doctrine of the freedom of the seas." But they "slice away" at our position in Berlin, which similarly reflects a legal doctrine, "the binding effect of agreements and rights derived from military conquest–comparable slicing tactics could be pursued on some sea autobahn that NATO can control–the Dardanelles or the Danish straits."

I recognized such a strategy would be dangerous and might trigger fighting. But, compared to the dangers, destruction, deaths, and overall cost of general nuclear war, or even limited war on a scale below that of Korea, the effects would be "relatively small in terms of destruction of population . . ." I believed it was "within our power to blockade the Soviet Union." While only extreme circumstances would warrant such a move, emphasis on that potential power made "in a manifestly nonaggressive manner, would be a limited technique to deter or deflect limited . . . aggression with the least risk of global war. . . . When the lesson sinks in, . . . a Cold War turning point of major proportions conceivably could be reached."

I suggested that the nonaggressive stress in such a strategy could be made clear by immediate, positive moves toward the integration of the United States with Western Europe in one oceanic community, which some other nations–Japan, for example–would be asked to join. Finally, I argued that "a sea pressure strategy would offer essential roles to a number of our allies" in NATO that were absent in the near-monopoly of nuclear weapons by the United States.

Applying this suggested new strategy to the problem created by the renewed Soviet threat to blockade West Berlin, I proposed in the "Minos" paper in 1961 that blockage of Western access to

West Berlin should be met by a naval blockade of Soviet access to the high seas. This clearly could have been taken by the Soviets as an act of war but, by the same token, so could their steps to deprive the allies of their legal access to West Berlin. I thought this was a much more moderate proposal than actually engaging in ground fighting on the access routes to Berlin. Before I rejoined the government, I gave a copy of the "Minos" paper to Arthur Krock of the *New York Times*. He wrote a complimentary column in late 1961 which quoted liberally from the paper.[4]

Not all the reviews were so complimentary, however. Former Secretary of State Dean Acheson wrote that, though he felt my suggestions were good ones, he believed I claimed too much for them. As Acheson saw it, control of the sea, while it had been a good weapon when used by a coalition against a European power, or group of powers, seeking hegemony of the continent, it was no alternative to being able to meet this power in Europe and to deny it success there. This he saw as the lesson of Louis XIV, the Kaiser, and Hitler, whose direct successor was Khrushchev.[5] Such thinking, I believe, was more the norm than my efforts to revisit the fundamentals of America's strategic concepts.

Despite the fears entertained at the time of possible nuclear war, and the numerous scares and ratcheting up and down of tensions which marked the unfolding of the Berlin Crisis in late 1961 and early 1962, the outcome was an uneasy truce. The Berlin Wall served to stem the tide of East Germans flooding to the West through the escape hatch of West Berlin, and thus met the immediate concerns of the communist regime ruling East Germany. Khrushchev, facing the undeniable military might and recognized nuclear superiority of the United States (the so-called "missile gap" having been revealed as a gap in our favor, as announced by McNamara's deputy Roswell Gilpatric in a public speech in October 1961), backed down yet again from threats to cut off West Berlin. This confrontation, however, left the Soviet ruler determined to rectify the strategic nuclear imbalance which apparently had constrained his designs over Berlin. This determination led to the most dangerous nuclear crisis of the Cold War–the Cuban Missile Crisis.

The Cuban Missile Crisis, 1962

My only connection with the Cuban crisis was during my work on the Multilateral Force, or MLF, to which I will return. The day that Dean Acheson came to Paris to brief de Gaulle on the Soviet missile deployments in Cuba, I was scheduled to brief the North Atlantic Council on the MLF, along with two colleagues– Abraham Chayes, the legal advisor in the State Department, and Admiral John M. Lee, who was Secretary of Defense McNamara's military advisor. First I had a call from "Squidge" Lee, who said that he was not going to be able to come to Paris and made a reference to the "pickles" in Cuba. Then I had a message from Chayes from the airport in Paris that he had been ordered back to Washington, where I understand he played a significant role in drawing up the quarantine provisions. I remember feeling a little forsaken as these two top colleagues were leaving me to make the presentation alone, but it didn't seem like a good time to argue. I felt somewhat awkward briefing NATO about a multilateral missile fleet which would be irrelevant if this new crisis led to war. About this time I received a cable from my worried daughter, Sheila, which somewhat plaintively asked, "Isn't it about time you were coming home?" As I remember, I finished the presentation to the North Atlantic Council and caught the next plane back to Washington.

Back in Washington, I was given a copy of the message that Khrushchev had sent to Kennedy which signaled that the crisis was coming to an end. It struck me as the product of a frightened Soviet leader who realized that his action had brought the world to the brink of nuclear war. At the time, I did not share the alarm of certain officials over the Soviet missile deployments because I was persuaded that the Soviets would follow their usual practice, seen when they deployed nuclear delivery systems in Eastern Europe, of keeping the nuclear warhead components securely under the Kremlin's control and in the Soviet Union. Although there was some debate in Washington then and since among scholars as to whether the nuclear warheads ever were deployed in Cuba, I understand that recent evidence indicates that they were.

A footnote to the Cuban Missile Crisis relates to my "Minos" paper, mentioned earlier. After the Kennedy administration had successfully navigated a safe course through the crisis, using the naval quarantine as the means to prevent further introduction of ballistic missiles into Cuba, an article by George Lowe in *Navy Magazine* in 1963 speculated that if the Soviets had read my paper "Minos," which Arthur Krock had discussed in his column in 1961, they should have realized what the U.S. reaction to their missile deployment in Cuba would be—a quarantine or blockade. By a circuitous route, a strategy that I had proposed to deal with the Berlin Crisis came to be the key to dealing with the Cuban Missile Crisis, which, as I noted earlier, can be seen as the direct result of Khrushchev's frustrations over Berlin and his desire to counter America's nuclear superiority.[6]

The "Minos" paper also reflected a search for new solutions to the overall strategic dilemma confronting the United States and its allies, and my growing interest in sea power as a possible answer. As I saw it, sea power held the potential for addressing both the strategic military and the political problems plaguing America's relations with its NATO allies under a collective security system which was then based upon a threat to use nuclear weapons. My efforts to sell our European allies on a NATO seaborne nuclear force as the answer to this dilemma had brought me to Paris during the Cuban Missile Crisis, and would involve my work for the government until 1965. This seaborne force was the ill-fated Multilateral Force, or MLF.

The MLF Saga, 1962-65

Background

In a sense, I felt like the midwife of the Multilateral Force. Confirming the adage that no good deed goes unpunished, I was fated to struggle to give it birth, and then be one of the mourners at its eventual demise. The roots of the MLF went back to the last years of the Eisenhower administration and the emerging dilemma which surrounded United States and NATO nuclear strategy. What began as a weapons system ended up as a highly inflammable political issue involving high stakes for the alliance, marking what I saw as a critical turning point in the alliance system.[7]

As discussed in the previous chapter, during my years as head of the Policy Planning staff, NATO's adoption of a strategy of nuclear deterrence in the Fifties had produced a number of serious and potentially divisive military and political strains within the alliance, which were exacerbated by the growing Soviet nuclear forces. As the Soviet ability to make nuclear strikes on Western Europe and the United States increased, doubts began to arise about the alliance's strategy, which was to rely on strategic nuclear strikes to meet Soviet attack on Western Europe. For some, the worry was that the United States would be loath to use its nuclear forces in defense of Europe, if this brought nuclear strikes down upon the American homeland. For others, fears centered on the devastation that would result from using nuclear weapons, either strategically or tactically, to defend Europe as called for in NATO's planning. In the minds of many, both fears coexisted uneasily, giving rise to a pessimistic belief that America's NATO allies were damned if U.S. nuclear forces defended them and damned if they did not.

Other developments added to these strains. Khrushchev's combination of threats and pressures during the Berlin Crisis, along with suggestions that he might be open to some sort of compromise, caused debate over the best way to deal with the Soviet threat, both immediately and over the long haul. America's allies in Europe were emerging from their postwar economic reconstruction and beginning to want a greater say in alliance decisions about strategy. De Gaulle's determination to chart an independent course in foreign affairs and the doubts he voiced about America's role in Europe's defense gave a powerful thrust to Europeans' desire to take greater control of their continent's destiny.

Within NATO, control over the use of nuclear weapons became a primary focus for these fears. Closely linked was the question of how to bring some flexibility into NATO's military strategy, so that our responses would not be limited to a stark choice between all-out nuclear war or surrender. Little progress was made on persuading the allies to spend more on nonnuclear forces, owing in large part to differences over economic capabilities, and to doubts that the

Soviets would risk limited war in Europe even after they had a sizeable nuclear arsenal. As discussed in the previous chapter, Eisenhower and Dulles sought to address these concerns by adopting Norstad's NATO atomic stockpile concept and offering to station Intermediate Range Ballistic Missiles (IRBMs) in selected NATO countries, subject to joint, so-called "dual-key" control by the United States and the nations where the missiles were based. Dulles also sought to persuade the allies of the need to maintain sufficient conventional forces to provide SACEUR with a range of responses to Soviet or East European threats that would not involve or require the use of nuclear weapons.

Creation of the atomic stockpile in Europe and the IRBM agreements with Great Britain, Greece, and Turkey served to ease some of the concerns, as well as to give the United States a ballistic missile capability to hit the Soviet Union in the time period before our Intercontinental Ballistic Missiles (ICBMs) came on line. The United States had proceeded with development of IRBMs because of the belief our ICBMs would not be available soon enough. When it was clear that the ICBMs were going to be operational on time, there was a good deal of discussion as to where to deploy the IRBMs. Eisenhower was not wholly convinced of their military utility–on one occasion I heard him say, "Why don't we throw them into the sea?" Given the problems these weapons based in Turkey caused during the Cuban Missile Crisis, when the Russians cited their existence as justification for the Soviet deployments in Cuba, that might not have been such a bad idea.[8]

I remained convinced that more was needed to reconcile the contending political and military needs pressing on NATO. One special worry was the prospect for proliferation of national nuclear forces if allied security concerns were not met in some other manner. Britain had already gone ahead with its so-called independent deterrent (albeit with considerable American aid after 1957), while de Gaulle had made clear his determination to do the same for France. At the same time, the prospect that NATO strategy and planning would bring nuclear weapons into the hands of German forces was creating some unease not only in the alliance, but also in Moscow. General Norstad, the current SACEUR, was pressing for a mobile ballistic missile force, an MMRBM, stationed on land and designed to strike targets in the Soviet Union. It was thought this MMRBM force might become the nucleus of an independent NATO nuclear force under SACEUR's command, but the proposal lacked details as to structure, composition, and control. I feared Norstad's scheme carried a heavy load of political and military difficulties, not least of which was the prospect that such a force could lead to West German access to missiles capable of reaching the Soviet Union.

Other schemes being discussed would have the United States provide the NATO allies with the necessary technology to produce their own ballistic missiles. The fact that a number of NATO allies expressed a strong interest in being able to obtain missiles for their national forces not assigned to NATO once the alliance's needs had been met revealed the dangers in this proposal. Again, some in the State Department felt that such open-ended offers could lead to a German national nuclear force in the long run (a fear that was shared by the British), as the acquisition of ballistic missiles would provide a strong, possibly irresistible, impetus also to acquire the warheads which would give them their ultimate value.[9]

Bowie Study

I had seen a chance to focus attention on the need for new thinking on these problems when NATO's tenth anniversary in 1959 led Secretary Herter to ask me for some proposals to mark this date. I suggested that he propose to NATO during the December 1959 NAC meeting that the alliance prepare a study laying out its goals for the next decade. Herter agreed, as did the North Atlantic Council. This meant that the U.S. government now had to make up its mind on some difficult issues and develop a vision of NATO's future in the 1960s. To do this, Herter (again following my suggestion) in early 1960 asked my predecessor as head of Policy Planning, Robert Bowie, to prepare a study on long-range NATO planning and make recommendations for the President's approval regarding the alliance's future goals and tasks.[10]

Bowie, who had left government in 1957, agreed to take on this task on the understanding the report would represent his own views and recommendations as a consultant. He was assigned a small staff of officials and consultants chosen by him, and was given access to the necessary classified information. He also held long talks with the Policy Planning staff, the Pentagon, and General Norstad. The final report, which was presented to the President in August 1960, was wide-ranging, presenting Bowie's recommendations on overall strategy for the United States and NATO in the coming decade, on the basis of what he saw as the major political, military, and economic issues confronting the alliance in the 1960s.

It was in his discussion of NATO strategy and nuclear weapons that Bowie laid out the rationale for what became the Multilateral Force proposal. He believed that the strategic nuclear deterrent against all-out war was quite robust, but he was worried that with the coming of nuclear parity, the Soviets might be tempted to use their ready, nonnuclear forces to seize key regions with quick, limited strikes that would confront NATO with a choice between accepting a fait accompli carrying dire political consequences, or escalating the conflict to the nuclear level, with all the risks that this would entail. To counter this risk, Bowie called for NATO to raise SHIELD forces of some 28–30 divisions (a goal Norstad was already pressing for) as well as to push for modernization of the alliance's conventional weapons.

If the alliance met this goal, Bowie argued the United States should make a proposal to meet the growing allied concerns over NATO's dependence upon America's nuclear arsenal. He argued that the United States must find some means of increasing the allies' role in decision making about the employment of nuclear weapons committed to their defense. Instead of Norstad's MMRBM force, Bowie proposed the creation of a seaborne multilateral force assigned to SACEUR's command. The first step would be a commitment of American Polaris submarines to NATO under SACEUR's command, subject to agreed control procedures. Second would be creation of a NATO seaborne missile force, to be jointly financed, owned, controlled, and manned by crews of various nationalities. As Bowie recalls, seabasing and mixed manning were key elements of the plan, aimed at assuring "joint control, [to] prevent national withdrawal of components, reduce vulnerability," and avoid other problems involved in Norstad's proposal. Overall, Bowie's concept had four objectives: "(1) to involve and reassure the allies; (2) to discourage national nuclear forces; (3) to meet the military need for MRBMs while avoiding the problems of land-based missiles; [and] (4) to encourage European integration by the prospect that the MLF might eventually become a European force as the European Community developed into an effective political entity."[11]

After Bowie briefed Eisenhower on his report and recommendations in August, matters moved quickly. The President endorsed the MLF idea because of his long-standing concern with finding a way to widen nuclear sharing within the alliance. He had already looked with favor on Norstad's ideas, and Bowie's proposal offered the means to reconcile national concerns with the need to prevent proliferation of national nuclear forces. Bowie's arguments impressed Eisenhower, though he was also well aware of the political obstacles the idea would face, both in Europe and at home. Bowie was told to develop the proposal further in discussions with Norstad, who also favored the MLF concept and believed it had a good chance of being welcomed by Congress and the Europeans (although not de Gaulle).

Further discussions that autumn led to Eisenhower's approval of Bowie's two-stage process to establish the proposed seaborne force. The timing seemed propitious. In July of 1958, the Assembly of the Western European Union (WEU) had proposed to its Council of Ministers that a study be made of what kind of organization would be needed to carry out a common decision-making function with respect to the strategic employment of nuclear weapons. A year later, this Assembly recommended that the power to decide on the use of nuclear weapons from ships, subject to NATO command, be placed under joint political control. By 1960, the WEU, decrying the fact that national control of nuclear weapons seemed to remain the preferred option, called for an alternative—a common strategic nuclear deterrent force giving to all partners a voice on its employment. That same year Chancellor Adenauer, NATO Secretary-General Paul-Henri Spaak, Dirk Stikker (who would succeed Spaak at NATO), and General Norstad talked about the creation of a NATO nuclear power. In the autumn of 1960, Eisenhower secured the approval of Spaak, who said that NATO's

European members (again minus de Gaulle) would welcome the seaborne force proposal.

Finally, at an NSC meeting in November 1960 the President announced his decision to submit the proposal to NATO in December. The United States would first offer five Polaris submarines as an interim NATO force, and then assistance to other NATO allies in creation of a permanent seaborne force, initially armed with 100 MRBMs, designed according to Bowie's criteria for mixed-manning and suitable control procedures. In a departure from Bowie's recommendations, the allies were only to be called upon to strengthen their conventional forces, but not required to do so before the United States moved ahead with the MLF offer.[12]

Kennedy Endorsement and Doubts

Herter put this offer before the North Atlantic Council meeting in December 1960. By this point the Eisenhower administration was on its way out after the November elections, so there was not a clear response. The NATO allies, naturally, wanted to wait to see if the Kennedy administration would adopt these proposals, and if so, with what changes. In the spring of 1961, President Kennedy announced in Ottawa that the United States would follow through on Herter's offer of five Polaris submarines to be committed to SACEUR's command, subject to agreed guidelines on their control and use, and then stated the eventual goal of a NATO multilateral seaborne force, provided the Europeans wanted it and NATO's conventional force goals had first been attained.[13]

Subsequent years would reveal that serious doubts and hesitations lurked behind Kennedy's endorsement of the multilateral force concept. As McGeorge Bundy, who then served as National Security Advisor, later wrote, support for the MLF under Kennedy (and I would add Johnson) was "broad but conditional."[14] The qualified nature of the proposal made by Kennedy at Ottawa involved a formidable set of preconditions: agreement on NATO guidelines for the use of the force, control arrangements that would be credible in a crisis, positive European indications that the force was both desirable and feasible, and prior attainment of NATO's nonnuclear force goals.[15] Bundy's phrase is a good indication of the ambiguity with which the White House viewed the MLF. When, in 1962, I was asked to succeed Ambassador Livingston Merchant as special envoy to our European allies to promote the MLF concept, I found myself caught between the ambiguities of the American position and the doubts of our NATO allies, a combination which ultimately sank this enterprise.

The troubled history of the MLF has been analyzed in detail by scholars. I will focus here on my involvement, and outline the arguments for the MLF as I saw them and presented them to American and European officials between 1962 and 1964.[16] My involvement with the MLF began with a call in the spring of 1962 from Howard Furnas of State. I had ceased being a consultant with the Berlin Task Forces and was taking a vacation. Furnas's call found me in a boat anchored off the island of Dominica in the West Indies. He asked if I would be interested in taking a hand in implementing the MLF concept with our NATO allies. I said I would be interested provided that I would receive the rank of ambassador, so that my voice would be given the necessary weight in dealing with our allies.

Assured that my position would be commensurate with my responsibilities, I returned to Washington to take up the brief for the MLF. Apparently, MLF had been somewhat dormant since Kennedy's Ottawa speech in 1961, only to be reawakened when the French government approached Washington with a request for U.S. aid to France's nuclear weapons program. This request set off a debate within the administration, with the opponents of such aid pointing to the dangerous precedent that U.S. aid for a French nuclear program could give to the Federal Republic of Germany. The U.S. government did not agree to aid France at this time.[17] Also part of this complex policy mix were efforts within the Pentagon under Robert McNamara to fashion a new strategic doctrine which would clarify U.S. control of NATO's nuclear deterrent. This new doctrine, announced by McNamara at the Athens NATO meeting in May 1962 (which I attended), amounted to a blunt condemnation of additional national nuclear forces as ineffective and destabilizing, and laid out the rationale for strong centralized (read American) control of NATO's nuclear forces. It involved a counterforce targeting strategy and called for a search for a wider range of options in response to threats, and led to the flexible response doctrine. Wanting to head off the French program, and fearing that McNamara's new doctrine might backfire and provoke proliferation of national nuclear weapons programs, a group of State Department officials, including my former colleague, Henry Owen, and my successor as head of Policy Planning, Walt Rostow, devised an alternative solution. It was detailed in a paper drafted by Owen, which proposed meeting France's (and by extension Germany's) nuclear concerns through the MLF.[18]

Owen and others in the State Department had kept the MLF idea alive, motivated in part by concerns that then-current policies threatened to lead to a proliferation of nuclear powers in Europe. These fears had been strengthened when Thomas Gates, Eisenhower's last Secretary of Defense, had presented proposals in 1959 and 1960 which contemplated the sale by the United States of ballistic missiles to the national forces of certain allies, presumably with retention of custody by the United States of the nuclear warheads. Such an open-ended offer seemed tailor-made to promote, not dampen, allied desires for national nuclear weapons programs, as was borne out when some Europeans argued that to be acceptable, the Gates proposal would have to allow the allies to obtain missiles for their national forces after alliance requirements had been met. Grasping the opening created by the French request for nuclear aid, Owen used the aforementioned paper to revive the MLF idea. It then became the basis for NSAM 147, a National Security Action Memorandum prepared in April 1962 which restated U.S. willingness to join a multilateral force. Kennedy's approval of NSAM 147 gave the MLF project new life and also authorized both further studies and preliminary negotiations with our allies.[19]

Rationale for MLF

Upon returning to Washington, I set about bringing myself up to date on MLF developments and getting my thoughts in order regarding the rationale behind the force. As I saw it, the MLF could be the means to address with one stroke the military and diplomatic dilemmas which had arisen to plague U.S. and NATO nuclear strategy over the past decade, as well as to promote key U.S. foreign policy objectives in Europe. And, I had continued to grapple with the issues surrounding the alliance's nuclear dilemmas even while no longer serving in the State Department. In a memorandum which I drafted in the summer of 1961, I set down some thoughts on the MLF proposal. This paper summarized the views which I brought to the new task of selling the MLF to our European allies.

An inexorable process of nuclear diffusion was under way, I believed, which in the absence of arms control agreements was bound to lead to the proliferation of national nuclear forces. U.S. policy had contributed to this spread of nuclear weapons knowledge by the programs of cooperation entered into with our NATO allies and the creation of the NATO atomic stockpile and bilateral agreements to base IRBMs in Europe in support of SACEUR's mission. The revision of the McMahon Act in 1958 liberalizing American technical assistance to allied nations that had made substantial progress in their own nuclear programs had been seen by some as a virtual invitation to embark upon nuclear weapons programs. I had been a persistent opponent of U.S. support to allied national nuclear weapons programs, with the notable exception of the United Kingdom. National forces seemed militarily insignificant and wasteful both politically and economically. Efforts to create such forces would likely distract our allies from the buildup of conventional forces called for by NATO planning, thus creating even greater dependence upon nuclear weapons and less flexibility in crises.

Washington had a spectrum of options to choose from in addressing the future shape of NATO's nuclear forces. It could try to maintain the existing setup; it could seek to place part of the U.S. (and the U.K. and in time the French) forces under the control of SACEUR; it could resign itself to the development of independent national forces; it could promote the development of some type of European force, such as a U.K.-French, a U.K.-French-German, or a six-nation force; or it could push for a full-fledged North Atlantic Community Nuclear Authority, or NACNA, which I had proposed to Foster Dulles in 1957. This Authority would determine the alliance's nuclear weapons requirements, have custody and control of the use of these weapons, and perhaps produce nuclear weapons for the alliance. Dulles had broached the NACNA concept with Adenauer in 1957 and obtained a favorable reaction, but the idea had not been pursued.

It had been the State Department's thesis that additional national nuclear weapons programs would not only be harmful to NATO unity, but also prejudicial to world stability and the possibility of international control of atomic weapons. There was also the danger, already noted, that such a diffusion could lead to the creation of a German nuclear force. To avert these dangers, we were convinced that some way had to be found to overcome the obvious hurdles in the path of a multilateral force. As I wrote at the time, we saw such a force "as constituting a substantial move toward political unity in the alliance, a less dangerous move than national force[s], a less provocative move and a move that would be subject to [tighter] 'control' than national force[s]."[20] As Owen argued, the MLF could advance our basic objectives of Atlantic partnership, European unity, increasing NATO's military strength, and the nonproliferation of nuclear weapons.

Washington had already made substantial moves towards European participation in a NATO nuclear deterrent. To this end the Eisenhower administration in December 1960 had made a flat commitment to maintain nuclear weapons in Europe at not less than their present levels, and had made the offer to deploy Polaris submarines as a first step towards a proposed multilateral force. As already noted, President Kennedy had reiterated Herter's offer in the spring of 1961, although with the important proviso (which Herter had deleted from Bowie's original recommendations) that the Europeans had to first build up their conventional forces before the United States would help them establish an alliance nuclear force.

Technical problems would weigh heavily in the analysis of MLF. It was still largely unknown how much it would cost, how it would operate, and how effective it would be. The critical question of how the decision would be made to actually employ the force seemed to defy solution. There was the danger that Soviet countermeasures might cancel out the force's effectiveness after great effort and cost had been put into its creation. There was the risk that after the

United States had shared nuclear weapons technology with the allies, the system might collapse. A potential for a number of national nuclear weapons programs might well survive.

Political Obstacles

There were also serious political difficulties to be surmounted. Officials just did not like to think about nuclear weapons, whether for strategic deterrent or tactical/theater defense purposes. There was a strong inclination in some quarters to let the Americans take the nuclear responsibility, bear its costs, and somehow manage to work out international nuclear arms control agreements with the Soviets. This did not strike me as a very tenable basis for the long-term, but it was difficult to find a consensus for new initiatives in American or European opinion. In Europe, it seemed that there was an unwarranted skepticism about the reality of any Soviet military threat. Doubts about the reality of the Soviet threat were underscored when the Kennedy administration admitted publicly in October 1961 that the "missile gap" was a myth, unless viewed in terms of America's large lead in ballistic missiles over the Soviet force. Paired with this European skepticism was a general feeling of hopelessness: nothing *could* be done if the Soviets did attack. There were periodic groundswells of concern over the continued effectiveness of the U.S. deterrent. These concerns were linked to the doubts that the United States would court suicide in order to carry out its commitment to Europe.

Domestic political uncertainties and competing economic demands also served to put obstacles in the way of the MLF. There was much more European interest in grappling with the economic problems of the emerging Common Market than in making the painful mental adjustments that would be required for the pooling of sovereign rights over life-and-death nuclear decisions. Other political dramas had to be played out before progress could be made on the MLF. In France, much depended on de Gaulle's fate, his decisions about returning the French Army from Algeria to Europe and his future moves with regard to the Western alliance. In the case of England, until Whitehall and Parliament decided whether the country's economic and political destiny lay in or out of the continent, there was little hope of establishing a collective nuclear arrangement, which would have to include the British nuclear deterrent. In Bonn, it was expected that Adenauer's long-lived government was nearing its end. For all three countries, there was the risk that MLF arrangements designed to meet current leaders' preconceptions could prove ill-designed to suit their successors. Was the only other option a policy of drift?

And there was still no strong consensus in Washington. The issue as presented to the United States was clear–should we further share the nuclear deterrent with NATO? There was no such clarity as to how this should be done if the answer was yes. Should there be shared decision making on nuclear weapons use in war? Should the United States move toward even greater sharing of weapons design information, or providing nuclear material or weapons, or some joint operation of a force? Military leaders generally believed the spread of nuclear weapons was inevitable, so the United States should share with its allies, thus avoiding wasteful duplication and producing satisfied allies who would cooperate with the United States in mutual defense (a viewpoint quite similar to that voiced by Eisenhower). There was the persistent opposition of the Congressional Joint Committee on Atomic Energy to any further sharing of America's "nuclear secrets" or control of nuclear weapons.

Key to the fate of the MLF was the spectrum of views of top officials, especially the uncertain views of the two presidents involved. There were a number of players in this competition for the President's mind. Secretary of State Dean Rusk appeared to be pro-British. His guideline seemed to be "don't cut away from the U.K. (or France)" until you have a better alternative in place. Beyond this, Rusk largely kept his own counsel. Others in State–George Ball, Walt Rostow, Robert Schaetzel, and Henry Owen–tended to view the MLF within the larger framework of preventing further proliferation of national nuclear forces within NATO, as discussed, as well as in terms of promoting Jean Monnet's vision of a United Europe.

On the military side, I had the impression that Defense Secretary McNamara, JCS Chairman Maxwell Taylor, and General Lyman Lemnitzer (who replaced Norstad as SACEUR) saw the

MLF as not first class and not really needed. It also threatened to complicate McNamara's efforts to impose rigorous centralized control of NATO's nuclear forces, which was part of his overall effort to bring rationality to America's defense planning. But the military leaders did not openly oppose the plan, and the Navy seemed to favor it, as might be expected. In the White House, McGeorge Bundy, a sophisticated and intelligent scholar with an acerbic wit, played a crucial role as National Security Advisor. Looking back, it seems that Bundy quite properly saw his role as making sure the President received a clear sense of the available options and did not become prematurely tied to any one of them. I also had a feeling that Bundy was somewhat sympathetic to de Gaulle's concerns, in contrast to the views found in the State Department.

Role of the Navy

Despite his doubts, McNamara allowed the Navy to take part in preparations for the MLF. While there were Navy officers in support of the MLF, Bowie's original idea of basing the force on Polaris submarines quickly ran into trouble. In 1962 an extensive Navy study of the MLF concept, directed by Rear Admiral Michaelis, had signed off on the legal, operational, and personnel feasibility of the proposed force, but had made a fundamental change in calling for a surface fleet instead of a submarine-based force. The MLF's supporters in the State Department feared the NATO allies would see such a force as inferior to the original plan, thus making our job of selling the force that much harder (especially after Kennedy agreed to provide Britain with Polaris missiles for its submarine force at the Nassau meeting in December 1962, to which I will return later).

It was well known that Admiral Rickover was a key opponent to the idea of allowing any foreign access to U.S. nuclear submarines, and so was believed to be behind this change. I had talked with the Admiral about the mixed-manning issue, only to be put off with the excuse that he would have to talk with his wife, an international lawyer, about the legalities involved. That was the only time in my career when an official of the U.S. government told me he wanted to consult with his wife about a policy question. An effort was made in early 1963 to deflect Rickover's opposition by arranging a meeting between him and Kennedy to discuss the submarine issue, in the hope that Kennedy would listen patiently to Rickover's critique and then state that political considerations had to override Rickover's technical concerns. But those who planned this meeting did not reckon with the Admiral's powers of persuasion. Though Rickover admitted that if forced to do so, the Navy could make the idea work, he then reportedly proceeded to make the following case to Kennedy: there are three key parts to a submarine system—the nuclear propulsion reactors, the missiles, and the communications. Rickover was ready to turn over the first two to our allies, but he asked Kennedy if the President really wanted to turn over the cryptology and codes necessary to operate the communications system for command and control of the missiles on the submarines. Apparently Kennedy had not considered that aspect, and came out of the meeting opposed to a submarine-based MLF, a decision he conveyed to the NSC that same day.[21]

So, we had to fall back on using surface ships for the MLF. Studies showed that surface ships would be sufficiently invulnerable to serve as a useful deterrent force. The ships would be indistinguishable from merchant ships, of which thousands were at sea every day. Any Soviet effort to locate and trail the MLF ships for years if necessary would fail. Though the object of some derision, the idea of basing the MLF on mixed-manned surface-ships proved to be quite feasible in 1964-65 when the mixed-manned frigate USS *Biddle* (renamed the *Ricketts* after the premature death of Admiral Claude V. Ricketts, a former Vice Chief of Naval Operations and one of the most enthusiastic supporters of the idea) made a tour of European and Mediterranean ports. Before leaving for its overseas ports of call, the *Ricketts* made a number of shakedown and training tours in 1964, including a stop in New York Harbor. This demonstration showed that mixed-manning could work. Unfortunately, by the time the *Ricketts* had finished its tour, the MLF was approaching its demise.[22]

Policy Debate

The larger debate over the MLF within the administration and with allies involved the linked issues of the proposed force's military and political utility. Much of my time and energies during 1962 to 1964 were spent refining the arguments in favor of the force in terms of these two criteria for presentation to my superiors and the NATO allies, all the while having to maneuver in the face of new countervailing influences, which unfortunately only continued to grow in strength.[23] I would be identified as part of a supposed "cabal" of MLF supporters. There was no such cabal, in the sense of a group trying surreptitiously to advance the cause of the MLF.[24] To the degree I was identified as one of those arguing the case for the MLF, I felt I was in good company, including Furnas, Bowie, Owen, Schaetzel, Ball, and Admiral Lee. The list could be expanded to include former President Eisenhower, Christian Herter, Dean Acheson, Walt Rostow, Livingston Merchant, Foy Kohler, Thomas Finletter, and C. Douglas Dillon.

Though members of this group could and did disagree on certain points, and would emphasize different aspects of the arguments in response to the changing criticisms, a clear and strong rationale for the MLF was developed which informed efforts to present the idea to skeptical politicians and military officers at home and abroad. This rationale addressed both military and political considerations, which I believed could not be separated, in an effort to find a way to share America's strategic deterrent responsibilities with allies and avoid promoting the proliferation of national nuclear forces, while at the same time advancing America's larger diplomatic objectives in Europe–European integration and Atlantic partnership.[25]

There were two alternatives to the MLF approach then under discussion: maintaining the U.S. monopoly over nuclear weapons operations, with some moves toward greater consultations within NATO about their use, or supplying medium-range missiles to our allies, who would have national control over them. The first, I felt, would not adequately address European concerns and appeared to perpetuate a dangerous discrimination, regardless of the degree of increased consultation, which of itself was a desirable goal. As I put it then, "The effectiveness of consultation is apt to be in direct proportion to the degree of participation by the consulting nations in the operations they are consulting about."[26] The second course risked creating new divisions within the alliance between the nuclear haves and have-nots, while producing new tensions in East-West relations. This left the MLF approach, premised upon a deterrent force jointly owned, manned, and controlled by the United States and its NATO allies, as the preferred course.

Refinement of Design

Following Kennedy's approval of a surface fleet as the basing mode for the MLF, the design which emerged called for a fleet of warships, armed with Polaris missiles, which would be under the military command of an allied officer and under the policy direction of the participating nations. No nation's share of the costs and responsibilities would exceed forty percent, and those carrying the larger shares would have greater influence over major decisions. Firing of the Polaris missiles would be by decision of a two-thirds majority of the participants, including the United States. This could only occur under two circumstances: in response to a Soviet nonnuclear attack so strong that NATO's conventional forces could not contain it, or in response to a Soviet nuclear first strike. Over a long term, control might devolve to the Europeans, a possibility which President Johnson and McGeorge Bundy alluded to in statements to the NATO allies, provided European unity and participation in the force had progressed sufficiently.

It was my position and that of the other supporters of the MLF that this approach would respond best to our policy objectives. Politically, it would meet European concerns about bolstering deterrence and frustrating Kremlin efforts at nuclear blackmail, strengthen the Atlantic bonds between the United States and its NATO allies, narrow the gap between nuclear haves and have-nots in Europe, promote and increase effective consultation within the alliance on NATO's nuclear forces, and provide the framework for a growing European role and influence in defense as political unity advanced. Militarily, by 1964 the U.S. Navy, the JCS, and the

The author as a young naval officer in 1941.

The Semenovs and the Smiths at a reception beginning SALT in Vienna, March 15, 1971. (*Photograph by USIS Vienna*)

The author discusses SALT instructions with President Nixon and Secretary of State William Rogers. (*Photograph by UPI*)

Ambassador Smith and his negotiating opposite in SALT I, Soviet Deputy Foreign Minister, Vladimir Semenov, with interpreter, in Helsinki in 1971. (*Photograph by Lehtikuza Oy*)

Sometimes accused of having an "Irish hangman" expression, the author was known nevertheless for his sense of humor and love of life. (*Photograph by Diana Walker*)

The author conferring with President Nixon. Relations between the SALT delegation and the Nixon-Kissinger White House were not always smooth. (*Official photograph of the White House*)

Ambassador Smith receives the Medal of Freedom in 1981 from President Jimmy Carter, his "student." (*Official photograph of the White House*)

The author in 1981 with his personal friends and professional collaborators, Henry Owen (left) and Robert Bowie (right).

The author remained active in private life during the 1980s, attempting to preserve the integrity of ABM Treaty commitments. Here he appears on *Meet the Press* with Robert McNamara.

In 1987, Secretary of State George Schultz convened a reunion of Directors of the State Department's Policy Planning staff. Those present included (left to right) the author, Paul Nitze, Henry Owen, George Kennan (seventh from left), and Robert Bowie (ninth from left). (*State Department photograph*)

The author, his wife Bernice, four children and spouses, and several grandchildren at a family wedding in 1985.

The author liked to entertain friends and associates at his Eastern Shore home, Ratcliffe Manor. Here he enjoys a visit in the late 1980s from Air Force General Royall B. Allison (at left), who served on the SALT delegation, and a former CIA Director, Richard Helms. (*Photograph by R. C. Hunt*)

Secretary of Defense now agreed the MLF would be militarily effective as part of NATO's strategic deterrent. Even General Lemnitzer, who had replaced Norstad as SACEUR, said he would welcome the force as a contribution to meeting SHAPE's requirements. The proposed missile, the Polaris A3, had effective penetration capability and thus could hit a wide array of targets important to SACEUR's planning. The surface ship deployment would permit survivability on the high seas, possessing the ability to evade Soviet defenses. Its survivability would serve to insure it would be used if necessary, thus making it a credible deterrent in the eyes of Moscow. Finally, in relation to existing and planned U.S. strategic nuclear forces, the MLF would serve as a substitute for some of these forces, not a net increase.[27]

The MLF was designed specifically with arms control considerations in mind. The multilateral ownership, manning, and control of the force would prevent any one nation from seizing control. There would be vigorous custodial procedures to guard against espionage, sabotage, or the unauthorized release of information which could compromise weapons design data. These considerations, however, did not prevent either the Soviets or arms control proponents in the United States from criticizing the MLF as an obstacle to arms control.

As for the fourth criterion–affordability–it was estimated that the average annual costs to European nations who would be major MLF participants would be between one and four percent of their average annual defense spending. As these costs were well below those of other major military programs underway, they seemed well within the realm of fiscal possibility. The general consensus which developed assumed that the United States would provide 35 percent of the funding, West Germany 32 percent, Britain 10 percent, Italy and the Benelux nations between 6-8 percent, and 2.5 percent each from the Greeks and the Turks. This division of support meant that, according to the control procedures described above, both the United States and West Germany could have a veto over use of the MLF's nuclear weapons. Finally, I and others were persuaded that the MLF would provide the genesis for a transatlantic nuclear defense relationship which would bolster Atlantic partnership and contribute to European integration, thus meeting the final criterion.

Beyond this set of arguments aimed at the common benefits of the MLF, I also felt there were some hardheaded benefits that would accrue to the United States if the force came into being. For one thing, it would save the United States money it would otherwise have to spend upon new missiles required for defense in Europe. Likewise, by promoting a growing European role in defense, it could ease the gold drain which was beginning to complicate U.S. relations with Europe, and in particular with West Germany. It would reduce the pressures upon the United States for greater nuclear weapons cooperation, and as Bowie had argued in 1960, create a pocket into which the British and French nuclear forces could ultimately fall. The project also would serve as a strong example of U.S. leadership to counter the troubling challenges to that leadership from de Gaulle in Europe, as well as his divisive criticisms of U.S. and NATO nuclear strategy. To the degree the MLF would bolster the deterrent in Europe, it would ease the burden upon the United States and reduce the opportunities for the Kremlin to put pressure upon individual allies. Moving the alliance deterrent out to sea could also defuse potential political tensions caused by the basing of ballistic missiles on European territory (a potential risk which became very real within two decades with the Euromissiles crisis).

It was this analysis and body of arguments that informed my efforts in presenting the MLF concept to our NATO allies, as well as in the ongoing struggle to keep the project alive within the Kennedy and Johnson White Houses. As part of a mission to Europe with Admiral Lee in 1962, then as a member of the Merchant Mission in 1963, and in 1964 as head of the special State Department task force on the MLF until early 1965, I fought the good fight to promote the MLF. I did so, however, under the somewhat artificial constraint, born of Washington's uncertainty about the idea, that I was only to present and discuss the MLF proposal to our allies, in the hopes of eliciting their support for it, not attempt to sell it to them (a dubious proposition, as Admiral Lee later noted, given that the MLF was a U.S. proposal, and I was part of an official U.S. delegation presenting it[28]). The various MLF task forces met many times with both Kennedy and Johnson, as well as with the NSC and senior diplomatic and military officials, to discuss the MLF and its prospects. Though the arguments presented above retained their cogency for me, I must admit that my enthusiasm ebbed and my doubts about the odds for success only deepened, as I experienced firsthand the formidable obstacles to the MLF at home and abroad.

Negotiating from a Position of Uncertainty

In hindsight, a key obstacle to the MLF was the uncertainty surrounding the U.S. position. The ambiguity and uncertainties surrounding Washington's position only served to encourage doubters and proponents of other options in Europe. The lack of firm commitment by Washington can be traced in large part to Kennedy's and Johnson's care not to be tied to a commitment that could prove troublesome with Congress and the NATO allies. It was the sensitivity to potential problems with Congress, and in particular the Joint Committee on Atomic Energy, which guarded its prerogatives in nuclear matters jealously, that produced the repeated demand that strong European interest in the proposal must precede any U.S. commitment. In the absence of a clear lead by the United States, the allies were hesitant to sign on to such a complex scheme which might create problems with their own publics and Parliaments, as well as cut across particular national aspirations in nuclear weapons. MLF diplomacy turned into a sort of Gaston and Alphonse routine, with each side waiting for the other to go through the door first.

The MLF also ran afoul of crosscurrents in America's relations with its major allies in Europe, in particular Britain, West Germany and France, as well as contending priorities being pushed in East-West relations and arms control. From my position on the front lines, I encountered most if not all of these crosscurrents.

In the fall of 1962, I had a discussion with U.K. Defense Minister Thorneycroft. These discussions gave me forewarning of how troublesome the French connection would prove to be, as well as of the different evaluations our British allies could make of NATO's nuclear problems. The British Defense Minister felt that it might be better to move toward a joint European force in the field of tactical, not strategic, nuclear weapons, and raised the idea that whatever force emerged should allow for national use in self-defense. Thorneycroft was accompanied by Lord Solly Zuckerman, chief science advisor to the Cabinet. For his part, Zuckerman was critical of tactical nuclear weapons (and so implicitly of Thorneycroft's idea), holding that he thought the Soviets would never waste time with large numbers of small nuclear weapons, but would plan to use thousand-megaton weapons as battlefield weapons. He was dubious of the ability to do any good political planning regarding these weapons, as the technical situation was changing so fast.

The British stressed French sensitivities and needs. I sensed behind Thorneycroft's remarks a desire to keep open the possibility that the United States would let London assign nuclear weapons to the French under whatever scheme emerged. Zuckerman seemed to feel there was a chance of getting the French to give up their nuclear weapons program if the British gave up theirs, but then the whole key would be back in Washington's hands. There were also concerns that U.S. policy could risk upsetting Anglo-French relations across the board.

As Thorneycroft bluntly summed up his attitude, "The way into Europe was through France, and all this worrying about Belgium, Dutch and German opinion was nonsense–or at least not relevant."[29] As the events soon would prove, these British fears were prescient. De Gaulle clearly was determined to prove that he was the gatekeeper into Europe, and he would exercise this power guided by his belief that the Anglo-American "special relationship" was merely a stalking horse for American, or at best Anglo-Saxon, interference in the affairs of the continent.

Skybolt

The first serious sign of trouble came in late 1962 with the Skybolt affair and the Nassau conference between Kennedy and Prime Minister Harold Macmillan in December. Many scholars, including Richard Neustadt who prepared a secret report for the Kennedy administration, have analyzed this episode in detail. Suffice it to say here that McNamara's sudden cancellation of the Skybolt air-launched ballistic missile created a crisis in Anglo-American relations, as London had counted on receiving this weapon to extend the life of its aging strategic V-bomber force. To salvage the situation, Kennedy, persuaded by Macmillan's presentation of Britain's plight, agreed at Nassau to provide Britain with Polaris missiles, to which would be mated British nuclear warheads and used on Britain's submarine force. In return, the British agreed to use the Polaris missiles in support of NATO defense, with a proviso allowing London to use them unilaterally in a supreme national emergency. London also agreed, as set down in the Nassau communiqué, that "the purpose of the two governments with respect to the provision of the Polaris missiles must be the development of a multinational NATO nuclear force in the closest consultation with other NATO allies." However, though at Nassau both the terms "multilateral" and "multinational" were used to describe possible ways of internationalizing the Polaris force America would provide Britain, Kennedy later told me there was no agreement on what those terms meant with regard to a NATO nuclear force. Such ambiguity, often helpful in reaching an agreement, can prove the source of confusion and recrimination later.

The Nassau agreement to provide essential delivery systems for a national nuclear force cut across the grain of the MLF effort, which sought to stem the spread of such national forces. It also cut across the expressed U.S. policy of not aiding national nuclear forces. Kennedy and his advisors, such as McGeorge Bundy, realized that something had to be done quickly to reconcile the situation, but once again the horse of U.S. policy managed to ride off in two directions at the same time. On the one hand, Kennedy authorized a new mission to Europe to discuss the MLF proposal. On the other hand, an offer was made to provide France with Polaris missiles on the same terms as were given to the British. De Gaulle, however, quickly refused, telling the U.S. emissary, George Ball, that the missiles would be of little use as France had neither the warheads or the submarines to give them utility. Then, to cap things off, de Gaulle soon thereafter vetoed Britain's application to enter the Common Market, though he professed to have made this decision before learning of the Nassau agreement.[30]

My aforementioned discussions with the British had also touched upon the other major player in European diplomacy— West

Germany. In the aftermath of Nassau, Adenauer told George Ball, it was only the prospect of the MLF that had prevented a serious rift between Washington and Bonn when Kennedy authorized a similar Polaris offer to France but not West Germany.

European Perspectives, 1963

The diplomatic constellation of forces clearly provided no wide or deep consensus in favor of the MLF as 1963 began. Only the Germans could be seen as anywhere near firmly on board, and this for their own particular reasons rooted in the desire for equal status within the Atlantic alliance, and the core security interest in maintaining the U.S. link to defense of Europe and West Germany. The British were just as plainly following their own national interests, which meant that any solution to NATO's nuclear dilemmas had to square with the survival of the so-called independent deterrent. This would lead the British to begin advancing an alternative to the MLF termed the Atlantic Nuclear Force, or ANF, which would be built upon contributions of nuclear forces from the United States and Britain, with the other alliance members (including West Germany) taking a secondary role, a course obviously at odds with German priorities. France under de Gaulle would become progressively more hostile to the MLF, tracking the deepening chasm between France and NATO, during 1963 and 1964. For de Gaulle, perhaps the key problem with the MLF was that it would tie West Germany and European defense ever more tightly to the United States, while he wished to pursue a European defense based upon the Franco-West German relationship. This in turn posed serious dilemmas for Bonn, which wanted to sustain U.S. engagement in European security without having to choose between the United States and France.[31]

Further stirring up the diplomatic waters was the anticipated opposition of the Soviets, who lost no opportunity to point out what they saw as the logical incompatibility between the MLF and the concurrent negotiations to reach agreement upon a nuclear nonproliferation treaty. While couched in general terms, the Soviet concern was rooted in the fear that the MLF would lay the basis for a nuclearized West Germany. This concern was reflected in the warnings issued by ACDA's head, Bill Foster, that U.S. efforts to advance the MLF would make his efforts to secure a non-proliferation treaty very difficult indeed.[32] The manner in which the MLF could become a bargaining chip in arms control talks was seen when, in the summer of 1963, Kennedy quickly agreed to the suggestion that Averell Harriman, on his way to Moscow for negotiations with the Soviets on a test ban treaty, should offer to abandon the MLF as a "sweetener" to the Soviets, adding that "it would be a great relief to get rid of that!" in light of de Gaulle's clear determination to pursue his own course in Europe.[33]

Domestic Uncertainty, 1963

The final obstacle to the MLF was rooted in domestic politics. First of all, there was the problem of Congress's Joint Committee on Atomic Energy, which would have to pass on any enabling legislation amending the McMahon Act to authorize the transfer of custody of U.S. nuclear warheads to the MLF. This body was fiercely protective of its prerogatives, and made its lack of enthusiasm and even opposition to the MLF clear on more than one occasion, such as a briefing of the JCAE in executive session which I attended in February 1963.[34] There were also serious doubts about the depth of support in Congress overall. I recall that Senator Scoop Jackson, after receiving his first briefing on the MLF, sarcastically commented, "Who dreamed up this nutty idea?"

This anticipated and firmly entrenched opposition to the MLF made Kennedy very cautious about pushing the MLF, as well as sensitive to the potential impact of election year politics upon his ability to get an MLF treaty through Congress. Similar electoral politics affected positions on the MLF in Britain and West Germany, where 1964 was likely to see national campaigns that the governments did not want to see entangled with debate over the merits of the MLF. So, if a treaty was to be secured, it had to be well in advance of the political campaigns.[35]

I was aware of all these intersecting, complex, and often frustrating crosscurrents as I continued my efforts on behalf of the MLF in 1963 and 1964. President Kennedy had given some impetus to MLF with a suggestion that a planned presidential trip to Europe in the summer of 1963 be the occasion for the signing of a preliminary agreement. This idea was shot down in June by a memo from Bundy detailing his concerns that the European allies were not really receptive to the MLF idea–he characterized European support as "slight and 'grudging'"–and that the United States was running the danger of forcing the proposal down our allies' throats. Arguing that the proponents of the MLF in the State Department and elsewhere had gotten ahead of the administration in pressing the idea in Europe, Bundy called for closer oversight of MLF activities and a shift to inquiry rather than pressure as the proper approach to discussing the matter with the NATO allies.[36]

Kennedy reportedly was quite responsive to Bundy's recommendations, which fit his own need to go slow in light of congressional attitudes and the upcoming election year. Trimming back the administration's investment in MLF also served the President's interests with regard to efforts to secure a test ban agreement and a nonproliferation treaty with the Soviets. As Glenn Seaborg has recorded, Kennedy at one point suggested that the United States might offer to trade MLF for a nonproliferation treaty with the Soviets.[37]

Johnson and MLF

Kennedy's assassination in November 1963 brought Lyndon Johnson into the White House. He brought a keen political sensitivity bred of his years in Congress which made him especially attuned to the obstacles the JCAE posed for the MLF, as well as to the problems a contentious treaty debate could pose for his efforts to secure election to the presidency in his own right in 1964. Johnson received a briefing on the status of MLF in early December 1963 which exposed him to the contending views within the administration on the issue. One briefing paper was prepared by Bundy, reiterating his analysis of the situation and recapitulating Kennedy's position, which Bundy said was characterized by a desire not to become tied to a complex treaty which might not survive Senate scrutiny, and the preference that the impetus should come from the Europeans, not as the result of U.S. pressure. Another paper reflected the more optimistic, pro-MLF viewpoint and sought to give a more positive assessment of the diplomatic and political situation facing the MLF at home and abroad.[38]

On the basis of these papers and discussion of them, Johnson authorized further briefings of congressional leaders as well as former President Eisenhower, to determine their current views. I took part in the briefing of Eisenhower, which elicited a strong statement of support from the former president.[39] A memo from Rusk to Johnson reporting on the results of these briefings (which did not include the JCAE leadership) gave a cautious endorsement to moving ahead in talks leading to an MLF agreement that year. A subsequent meeting involving Johnson, George Ball, Thomas Finletter, McGeorge Bundy, and myself thrashed out a decision that again was read differently by those on each side of the issue. Johnson gave the go-ahead for expanded briefings of Congress and continued talks with the Europeans on the basis that the United States believed the MLF was the best solution, and for seeking an MLF agreement by the end of 1964. Despite this seemingly strong endorsement, however, the cables giving Finletter and others their guidance on carrying out this decision stressed the importance Johnson gave to insuring that the MLF was not shoved down the Europeans' throats. Again, U.S. advocacy was put on a short leash, with the onus being placed on the Europeans to provide the impetus and drive for the MLF. For MLF supporters such as Finletter, such an approach would only deepen European doubts about the depth of U.S. commitment to the MLF.[40]

Demise of MLF

Given the lack of consensus in Europe on the MLF, as discussed earlier, in the absence of a strong U.S. lead, which Kennedy and now Johnson, guided by Bundy, equated with the politically unacceptable forcing of the MLF upon NATO, matters were doomed to drift. Outside events, such as the Chinese detonation of an atomic bomb, also affected the balance of forces, in this case giving a higher priority to obtaining a nonproliferation agreement, which within the administration meant lowering the priority for MLF. The final *coup de main* came after Johnson's election victory in November 1964, as preparations went forward for a meeting between Johnson and Harold Wilson, the newly elected Prime Minister of a Labour government existing on the narrowest of majorities in Parliament. As Glenn Seaborg has recounted, it was this visit that spelled the end of the MLF, though the venture stayed alive briefly, in part to avoid too great a shock to our German allies who had given the strongest support to the project. As Johnson focused upon preparing for his talks with Wilson, the forces and factors standing against the MLF were once more rehearsed for the President by Bundy. The JCAE had again made clear its deep concerns in a letter sent to the White House the previous September. The diplomatic scene was likewise unchanged. Never one to bet on a losing horse, Johnson signaled the U.S. willingness to discuss alternatives to the MLF during his meeting with Wilson. From this point on, discussions within NATO about nuclear forces and strategy would proceed on a different track, facilitated by de Gaulle's withdrawal of French forces from the alliance, culminating in the creation of the Nuclear Planning Group as the means to secure greater allied involvement in NATO nuclear matters.[41]

Seeing the handwriting on the wall following the Johnson-Wilson talks, I submitted my resignation to Secretary of State Rusk on December 15, 1964, as head of the State Department's MLF Task Force. In my letter to Rusk, I noted that my assignment had always been seen as a temporary one, and I based my decision on the fact that it now appeared the MLF matter was evolving into much broader NATO nuclear negotiations better conducted by a regular State Department official.[42] I was not the only person to resign in the wake of this shift in policy. Thomas Finletter was particularly embittered by this shift, and resigned his appointment as U.S. Ambassador to NATO, feeling quite naturally that the administration's actions had placed him, a prominent supporter of the MLF, in an untenable position.[43] I had advised Finletter of my plans in a letter sent the same day as my resignation letter to Rusk. In this letter, after noting again the altered nature of the negotiations with NATO, I also mentioned that in talking with George Ball, I had gotten the impression that all of the talk in the press about the MLF "zealots" in the State Department had some effect on high officialdom, and that in light of this I felt my decision would not be unwelcome to the Johnson administration.[44]

My resignation elicited the usual letters of regret seeking to cover over the policy differences leading to my decision. Mac Bundy wrote a gracious note which acknowledged our different "tactical" estimates from time to time, but which also stated that Bundy shared my view that the general concept remained valid.[45] Dean Rusk wrote in a similar vein, noting that my work had "shaped up in great detail an idea which demonstrated that the United States is prepared to share in nuclear responsibilities with allies who are joined with us in such safety as there is in nuclear protection and in such devastation as there would surely be in the event of nuclear conflict."[46] An interesting letter, in light of subsequent events, came from Henry Kissinger, who wrote that though he differed with me on the MLF, he was greatly impressed by the "dignity, efficiency and sense of honor" with which I performed my task.[47]

In writing to Henry Owen a few years later, I listed what I saw as the reasons the MLF did not succeed. As the foregoing discussion makes clear, my views in this regard have changed little. Among the primary reasons I listed were: (1) the U.S. government did not pull together as a team; (2) the weakening of the National Security decisional machinery with the advent of the Kennedy administration engendered this lack of teamwork; (3) the built-in bias on the part of U.S. leaders in favor of Britain, which worked on several occasions to the detriment of a multilateral solution; (4) the Congressional consultation restraints under which we were required to operate; (5) the fact that Secretary of State Rusk apparently never put the full thrust of his office behind the project and, in effect, allowed dissenters in various parts of the administration to operate rather freely; (6) the concern that de Gaulle would prejudice NATO and that the Soviet Union might cease some cooperation with the United States; (7) the fact that 1964 was an election year; (8) the fact that much of the responsibility was thrust upon consultants, not officials, *i.e.*, myself, Merchant, Neustadt; and (9) the unreasonably large power that the JCAE possessed. Among these, Owen felt that the adverse congressional opinion, linked to a similar public attitude, was decisive; the other factors, he felt, could have been overcome.[48]

After resigning from the MLF position, I remained as a consultant to the State Department's Policy Planning Council on a range of issues, many relating to disarmament and nuclear weapons. I stayed in touch with Henry Owen, who continued to carry the torch for a multilateral approach to resolving NATO's nuclear problems, at one point responding to a request from him for suggestions on a possible alternative to MLF with some ideas about a multilateral antiballistic missile force. Explicitly leaving aside the concerns some were beginning to raise about the destabilizing effect of ABMs, I felt that such a project would avoid most of the pitfalls inherent in the MLF and to the degree that a regional ABM proved effective, it would be a spur to nuclear disarmament and non-proliferation.[49] My suggestion of a NATO ABM would prove to be quite ironic, given the course my life and efforts would take when Richard Nixon chose me to be the director of the Arms Control and Disarmament Agency following his election in 1968. This appointment would result in my becoming head of the U.S. delegation to the first Strategic Arms Limitation Talks, in which role I would take quite a different position on the desirability of ABMs. It would also mark a culmination of sorts for a lengthy trajectory in my public career, as I took up the challenging responsibility of engaging the Soviets in a dialogue seeking to curb the mad spiral of the nuclear arms race.

Chapter Five

ACDA and the SALT Negotiations, 1969–72

In early 1969, I returned to public service as the director of the Arms Control and Disarmament Agency (ACDA) and as the chief U.S. negotiator for the first Strategic Arms Limitation Talks, or SALT. By this time, I had been involved in nearly all aspects of nuclear planning, policy, and arms control. I had thought about, written about, and worked on nuclear problems for each of the post-World War II administrations. The ACDA position, and SALT in particular, now offered a unique opportunity to take direct action on my concerns about nuclear weapons. I believed that the chance to place significant controls on strategic arsenals would improve U.S.-Soviet relations. But more important, I thought a superpower agreement would also have a major impact on what I considered the gravest danger, proliferation. As I later summarized before a Senate congressional committee, "[I]f we do not make progress with the Soviets, our prospects of getting other countries to stay away from this [nuclear] business are substantially lessened."[1]

Scholars, former policymakers, and pundits all have written extensively on the SALT story,[2] although much of the official record of the negotiations remains classified. My own impressions and analysis appear in my book *Doubletalk*, which was published in 1980. This chapter does not attempt to duplicate that effort; instead it uses some newly released documentation to reemphasize and elaborate several issues that I consider important: (1) the nature of negotiations, both with the Russians and in Washington; (2) missed opportunities to slow the arms race, especially regarding MIRVs; and (3) the importance of the stability of treaty regimes, as challenged by the quasi-legal Reagan attack on the ABM treaty.

Appointment to ACDA

In January 1969, Secretary of State William Rogers advised me that newly elected President Richard Nixon wanted me to head up ACDA. I was surprised by this news in light of my previous high profile role in MLF planning, which ACDA had viewed as a serious obstacle to negotiating the Nonproliferation Treaty (NPT). Despite my advocacy of the MLF (which I viewed as a complement rather than a barrier to the NPT), the first and only director of ACDA to that time, William C. Foster, recommended my appointment. Foster, a former Defense Department official and chief of the U.S. delegation to the 1958 Surprise Attack Conference, was a close friend with whom I had worked on arms control issues during the Eisenhower administration.

Initially, I had my doubts about accepting the ACDA job. When John McCloy first proposed creating the separate agency under President Kennedy in 1961, one congressman reportedly voted favorably for establishment because it would be good to have all the "arms control nuts" under one roof where they could be closely scrutinized. Some of this shortsighted thinking that arms controllers were all "screwballs" or "do-gooders" continues. I sought advice from three friends and colleagues before taking the ACDA position. Douglas Dillon, former Secretary of the Treasury and Ambassador to France, Senator Henry "Scoop" Jackson, and Admiral Rickover all recommended that I accept. I particularly remember the admiral's counsel. "It's time you settled down," he said. "If you take the ACDA job, be prepared to work on it for twelve to sixteen years." Later, I found out that another good friend, Henry Owen, my close colleague on the Policy Planning staff, had put my name, as well as two others, forward as possible candidates for ACDA at the time that the agency was created. About me he said, "He's a good executive, knows arms control thoroughly and has right ideas, and [he] gets on well with the military."[3] I am sure that at least Henry's last point had something to do with my eventual appointment to the post in 1969. I later found out (by way of the JCS representative on the SALT delegation) that when JCS Chairman General Earl Wheeler learned of my appointment to head the SALT delegation, he was reported to have said, "This is good news."

Even though ACDA was under funded, under staffed, and under represented in the Washington bureaucracy, I never regretted taking on this responsibility. Despite such problems, I believed that it was a sensible idea to set up a separate group within government to deal with arms control matters. The existence of a separate agency, whose director at least had nominally direct access to the President, has assured for arms control an independent voice in decision-making circles, one that probably could not be guaranteed with simply an arms control section or division of the State Department or some other similar arrangement. ACDA should be an activist proponent of realistic arms control measures; it should be a participant in government decisions about both arms and arms control; and it should inform the public, Congress, and the President about arms control matters. As I once wrote, "ACDA as the needle, the catalyst, the conscience of an administration can produce results."[4]

In making choices about staffing ACDA, I attempted to adhere to this activist philosophy. One choice appeared obvious. As my deputy and right arm, I selected Phil Farley, my former State Department associate who had vast experience in making and carrying out arms control policies. I trusted Phil with many of the administrative duties of running ACDA as well as with backstopping all major negotiations while I was abroad. Other appointments reflected my sense of maintaining a high level of bureaucratic and technical expertise within the agency: Larry Weiler as counselor; Spurgeon Keeny as head of the Science and Technology Bureau, with Sid Graybeal as his deputy; James Leonard, a career foreign service officer, for International Relations; and Admiral John M. Lee, who had worked with me on the MLF effort, in charge of Weapons Evaluation and Control.

In naming Farley as my deputy, I had my first (but definitely not last) minor run-in with the Nixon White House. Shortly after I was appointed, the White House "advised" me that my deputy would be William Casey, a close friend of Nixon's and the same Bill Casey who later would become CIA director under President Reagan. I had known Casey when he was a practicing lawyer in New York, and I politely but firmly rejected the recommendation. The White House insisted. I then spoke to Secretary of State Rogers, and he said, "You mean that New York lawyer?" I said, "That's the man." Rogers then called the President and had the designation canceled.

Why SALT?

U.S. and Soviet interest in SALT in 1969 stemmed from one basic premise. By this time, stockpiles of nuclear weapons and the means to deliver them had reached such levels that the two sides could agree that their national security lay in some degree of mutual restraint. In essence, both sides had reached a new level of strategic maturity. Washington and Moscow each cited the risks of nuclear war and the prohibitive costs of carrying on an unbridled strategic competition as reasons to enter into negotiations.

Each side had its own slant on the common theme of mutual security through arms control. For the United States, arms limitation had become more palatable because of fundamental changes in the strategic environment brought on by a determined Soviet buildup following the 1962 Cuban Missile Crisis. U.S. nuclear dominance had clearly and irrevocably ended. Despite his tough campaign rhetoric, Nixon accepted this nuclear fact of life once in office, moving away from a doctrine of "superiority" toward one of strategic "sufficiency" or parity. The President indicated this shift in his first annual foreign policy report to Congress. The report emphasized that each side now possessed a retaliatory force that could inflict unacceptable damage even after it had been attacked in a first strike. "Thus," it concluded, "both sides have recognized a vital mutual interest in halting the dangerous momentum of the nuclear arms race."[5] The fear, however, was that the Soviets would not stop at parity, but would continue to build.

As I noted in *Doubletalk*, and as I have indicated in previous chapters, the notion of nuclear capabilities as a wasting asset owes much to the legacy of the Eisenhower administration. Eisenhower was consistently an arms control advocate within his own bureaucracy, and he encouraged those of us working on the problem on a day-to-day basis. His administration considered the doctrine of sufficiency fully thirteen years before Nixon came into office. An interesting early statement of the basic premise of negotiations is contained in former AEC Chairman Gordon Dean's preface to Kissinger's influential 1957 study on *Nuclear Weapons and Foreign Policy*:

> For all practical purposes we have in terms of nuclear capabilities reached a point which may be called "parity." We have long known that such a time would come. It is now upon us. I do not mean necessarily parity in numbers of large bombs. Numbers become less important when the point is reached where both sides have the capability to annihilate each other.[6]

For the Soviet Union, negotiations were attractive for slightly different reasons. The Soviets traditionally had been haunted by feelings of national inferiority and inequality with the West. The leaders who took over in 1964 in the wake of the Cuban Missile Crisis, Leonid Brezhnev and Alexei Kosygin, viewed SALT as one way to redress the situation. U.S. recognition of the Soviet Union as a full negotiating partner meant recognition of Moscow's status as a superpower as well. The Brezhnev-Kosygin regime also recognized an opportunity to check U.S. technological development through SALT.[7]

Beyond strategic considerations, Nixon and Kissinger had other, grander rationales for SALT. In proclaiming an "era of negotiations" in his inaugural address, Nixon and his national security adviser hoped to place SALT in a broader strategy of détente. Their idea was to negotiate zones of stability separately with the Soviets and the Chinese. They hoped to get these communist powers to control nationalist movements and refrain from global adventurism in partial return for an agreement on strategic nuclear forces. Nixon hinted at such linkage in his first press conference in January 1969: "What I want to do is to see to it that we have strategic arms talks in such a way and at a time that will promote . . . progress on outstanding political problems at the same time."[8]

My own views on SALT corresponded much more with those of military planners and arms controllers who stressed classic objectives of strategic stability and nonproliferation. In November 1968, anticipating a Nixon victory at the polls, I wrote an article in *Interplay* magazine (a journal which I had a hand in starting, as I will discuss in the next chapter) speculating on foreign policy directions under the new administration. Noting that all the candidates seemed to be prudent men of the center on foreign affairs, I argued that the first priority for the new person in the White House would be to end the war in Vietnam. Following a close second and third, however, were relations with Europe and our allies and negotiations with the Soviet Union. The time was ripe, I maintained, to press arms control in general and controls on ballistic missiles in particular. "It may well be now or never in the case of anti-ballistic and multiple warhead missiles," I concluded.[9] Moreover, I strongly believed that a major by-product of any East-West restriction on strategic weapons would be to help control the spread of nuclear weapons to other countries.

SALT Negotiations: Setting Up the Process

Remarkably, one year after the *Interplay* article appeared, I found myself in Helsinki, Finland, sitting across the table from Soviet representative, Vice Minister of Foreign Affairs Vladimir S. Semenov, at the opening round of the SALT talks. My personal road to this position had gone through a number of direct interactions with the Soviets as well as my own private "negotiation" with the Russian language. I had had discussions with the Russians in a number of multilateral forums: the 1955 Geneva international scientific conference on peaceful uses of atomic energy, the 1955 atomic safeguards conference, the 1956 U.N. conference on the IAEA, the 1957 London Disarmament Conference, the 1958 Surprise Attack Conference, the 1958 Geneva international scientific conference, the 1959 four-power conference on Berlin, and the 1960 Paris summit.

My study of the Russian language had begun even earlier, in 1948, and had continued sporadically throughout my government career. I had the good fortune to have available in Washington a member of the Foreign Service Language School, Madame De La Cruz, to help direct my studies, which included innumerable lunchtime sessions. At first I was told that I would have to go over to the Foreign Service School. When I asked if exceptions had ever been made, I was told that a language expert had gone to the White House to help President Kennedy. With this precedent in hand, it was finally agreed that I could have my lessons at ACDA. My occasional use of the Russian language in the negotiations seemed to be appreciated by the Soviet side.

When I became the director of ACDA and strategic arms control became a leading item on the agenda, I naturally assumed, almost as a matter of course, that I would be selected as the head of the U.S. delegation. This would lead, I believed, to more coherent policy formulation on the issue. This practice of combining the positions of ACDA director and chief negotiator continued to work well up to the Carter administration, but became so contentious and consumed by politics during Paul Warnke's tenure as director, as well as SALT II and comprehensive test ban negotiator, that it was stopped. From that time, it has been very difficult to achieve the type of bipartisan consensus that existed for arms control during the 1960s and early 1970s, although we are again approaching that ideal in the post-Cold War environment.

The negotiating team assembled for SALT was an experienced and distinguished group. While not able to go abroad very often because of his involvement in the day-to-day operation of ACDA, Phil Farley served as the formal deputy on the delegation. With my full cooperation, the administration actively recruited people with varied backgrounds–political, diplomatic, technical, and military–to deal with the inherently complex issues of SALT. Scientists no longer dominated the process, as they had during earlier negotiations over a comprehensive test ban, although they continued to contribute important technical input on such crucial questions as verification. The physicist Harold Brown–president of Cal Tech, former director of the Livermore Laboratory, and test ban negotiator–served as the primary technical person on the delegation. Brown, who later served as President Carter's Secretary of Defense, split time between Cal Tech and the negotiations. He combined a keen scientific intellect with an uncanny affinity for international politics.

The State Department designated individuals who had demonstrated special expertise in U.S.-Soviet relations. Secretary Rogers's first appointment, Ambassador Llewellyn "Tommy" Thompson was, in 1969, the top American diplomat dealing with Moscow. Thompson had been a major actor during the Cuban Missile Crisis and had advised four presidents on Soviet-American relations. The Soviet leadership apparently had a high regard for him as well. Semenov once told me that Thompson was referred to as a "cheesti chelovek"–an honest man. Unfortunately, Thompson became ill in 1970, and died in 1971 before the negotiations ended. James Graham "Jeff" Parsons, a senior foreign service officer who had been ambassador to Sweden, replaced Thompson as the State Department representative. Another Soviet expert, Ray Garthoff of the State Department, served as liaison with the Russian delegation. Referred to as a "wizard" by Semenov, Garthoff once wondered to me what the Soviets might think if they knew that his wife's grandfather had been a minister for the Czarist navy.

A key member of the SALT team was Air Force General Royal B. Allison. I did not directly recruit General Allison, who was designated by the JCS chairman, but I readily agreed with his appointment. Allison's presence on the delegation indicated an attitude of seriousness on the part of the U.S. uniformed military toward arms control. During the Johnson administration, JCS Chairman Earl Wheeler, with whom I worked closely while I was in the State Department, had set up a special Office for Strategic Arms Negotiations, and named Allison to direct it. Allison, a World War II fighter pilot and longtime Pentagon strategic planner, helped lay the groundwork for SALT, and helped assure military understanding and support for the process. Secretary of Defense Melvin Laird designated Paul Nitze to represent the civilian side of the Pentagon. Nitze was also a former director of Policy Planning in the State Department, and he had worked on nuclear matters in the government for over twenty years.

The head of the Soviet delegation, Vladimir Semenov, was a senior diplomat, who, by his own admission, had little background in arms control issues. A graduate of the Moscow Institute of History, Philosophy, and Literature, Semenov joined the Foreign Service in 1939 and specialized in Central European and Middle Eastern affairs. Semenov was quite an interesting character. On December 6, 1969, I described him in a letter to my brother, coining a new word in the process. "My opposite number," I wrote, "is very 'culturny'–fond of Bach and Goethe, full of references to musical analogies and old Russian proverbs, which apparently are useful in the arms control dialogue."[10] Interested in history, philosophy, and art, able to understand German and English, Semenov was a true Russian renaissance man. He liked to quote from the classics, including the Bible and the Koran, and was very precise in choosing his words in both official and unofficial settings. During our long hours together, I came to respect him.

Semenov had been a political adviser to the commanding general during the 1945 Battle of Berlin. He also played a major part in negotiating the end of the Finnish War. The top Soviet military delegate was General Ogarkhov, who subsequently became a Marshal of the Soviet armed forces. On his death in 1994, it was reported that Ogarkhov had been the only remaining Soviet Marshal.

An unusual arrangement that I insisted upon was that wives could accompany the delegation. The Soviets soon imitated this idea. At first, the administrative people at State refused my request, but when I pointed out that if ever a U.S. delegate was seduced by a Russian agent, I would know where to place the blame, I quickly got permission to have the wives go with us!

Although Semenov and I got along well personally, we knew our job would not be an easy one. My office in Vienna during SALT had a plaque on the wall which said, "In this room the ultimatum leading to World War I was signed." We hoped to do better. As one of my aides said at the time, "It was the room where World War I began. Let's hope World War III is averted there."[11] But years of distrust and Cold War conflict had led to what was called a "binocular view" of each other's nuclear arsenals. We looked through the end of the binoculars which magnified their programs, and we looked at our own programs through the other end. I assumed the Soviets did the same. I wish that there were a better public understanding of this rather distorting optic–what is usually called worst case analysis–which not only takes liberties with the past but results in possibly unnecessary overinsurance for the unknowns of the future.[12]

At least on the big questions, Ambassador Semenov and I seemed to have similar perspectives. Semenov's opening statement, cleared by Moscow, offered what I thought were encouraging signs. As I reported back to President Nixon:

> The first business session this morning went off slightly better than I had expected. Semenov's statement had a minimum of polemic . . . clearly intended to lay the basis for a serious exchange of views. He spoke of nuclear war as a disaster for both sides–of the decrease of security as the number of weapons increases–of the costly results of rapid obsolescence of weapons–of the dangers of grave miscalculations–of unauthorized use of weapons–and of hostilities resulting from third power provocation.[13]

Throughout the negotiations, I found Semenov and the other Soviet delegates to be very serious and businesslike in their approach. I remember contrasting that style to many of my earlier encounters with Russian negotiators who would simply repeat propaganda harangues.[14]

In this spirit of carrying on in a serious and businesslike manner, I prided myself on keeping things under control within the U.S. delegation, and as much as possible, with our Soviet counterparts. I recall one instance when one of Paul Nitze's assistants wired the Pentagon that I had been negotiating face-to-face with Semenov without instructions. This was not true and General Allison, who saw the cable traffic, reported it to me. I had to admonish Nitze for this breach of delegation rules regarding separate communications to Washington. Allison, Nitze, and I flew to Brussels soon after to have breakfast with Secretary of Defense Laird, and the matter was quickly straightened out. But since Nitze had also engaged in a previous breach of the communication rule, I told him that he had two strikes against him. He knew what three strikes meant. He seemed appropriately subdued.

Another incident involved an attempt by a Soviet official to recruit a member of the American delegation who had a Russian name and who was a famous interpreter. I received a report that this had occurred at the very first Soviet-American reception before formal negotiations had started. I got word immediately to Semenov that this sort of tactic would not be tolerated. No other attempts (at least that I know of) were made by the Soviets.

Semenov and I agreed on the principle of confidentiality with regard to our discussions. "Secrecy was immaculate," one prominent historian of the process has noted.[15] Leaks occurred, but they came out of Washington, not Helsinki or Vienna. Before SALT, I think I had a deserved reputation of not revealing inside information to newspaper people. Arthur Krock once referred to me as "the tomb." The one exception was when I was directed to hold a background briefing for a *New York Times* reporter on President Eisenhower's Atoms for Peace proposal. A few days later, a headline story in the *Times* disclosed much of Eisenhower's thinking on the issue. I quickly informed AEC Chairman Strauss that I was to blame. Strauss told me to forget about it; some crisis would come along and take the story away. That in fact happened, but it taught me a lesson that I carried with me throughout my government career.

Negotiations at Home: The Infamous Back Channel

Another principle that I attempted to adhere to throughout the negotiations was to stay strictly within my instructions from home, to not embarrass Washington, and yet fight hard within the bureaucracy for positions I thought important. Ultimately, however, I found it extremely difficult to deal with the White House because of the machinations of Kissinger and Nixon. As I and others have recounted, Kissinger took absolute authority over national security decision making within the administration. Obsessed with secrecy, distrustful of nearly all within the Washington establishment, Nixon was a willing partner in this process. In effect, as John Newhouse characterizes it, Kissinger "functioned as a kind of prime minister rather than a senior adviser."[16]

I later learned that Nixon and Kissinger had a particular distrust of ACDA and arms controllers that extended to me as the director of the agency. Apparently, as Paul Nitze tells it in his memoirs, the White House viewed both me and Secretary of State Rogers with suspicion, as being too liberal and perhaps too eager to reach agreement with the Soviets. According to Nitze, Nixon and Kissinger called him into the President's office before the negotiations began. They asked him to keep an eye on me and report anything that he did not agree with directly to the White House. Nitze refused, but Nixon repeated the suggestion and spoke of a special JCS back channel communication that would remain open to him throughout the talks.[17]

When the negotiations began, Kissinger, in characteristic fashion, set out to gain total control of SALT policymaking and planning. He did this first by dominating the so-called National Security Council system. He was the special assistant to Nixon for national security affairs, but he also directed the NSC staff and chaired the Verification Panel, the special committee charged to deal with arms control, with representatives from all the major agencies. I was a member of the Verification Panel. In fact, I had originally suggested that the Panel be set up in June 1969. But as its chair, Kissinger came to use the Panel–and the entire NSC machinery for that matter–as little more than an information funnel and debating society rather than a problem-solving body.

More important, Kissinger set up a separate negotiating channel between Washington and Moscow completely independent of the official diplomatic talks. At the time, this parallel negotiation between Kissinger and Soviet Ambassador Anatoly Dobrynin was known to no one on the U.S. side except the President. Information was so closely held that Secretary of Defense Laird attempted, unsuccessfully, to have Kissinger's back channel traffic read by the admiral in charge of the National Security Agency, with the promise of a significant promotion at the end of his tour. No less than an effort to "restructure the bureaucracy to serve their ends,"[18] to borrow the words of George Bunn, former general counsel of ACDA and NPT negotiator, the Nixon and Kissinger back channel had many more negative than positive consequences. It imposed an additional set of negotiations on a process that already had many complex layers. It placed an extreme burden on the diplomatic negotiations and on our relations with allies and Congress. As I described the back channel in *Doubletalk*:

> It was a one man stand, a presidential aide against the resources of the Soviet leadership. There were no building blocks, no analytical work, no strategic analysis in the agencies concerned. There were no Verification Panel or National Security Council discussions. There were no consultations [by Kissinger] with congressional committees or with allies. . . . It is not a pleasing contrast—one American (presumably keeping the President informed) ranged against the top Soviet political and technical authorities.[19]

In his memoirs, Kissinger has touted the back channel as providing significant breakthroughs in SALT. One major example he cites is the May 20, 1971, understanding that he achieved with the Russians on the key issue of the interrelationship of offensive and defensive systems, and the need to achieve limits on both at the same time. According to Kissinger, the May 1971 accord represented "a milestone in confirming White House dominance of foreign affairs."[20] In reality, this Kissinger "non-negotiation," as I prefer to call it, resulted in bringing Moscow to a position that Soviet officials had indicated to me and the U.S. delegation as early as December 1970. I reported this development in the Soviet position to Washington but received no instructions for follow-up. Presumably, Kissinger was preoccupied with the back-channel negotiations. I regret that when Kissinger finally called me into his office to tell me about the "great breakthrough" that he had personally achieved, I did not point out to him that he had been pushing on an open door, that the Soviets had proposed a similar arrangement many months before.

The back channel not only cost us time; in some cases it actually worked to the detriment of U.S. interests and the long-term interests of arms control. One important instance related to Submarine Launched Ballistic Missiles (SLBMs). In the midst of a major buildup, the Soviets showed no interest in including SLBM launchers in any offensive force agreement. Kissinger, in his private negotiations, told Dobrynin that limits on offensive forces would not have to include SLBMs. This decision, which all U.S. government agencies opposed, eventually was reversed in 1972, but only at a price. The final terms of inclusion allowed for a differential in the Soviet favor of 950 to 656 launchers. Although this compromise did not in any way jeopardize our strategic deterrent, as some have argued, I believe it was nonetheless unnecessary and costly in a political sense. Because the strategic balance has such a large psychological component, I knew that the perceived Russian advantage would create severe political problems for SALT down the road.

Forward Based Systems: A Soviet Obsession

At the beginning of SALT, the delegation and I still did not have a clear-cut picture about where Washington wanted to carry the negotiations. Because of the issue of linkage, I personally remained somewhat at odds with Nixon and Kissinger on overall goals and objectives. Just before the talks started in Helsinki, Nixon wrote to me and reiterated that he had broader political intentions in mind for SALT:

> I should like to make clear that I view arms limitation talks in the context of our overall relations with the Soviet Union. . . . I do believe that, to be meaningful, progress in arms limitation must be accompanied by progress in the solution of critical political problems. . . .[21]

I continued to have a more limited view, hoping to achieve a more secure strategic deterrent as a result of the talks. Publicly the administration endorsed such a perspective. On November 13, 1969, Secretary of State Rogers announced the U.S. SALT objectives: (1) to promote a stable U.S.-Soviet strategic relationship, (2) to dampen the arms race, and (3) to reduce the risks of nuclear war.[22] But Kissinger and Nixon continued to press the idea of linkage on me, and, as I later learned, on the Soviets through the back channel.[23]

The opening round of talks was necessarily exploratory in nature. In an effort to establish at least a framework for negotiations and to define a work program, we put forward a set of "Illustrative Elements." Specifically *not* a set of formal proposals, the Elements identified possible categories of systems to be controlled and suggested certain negotiating principles. They advanced the idea of limitations on ABMs and called for a freeze on offensive missile launchers, both ICBMs and SLBMs, with freedom to mix. They did not say anything about aircraft or MIRVs, which certainly Semenov must have mentally noted but did not comment on openly.

The specifics of the Illustrative Elements, and SALT generally, owe much to the excellent preparatory work done by the Johnson administration. Several members of our delegation–General Allison, Harold Brown, and Ambassador Thompson, for example–had been in the middle of those initial studies. Johnson, moreover, had taken a personal interest in the subject. He and his national security advisor, Walt Rostow, kept alive until quite late the possibility of a summit meeting with Moscow on arms limitation. Exchanges took place up until the late fall of 1968, when the Soviet invasion of Czechoslovakia ended all possibility of starting talks.[24] I was briefed on those exchanges, and I had a chance to go over the written record, but only after requesting that the documents be sent back to Washington. The papers had already gone down to the University of Texas in anticipation of being placed in the new Johnson presidential library.[25]

The Illustrative Elements proved very useful as a starting point in the talks, and in fact anticipated most components of the final SALT product two-and-one-half years later. Their introduction, however, also foreshadowed how difficult the negotiations would be. One of the members of our own delegation, only slightly with tongue-in-cheek, observed that our offer was so complicated he would have to build a slide rule to explain it, which he did. Certainly, we were not prepared for the Soviet response, which took us very much by surprise and down a path that presented major obstacles to progress.

On November 26, 1969, Semenov, arguing that geographic asymmetries should be accounted for, introduced the contentious issue of forward-based systems (FBS), by which he primarily meant U.S. land and carrier-based aircraft capable of delivering atomic weapons on Soviet soil. Tommy Thompson, representing the State Department on our delegation, immediately recognized the gravity of the problem posed by FBS. Thompson came up to me right after the session and emphasized that Semenov's remarks were a particularly bad omen for the negotiations. He stressed that I should at the earliest opportunity take the position that FBS were clearly not intended to be covered by SALT. Of course, Thompson was right since this matter plagued the negotiation directly for many, many months, and indirectly for years throughout SALT I and II.

The Soviets brought up FBS every chance they could. Semenov raised it over and over, to the point that, as I reported in *Doubletalk*, "the subject was drilled into us ad nauseam."[26] I have recently had the opportunity to review newly declassified ACDA documents on SALT and FBS. This interesting set of materials, put together by ACDA's historical division, has reconfirmed my strong sense of the centrality and intensity of the FBS question for Moscow. Semenov first demanded that any agreement on offensive forces should ban all foreign deployment of nuclear capable systems, the so-called "radical solution." He later offered an alternative proposal that called for "compensation"; that is, partially withdrawing FBS and allowing the Soviets an advantage in the number of central systems.[27]

Soviet motives for raising and pressing the FBS issue cannot be known with any real certainty until Russian archives are fully opened to historians. At the time I wrote *Doubletalk*, I speculated that Moscow perhaps wanted to use FBS to drive a wedge between us and our NATO and Pacific allies. But I also added that the farther their position evolved, it seemed from my perspective that Semenov was expressing a genuine concern about a perceived U.S. strategic advantage.[28] Clearly, the Soviet military was a driving force behind the Kremlin's FBS position. To illustrate their concerns, one Soviet general at the negotiations told the following anecdote. During World War II, he recounted, the Germans bombed his unit while he was in the hospital, and he was wounded a second time. He did not stop to ask whether it was a strategic weapon or a bomb from a fighter plane that had hit him. Semenov would also vividly illustrate the military's uneasiness by bringing out maps of American bases around the Soviet Union. He would then ask, how could it be denied that the bases represented a "threat of a strategic nature for the Soviet Union?"[29]

In retrospect, and even at that time, I could see the logic of the Soviet argument. I remember seeing some figures, for example, that indicated that U.S. fighter and carrier bombers in the Mediterranean could knock out as much as one-third of the whole Russian navy. Still, for obvious reasons, these private sentiments could not and were not brought into the formal negotiations. I made a strong case that the talks should focus on central strategic systems. As I said at the time, ICBMs and SLBMs were the true "time urgent systems." Tactical aircraft were strategically insignificant by comparison and were not a driving force in the U.S.-Soviet arms competition. In addition, I noted the definitional problems in attempting to bring FBS into the talks.[30] Finally, I separately reassured our allies that the United States would not compromise on this issue. In fact, the U.S. position never changed.

Although the Soviets ultimately agreed to defer FBS, truly comprehensive limitations on offensive strategic forces could not be achieved in SALT I because of this issue. We learned the hard way that grave problems are raised for arms control by systems that can perform more than one function, and that basic asymmetries between the two sides, caused by inherent geopolitical differences, require a great deal of attention.

MIRV: A Missed Opportunity?

In addition to FBS, SALT I also set aside the issue of limits on a critical emerging technology—multiple missile warheads, or more formally, multiple independently-targeted reentry vehicles (MIRVs). MIRV technology evolved within the U.S. research and development community in the late 1950s and early 1960s. Handled at a higher than usual level of secrecy, MIRV programs moved forward with little controversy or debate during the 1960s. The first MIRV tests took place in 1968. Analysts justified MIRV internally as a hedge against growing Soviet ABM capabilities and as a cost-effective offensive force multiplier. MIRVs had a potential downside, however, that many recognized early on. Highly accurate MIRVed systems, predicted for the 1980s, posed a threat to fixed land-based ICBMs, thus putting a premium on surprise and preemption in a crisis. Such "crisis instability" could in turn lead to more long-term "arms race instability" as each side made efforts to deal with the problem. Although highly theoretical, depending on the relative importance of ICBMs in a given strategic arsenal, these instabilities could be potentially troublesome.[31]

Why, then, did we not make more of an effort during SALT to get at this problem? In 1974, after both the United States and Soviet Union had developed MIRVs, Secretary of State Kissinger suggested that it had been a matter largely of oversight and neglect. "I would say in retrospect," Kissinger lamented at a December press briefing, "that I wish I had thought through the implications of a MIRVed world more thoughtfully in 1969 and 1970 than I did."[32] Yet, as Kissinger himself later acknowledged in his memoirs, the reasons that MIRV went forward go far beyond such a simplistic explanation.

As ACDA director and SALT chief negotiator, I strongly believed that the United States should make a concerted effort to control MIRVs within the context of a strategic arms limitation agreement addressing both offensive and defensive systems. During 1969 and again in 1970, I did my best to get the President and Kissinger to press for a ban on MIRV deployment as a complement to limitations on ABMs. In letters to Secretary of State Rogers and to President Nixon and in presentations before the Verification Panel and NSC, I argued that a MIRV ban would be in the long-term interest of the United States because of the larger capacity (throwweight) of Soviet ICBMs. As I summarized in one letter to Secretary Rogers of June 1969:

> It may be that our giving up MIRVs would be the only quid pro quo that the Soviets would be interested in for their halting deployment of ICBMs, SLBMs, [and] ABMs. I believe that a strong case can also be made that in the long run it is not in U.S. interests to see

> MIRVs enter U.S. and Soviet arsenals. Certainly it will bring increased instability.[33]

The driving intellectual and scientific force behind my position at this time can be traced to one of my colleagues at ACDA, Ben Huberman. Huberman was in the ACDA scientific bureau, and would later go on to become deputy scientific advisor in the White House. Earlier, he had worked on nuclear propulsion problems for Admiral Rickover. Huberman did all the number crunching that demonstrated, at least to me, how a U.S. MIRVed force could appear as a real threat to the Soviets and how MIRVed arsenals on both sides would bring increased strategic instability. He wrote the basic papers which I used in making my arguments to the President and NSC.

At the suggestion of another ACDA official, Sidney Graybeal, who would later go on to distinguish himself as the first head of the SALT Standing Consultative Commission, I incorporated my MIRV proposals into a broader package called "Stop Where We Are" (SWWA). In January 1964, President Johnson had proposed a "verified freeze" on strategic launchers (at a time, however, when the Soviets were so far behind in numbers as to not seriously consider such a proposal). I now made a case to freeze forces at the 1969 level with a moratorium on all strategic construction programs, including MIRVs.

Storm warnings about MIRVs were reaching the White House from a number of other sources as well in 1969-70. Studies by the JASON group–a special advisory body of scientists and other specialists who gathered together each summer to examine national security and defense issues–and a separate report of ACDA's General Advisory Committee cautioned against headlong MIRV development. Both the JASON group and the GAC/ACDA reports recommended instituting a test moratorium until the question could be raised in SALT. Even more directly, Kissinger during this period met on a regular basis with a group of expert former officials and advisers–including Jack Ruina, Sidney Drell, Richard Garwin, Wolfgang Panofsky, and Paul Doty–to discuss strategic and arms control issues. Most of this group were former colleagues of

Kissinger from his Harvard days. MIRV was a frequent topic at these informal meetings, which were arranged by Doty.[34]

Most of the early official documentation on MIRVs and ICBM vulnerability remains classified, but one interesting report of MIT physicists George Rathjens and Jack Ruina has come to my attention. Rathjens sent the report, entitled "A Moratorium on the Testing of Multiple Warheads," to Kissinger on June 2, 1969. Although asked by Kissinger to develop "several formal alternative proposals" on MIRVs, Rathjens and Ruina saw only "two meaningful alternatives: a simple moratorium . . . or waiting until the Strategic Arms Limitation Talks to deal with the problem as a matter of high priority." "We are concerned," the authors maintained, "that if tests are permitted to continue on these first generation systems, the point will have been passed where we could have the required high confidence that the Soviet Union might not develop a counter-force capability some years hence without it being obvious to unilateral intelligence collection efforts." Rathjens again reminded Kissinger about the potential problems of ICBM vulnerability and MIRVing in yet another letter of April 13, 1970, just before the reopening of SALT negotiations.[35]

In the meantime, Ruina and other specialists brought many of their arguments into the public domain in testimony before Congress. A congressional effort to achieve a MIRV ban, led by Senator Edward Brooke of Massachusetts (and his national security advisor Alton Frye), was already well under way by mid-1969. Brooke, with strong support both in the Senate and the House, introduced Resolution 211 for a mutual suspension of MIRV testing. Several major newspapers, including the *New York Times*, *Wall Street Journal*, and *Washington Post*, added their voices to the anti-MIRV agitation. In August 1969, Senator Hubert Humphrey, after a visit with Soviet officials and scientists in Moscow urged a unilateral U.S. MIRV test suspension.[36]

I did not favor a unilateral suspension, but I did continue to push for a negotiated moratorium. The response by Nixon and Kissinger to all of these overtures on MIRV left much to be desired. After much interagency discussion and consideration, the President authorized me to make only one-sided, nonnegotiable "approaches" to the Soviets. The principal "approach" called for a ban on testing and deployment of MIRVs but not on production, and contained requirements for on-site inspection that went far beyond anything the Soviets might accept. The verification provisions asked for inspection not only of MIRVed systems but also of antiaircraft and ABM sites. It was perfectly clear that this proposal was a complete nonstarter, meant primarily to placate domestic opponents of MIRV. As for my SWWA proposal, Nixon never saw it as anything more than a propaganda ploy.[37]

Rather than any dearth of analysis of the problem, as suggested by Kissinger's deceptive 1974 statement, I am convinced that the White House did not make serious proposals because of internal opposition to a MIRV ban, in particular from the JCS and Secretary of Defense Melvin Laird. While the military generally supported the arms control process as represented by SALT, they drew the line at setting qualitative as opposed to quantitative limits on U.S. forces. They made this position clear within the bureaucracy early on. A draft treaty prepared in the summer of 1968 for President Johnson by the Pentagon, CIA, State Department, and ACDA contained only references to quantitative limits on ABMs and missile launchers. "*There were to be no numerical restrictions on MIRVs* [then undergoing their first test]," Glenn Seaborg reports. The JCS "insisted on this."[38]

The military continued to say no to MIRV restrictions in 1969–70 for a simple and all too familiar reason. The United States was ahead in MIRV technology at the time of SALT and did not want to relinquish this short-term advantage. To the Pentagon, MIRV represented America's technological "trump card." In addition, the administration could not get satisfactory assurances from the intelligence community regarding Soviet compliance with any potential MIRV ban. Many months before Nixon's final decision on this score, as an exception to my usual practice, I had had a conversation with the prominent *Wall Street Journal* reporter Robert Kleiman that foreshadowed the government's concession to the Pentagon's position. Prominent defense officials David Packard and John Foster had flatly told Kleiman that there would be no MIRV ban without on-site inspection. Kleiman said to me that Nixon would be loath to propose a ban without on-site inspections because of the necessity to maintain such conservative support.[39]

The Soviet MIRV position turned out to be as untenable as ours. Moscow countered with a plan to prohibit deployment and production but not testing, which they had not yet started. They knew full well that no real way existed to monitor a production ban. Undoubtedly, a similar process to our own was taking place in the Kremlin bureaucracy, with the Soviet military opposed to a ban because they were behind in MIRV development. Reflecting this lack of interest, Semenov told me privately that controls on MIRVs probably would "complicate" an already difficult negotiation.[40] It was almost as if there existed a silent conspiracy to make it look as though we were striving for a MIRV ban when in fact neither side was.

But the fact remains that however unlikely a positive outcome might have been, the onus must go to the U.S. side for not putting forward a realistic MIRV proposal. We never gave a MIRV ban a real chance. Since we had tested MIRVs and were about ready to deploy, the Soviets expected the United States to take the lead on this subject. In June 1970, my deputy Farley and Ronald Spiers, a veteran arms controller in the State Department, indicated to Secretary of State Rogers that we should at least consider the Soviet offer of a production ban if Moscow would accept a flight test ban.[41] This never happened, and I personally regret not making another, more concerted effort on MIRVs during the ensuing stages of SALT.

After the American decision not to attempt to ban MIRVs in 1970, the United States and Soviet Union went forward with extensive modernization programs of all strategic systems, resulting in a tenfold increase in strategic warheads. It is perhaps not surprising that short-term considerations for both sides–for Washington to stay ahead and for Moscow to catch up–should triumph over long-term questions of stability. Short-sighted thinking has been the general pattern in the history of the superpower competition. Just as we led the way with MIRVs and then worried about the vulnerability of our own strategic forces, so too we led the way with cruise missiles and, when the Soviets imitated us, only then began to worry about the greater vulnerability of our Navy to such weapons. As I noted in 1985, we have played the card of technological leverage again and again to little avail, "believing that our new weapons developments would make us more secure. In every case, the Soviets matched our developments, and we ended up less secure."[42]

ABMs: The Treaty and the Challenge

Despite all of the trials and difficulties we had with the offensive components of SALT, we did manage to achieve an Interim Agreement that at least set a numerical cap on strategic systems. The offensive force threat remained, however, most visibly represented by the proliferation of MIRVed launchers.

On the defensive side, we did much better. Although we missed a chance to ban ABMs entirely, the 1972 ABM Treaty was a solid accomplishment. The treaty severely restricted nationwide ballistic missile defenses, closing off an entire area of strategic arms competition. Without it, there would be many more strategic weapons of all kinds, both defensive and offensive. As I said in 1980, this was the "great prize" of SALT I.[43] Most arms control and national security specialists still regard the treaty as the centerpiece of the entire arms control regime.

It is interesting to chart the strange odyssey of defenses since the treaty was signed. As an indication of the fluidity in arms control thinking, the Soviets wanted only offensive controls in 1968; we wanted both offensive and defensive limitations. Then, in Salt I, until late 1970, the Soviets wanted to control defenses only; we said we wanted both. In 1985, when the Soviets wanted both offensive and defensive limitations, we had reversed gears and wanted only offensive controls. Again as I have noted elsewhere, "how quickly the strategic orthodoxies of one decade become the heresies of the next!"[44]

The original rationale or premise behind ABM control, with which I fully agreed, was that ABMs would add a particularly destabilizing component to the arms race by acting as a stimulus to offensive countermeasures. Within the U.S. government, Jack Ruina, while director of the Pentagon's Advanced Research Projects Agency (ARPA), in the early 1960s, was one of the first to seriously urge limiting ABMs by agreement. Jerome Wiesner, while science advisor to Presidents Kennedy and Johnson, did the same in the

White House.[45] The ABM became the special concern of Defense Secretary Robert McNamara, who gradually conveyed his concerns about ABMs to President Johnson. This or any other technological fix, he argued, offered no sure security guarantees and might completely unsettle the deterrent system. To help bolster his case, McNamara in January 1967 arranged a special meeting of the President and all past and current White House science advisers and defense directors of research and engineering. This distinguished group–Donald Hornig, John Foster, Harold Brown, Jerome Wiesner, James Killian, George Kistiakowsky, and Herbert York–unanimously recommended against ABM deployment.[46]

It was difficult for the Soviets to accept the logic of the McNamara argument. During the 1960s, U.S. officials and scientists expended a great deal of intellectual capital to educate the Soviet leadership about the potentially destabilizing consequences of defenses. After leaving government, Ruina, at a 1964 Pugwash conference, first introduced the idea of an ABM ban to the Soviets, who had begun construction of a system around Moscow. (Inaugurated in July 1957 in Pugwash, Nova Scotia, these unique annual meetings attracted some of the top scientific and technical minds from East and West to discuss international security issues.) Western scientists continued to promote ABM limits at subsequent conferences, providing, in the words of Paul Doty, a "sort of tutorial" for their Russian counterparts.[47] In 1967, at the Glassboro summit, McNamara and President Johnson attempted, unsuccessfully, to persuade Soviet Prime Minister Alexei Kosygin of the security dangers posed by ABMs. Unlike offensive systems, Kosygin reasoned, defenses were humane, meant to protect rather than to destroy. By the time of SALT, however, the Soviets had changed their minds. In addition to accepting the destabilization argument, Moscow clearly was worried about the nascent U.S. ABM program, begun as a hedge against Soviet efforts.

Things changed yet again in 1983 when President Reagan introduced his flamboyant Star Wars proposal, the Strategic Defense Initiative, and in 1985 when the administration made its incredible and ultimately ill-fated attempt to "reinterpret" the ABM Treaty. On October 6, 1985, Robert McFarlane, the President's national security adviser, announced to the nation on television that "[r]esearch involving new physical concepts . . . as well as testing, as well as development indeed, are approved and authorized by the treaty. Only deployment is foreclosed."[48] In effect, the administration said, "Guess what? We are much freer to develop anti-ballistic missile systems than we had thought. The treaty has been misinterpreted for thirteen years and we are free to do all the development and all the testing we want. We can even build these systems and label them 'test systems' and put them up in the sky and say we are living up to the treaty."[49]

The procedure by which this conclusion was reached was rather exotic, even for the Department of Defense, where it originated. An assistant secretary for international security policy, Richard Perle, said, "Get a lawyer and have him look at the treaty and see if there isn't some loop-hole." The department got a young gentleman, Philip Kunsberg, an expert on pornography law with no background in arms control issues. Kunsberg, in a week, reached the conclusion that we all had been wrong in thinking that the treaty banned the development and testing of new technology defenses. In the State Department, Abraham D. Sofaer, previously a judge on the federal district court in New York, supported the new interpretation and defended it publicly.[50] Other lawyers in the State Department who had actually worked on the treaty were not permitted to take part in Judge Sofaer's review.

When the administration started to feel the inevitable heat generated by the new "broad" interpretation, officials took the position that the new interpretation was "legally correct" and "fully justified," but that SDI research would continue to be conducted within the old "restrictive" interpretation. In particular, Secretary of State George Shultz pushed this compromise approach in order to deflect criticism from our NATO allies that they were being ignored and abandoned under the new SDI plans.[51] So we were left with two versions of the treaty, one adopted unilaterally without any reference to the Senate which ratified it, and without talking to our allies or the Russians. Although the treaty has machinery to resolve ambiguities, Reagan officials decided not to use it.

I was particularly disappointed by the role that Paul Nitze played in the reinterpretation scandal. Not coincidentally, Nitze was the sole survivor in government of the U.S. delegates who had negotiated the ABM Treaty. During Judge Sofaer's review, Nitze, who earlier had had no doubts about the traditional or narrow interpretation of the treaty, now said that the agreement allowed development of spaced-based defenses. All of the other SALT negotiators disagreed. Reagan's move to annul a solemn international commitment would, I believe, have been much more difficult for the administration had Nitze joined the rest of us in objecting.

It seems that Nitze's acquiescence in the Reagan administration's effort to revise the treaty was motivated by a feeling that, since he was the main voice in Washington for sensible arms control measures, he would do greater service to his country by remaining in government rather than resigning. From his position as special arms control advisor, he supported the idea of keeping SDI research within the restrictive interpretation, and he later elaborated strict criteria which SDI should meet before any deployment took place. Nitze's sensitivity about his peculiar conversion is evidenced by his devoting the only annex of his memoir to an elaboration of his reasons for switching.[52]

In mid-1984, even before the reinterpretation fiasco, I started a national campaign to save the ABM Treaty since it was obvious that the ultimate goal of Star Wars directly challenged the treaty's premise. In fact, six days after Reagan's March 1983 speech, I staked out the case that SDI would make the treaty a "dead letter."[53] Throughout 1984, I continued to lobby strongly against Reagan's plan. Late in the year, I joined with my friends and colleagues Robert McNamara, McGeorge Bundy, and George Kennan to write a *Foreign Affairs* piece arguing that SDI set up a major obstacle to progress in arms control. We maintained that the President's initiative constituted "a classic case of good intentions that will have bad results because they do not respect reality." We concluded, "To lose the [ABM] Treaty in pursuit of the Star Wars mirage would be an act of folly."[54] I noted in my diary at about the same time that with SDI, "We have shot ourselves in the foot."[55]

Many others joined in the campaign to rebut the new interpretation after it was introduced in 1985. Abram and Antonia Chayes, for example, two Harvard lawyers and former legal advisers at State with extensive arms control expertise, termed the effort the "great reinterpretation caper." In addition to a point-by-point rebuttal of the Sofaer position, the Chayeses noted that higher concerns were at stake:

> The issue is not simply a lawyer's quarrel or an academic exercise in textual analysis. The ABM Treaty is the only bilateral arms control agreement in full force and effect between the superpowers. It is central to the present strategic arms control regime. Its demise would end the era of arms limitation by agreement, for if this treaty collapses, it is hard to see why either country would want to enter another one.[56]

Ray Garthoff, who had spent so much time on the language of the treaty itself, wrote a scathing critique of the Reagan administration position and its political, international, diplomatic, and constitutional implications.[57] It is also significant that six former secretaries of defense, three Democrats and three Republicans, publicly supported the traditional interpretation.

Thankfully, the 1985 reinterpretation scheme has finally been laid to rest by the Clinton administration. Taking the issue full circle, Thomas Graham, Jr., then acting director of ACDA, sent a written statement to Congress in July 1993 that formally rejected the new interpretation of the ABM Treaty. Senate Foreign Relations Committee Chairman Claiborne Pell responded that the decision "closes, on a high note, a sad chapter in United States arms control treaty relations."[58] Certainly, it is a long overdue affirmation of international law and the notion that treaty stability is just as important as ballistic missile stability.

Secondary SALT Accomplishments and Other Arms Control Measures

I believe a major part of the problem with the final SALT accords related to the penchant of Nixon and Kissinger to oversell the agreements. The "aura of jubilee" created in the White House, which stemmed from the two leaders' more grandiose notions about what arms control could achieve for general East-West relations, led to exaggerated expectations on the part of Congress and the public.[59] We on the delegation tended to take a more circumspect, businesslike approach to the process and, both during and after the negotiations, urged the administration to check its unbridled optimism about SALT.[60]

Stability, predictability, management–these were the watchwords by which those of us on the delegation lived. Judged in these terms, our accomplishments at Helsinki and Vienna, and those of the subsequent SALT II negotiations, were modest but useful steps in the right direction. As I commented in *Doubletalk*, the "results [of negotiations] will not be all good or all bad."[61] Or as I said on another occasion, "It was clearly not arms control that went awry, but our political expectations of arms control."[62]

The flood of publicity about the major agreements of SALT has overshadowed a number of modest but nonetheless important secondary achievements of the negotiations. In 1971, to very little fanfare, the superpowers signed two complementary accords on what are now key questions relating to nuclear weapons. The first, "Measures to Reduce the Risk of Outbreak of Nuclear War," aimed to minimize the chance of accidental nuclear war by setting up arrangements for information exchanges and establishing standards of conduct to prevent accidents. The second, "Measures to Improve the U.S.A.-U.S.S.R. Direct Communications Link," sought to upgrade and modernize the 1963 Hot Line agreement, which I had also played a role in promoting.

During the talks, Semenov displayed a particular interest in the possibility of accidental or unauthorized use of nuclear weapons, especially by a third party. He and the Soviets raised the question in an interesting and somewhat peculiar context, one that showed their deep and growing concerns about the People's Republic of China. Although China was never explicitly mentioned by name, it was clear Semenov had the Chinese in mind when he introduced the so-called "provocative attack" problem, the idea that one nation might deliberately attempt to get the superpowers involved in a nuclear conflict so that it could somehow reap the benefits and emerge as the world's dominant power. Semenov first mentioned the notion of provocative attack by "some third country possessing nuclear weapons and means for their delivery," a very thinly veiled reference to China, at our initial private discussions at Helsinki.[63]

He followed up at the next round in Vienna with a formal proposal that would commit the superpowers to joint retaliation against any country launching such an attack.[64]

Although it seemed to me that the chances of accident were much greater than provocative attack, I took the position with Washington that we should not reject Semenov's proposal out of hand, but wait to see another card. At the time, I do not believe that any of us was aware of earlier discussions of the Chinese problem by Washington and Moscow. During the limited test ban negotiations in Moscow in 1963, President Kennedy apparently had instructed Ambassador Averell Harriman to explore with Khrushchev possible means of inhibiting Chinese nuclear development. This U.S. feeler never got beyond the talking stage.[65]

Ultimately, after much internal study and debate, the United States used the Soviet preoccupation with provocative attack to push for the separate Accidents and Hot Line agreements. I took a special interest in the latter, since I had proposed the original Hot Line idea ten years before. Today, by way of the 1987 INF Agreement and START, we have further improved our communications' capabilities with the establishment of risk reduction centers, which directly link each side's defense establishments.[66]

Another unheralded area of progress in SALT related to the thorny issue of verification. While it became apparent early on that such breakthroughs as on-site inspection would not be a realistic goal at the negotiations, SALT institutionalized and legitimized two important compliance techniques. First, Article XII of the ABM Treaty authorized so-called "national technical means of verification," a euphemism for satellite reconnaissance. From my early days in government, I had had a strong interest in overhead reconnaissance and what it could contribute to arms control. In 1957, for example, after Sputnik I spoke to Secretary of State Dulles about the subject. Dulles seemed fascinated with the idea, both as a practical concept for replacing aerial reconnaissance (the U-2) when it became obsolete and as a potential element of a general verification system. Also, in part because of my advice, James Killian, President Eisenhower's science advisor, extolled the value of satellite reconnaissance in his seminal *Introduction to Outer Space* report.[67] Soviet acceptance of National Technical Means, which was by no means assured before SALT began, indicated to me that they had a real and serious interest in making strategic arms control work. As I wrote in 1984, "In the annals of espionage there has never been such a formal, explicit endorsement of spying."[68]

A second constructive outcome of SALT I was the creation of the Standing Consultative Commission. The SCC was a forum for continuing dialogue on SALT in particular and arms control in general. Meeting at least once a year, it was the one place where the parties could raise compliance questions and discuss misunderstandings in a businesslike and nonpolemic setting. A clearinghouse for useful information, the SCC operated well throughout the 1970s and 1980s, even during the most trying times of East-West tension.

As always, one of my central personal concerns was with nonproliferation. As I mentioned earlier, I believed that SALT would have a major impact in this area. I agreed wholeheartedly with Henry Owen's assessment in 1969 made while he was director of Foreign Policy Studies at the Brookings Institution. "It will be hard to avoid atomic proliferation," Owen maintained, "if the superpowers keep on marching toward ever large strategic forces, other countries will then see atomic weapons as an increasingly important aspect of world power and status."[69] Accordingly, I urged Semenov in private talks to encourage his government to ratify the NPT, which Moscow finally did in 1970. Also in line with Owen's recommendations, I promoted within the U.S. bureaucracy a country-by-country approach to the problem of proliferation. At the time, I did not know that I would later have a chance to test this approach personally, when I was named presidential representative and ambassador-at-large for nonproliferation during the Carter administration.

Aftermath: My Resignation and the Purge of ACDA

In 1973, there were rumors and some talk in the media that, after the SALT I accords were signed in Moscow in May 1972, I was "forced out"–in essence fired–by the Nixon administration. This was not true; the initiative for leaving government was my own. Anticipating the White House might play it this way, I made a diary entry on October 25, 1972: "Advised the Secretary [of State Rogers]

I wanted to resign but wanted to handle it in a way most convenient for the administration."[70] I asked Rogers's advice about whether I should offer to stay on until January 20, 1973, when the new President would be taking over, whether it was Nixon or Humphrey. Rogers appreciated my wish to make the resignation harmonious. He advised that it would make for a better image if I stayed the course in Geneva, where the talks had resumed. He praised my work, but he added that Kissinger had poisoned the waters in the administration and with the president. If it seemed that I was not in Nixon's good graces, I was not alone.

On November 1, 1972, I had a session with Kissinger and told him I thought it was time to move on. In an oblique reference to the back channel, Kissinger said he understood that I had worked under very trying conditions. Somewhat disingenuously, he added that this would be his last negotiation without State Department people. He planned in the next round of SALT to do business differently. His last words to me were "You behaved very well." Some time later, Secretary of Defense Mel Laird told me, "You were shafted." I think that was correct when speaking about the SALT back channel negotiation, but it was not correct in the sense that I had been fired.

To my chagrin, in 1973, immediately after my departure, the White House fired nearly all of the most senior people remaining in ACDA. In what became known as the "great purge," Fred Iklé, former RAND strategist, became the new director but not the chairman of the SALT delegation. A career diplomat, U. Alexis Johnson, became the new chief SALT negotiator. The ACDA budget was cut by one-third, and, according to newly appointed Ambassador Johnson, an intragovernmental debate "in which everybody had a veto over everything" began to dominate the negotiating process.[71]

The Nixon White House made these changes in large part at the instigation of Senator Henry "Scoop" Jackson. Senator Jackson, even though he voted to ratify the ABM Treaty, was highly critical of the unequal force levels set by the Interim Agreement. He apparently blamed this situation on the influence of "arms controllers" and "disarmers" within the administration, when in fact the final freeze agreement numbers were largely the responsibility of Kissinger and the back channel. The man who I hoped would succeed me as ACDA director, Phil Farley, also became an indirect victim of the purge. Although asked to stay on, Farley felt compelled to retire as friends and colleagues fell around him.

One other victim of this unfair purge was Air Force General Roy Allison, who had served ably as the representative of the Chairman of the Joint Chiefs of Staff on the SALT delegation. The White House allowed Senator Jackson to handpick Allison's successor, Army General Edward G. Rowney, in preference to a highly knowledgeable Navy officer nominated by Thomas Moorer, the Joint Chiefs Chairman.[72]

Despite this bittersweet conclusion to my ACDA service, I took pride in what we had accomplished over a few short years. On October 27, 1972, I reflected in my diary, "It's over. The waiting for guidance, the split positions, the hotel room life, the suspicions and squabbling, the congressional hearings, the North Atlantic Council briefings and Atlantic crossings–at least twelve, the President seeing us for public relations purposes." I then added, "Yet I should not have much to complain about–a part in an important bit of current history, an adventure into the unknown."[73]

Chapter Six

New Ventures in Diplomacy: The Trilateral Commission and Special Ambassador-at-Large for Nonproliferation under Carter

As I indicated at the close of the previous chapter, my sense of accomplishment at the results of my labors as head of ACDA and the U.S. delegation to the SALT I talks during the first Nixon administration was overshadowed by growing frustrations at the intrigues and maneuvering of Nixon and Kissinger as they practiced their highly personalized form of diplomacy. My deep concern for the issues of foreign policy and national security to which I had devoted much of my adult life was undiminished, and I found myself soon involved in a new venture, outside of government, dedicated to promoting greater dialogue among North Americans and our primary allies in Europe and with Japanese leaders. This new venture, the Trilateral Commission, would have as one of its inspirations the desire to create a counterweight to the foreign policy of Nixon and Kissinger, which many believed had tended to undermine U.S. relations with Europe and Japan. As head of the U.S. SALT delegation, I perhaps could be saddled by some with part of the responsibility for this estrangement, to the degree that these negotiations fed concern in European capitals that Washington was looking to establish a condominium with Moscow over the heads of its Cold War allies, and possibly at their expense. The Trilateral Commission would seek to ease these worries and present policy recommendations to strengthen America's relations with its allies.

The Commission would also serve as my unexpected route back into government service. Jimmy Carter, an early member of the Trilateral Commission, upon reaching the White House looked to people he had met through the Commission to advise him on foreign policy issues. President Carter would give me another chance to curb the dangers of nuclear war by appointing me his special representative for nonproliferation negotiations. Having spent two decades struggling first to reconcile nuclear weapons with U.S. and allied security, and then working to bring some stability to the U.S.-Soviet arms race, I would now try to persuade other nations not to develop nuclear weapons.

Prior Venture: *Interplay* Magazine.

My involvement with the creation of the Trilateral Commission and its first years can best be seen against the backdrop of activities I had pursued after leaving the Johnson administration in 1965. After leaving the MLF project, I was persuaded by my friends Henry Owen, Robert Bowie, and J. Robert Schaetzel to become publisher of a new European-American magazine called *Interplay*. Its goal would be to strengthen the relationship between Western Europe and North America by publishing articles highlighting the interplay of ideas and interests of Europeans and North Americans. *Interplay* was published from July 1967 to November 1970. I stepped down as the publisher with the March 1969 issue upon becoming the director of ACDA.

Interplay's international advisory board was a veritable "who's who" of the American and European scholarly and policy-making worlds: from Canada, Douglas LePan, who was principal of the University College, University of Toronto; from Great Britain, the Earl of Cromer, former governor of the Bank of England, Lord Harlech, who was former ambassador in Washington, and Kenneth Younger, who subsequently served as a minister in the British government; from France, there was Jean Claude Casanova and Jean Laloy, who were from the School of Political Science, and

Marc Ullmann, who published *L'Express*; from Germany, Kurt Birrenbach, who was a famous German politician, Marion Donhoff, who became editor of *Die Zeit*, and Helmut Schmidt, who was subsequently prime minister of West Germany; from Italy, there was Aurelio Peccei, who was a key figure in Italian industry, and Altiero Spinelli, who was director of the Institute of International Affairs; from the Netherlands, we had Max Kohnstamn, who was vice president of the European Action Committee. From the United States, we had George Ball, Christian Herter, Jr., Anthony Knoppers, who was senior vice president of Merck, Robert Manning of *The Atlantic*, Benjamin Moore, who was the executive director of the Tocqueville Center, Arthur Schlesinger, and Marshall Shulman, who was the director of the Russian Institute at Columbia University. We were fortunate to recruit a distinguished British journalist, Anthony Hartley, as editor.

Our list of contributors was equally formidable. For example, the first issue contained articles by David Broder, Ronald Steel, and Charles Kindleberger. *Interplay* published articles and book reviews by Max Beloff, William Pfaff, Harlan Cleveland, Joseph Kraft, Drew Middleton, Pierre Hasner, John McCloy, Alfred Grosser, Alastair Buchan, John Newhouse, Zbigniew Brzezinski, Adam Yarmolinsky, and Jacques Ellul. I made a few contributions: reviewing a book on John Foster Dulles, giving some observations on French foreign policy, and contributing to an article discussing U.S. foreign policy issues on the eve of the 1968 presidential election.

As this list suggests, the magazine reflected a decidedly "Atlanticist" orientation, giving voice to those who argued the need for the United States and Europe to cooperate in facing the array of dangers and problems which faced the Atlantic world. Anthony Hartley laid out our '*raison d'être*' very clearly in the first issue. He noted that interaction and interdependence were increasingly needed between the United States and Europe. This process of political, economic, and social integration was producing overlapping problems not only in the Atlantic world, but also in Eastern Europe, Russia, and Japan. Hartley stated that "this supranational convergence of problems" would be *Interplay*'s main theme. The primary focus would be upon the Atlantic world, where this process of integration had proceeded to the stage that posed serious political problems.

Key to this process was the ongoing integration of Europe, and the necessary changes in U.S.-European relations that this process would dictate. It was our hope and purpose that *Interplay* would provide a forum for both dialogue and the clash of ideas on these issues. It was also hoped that this dialogue would lead to discussions on the mutual responsibilities which the industrialized West held for the developing regions of the world in Africa and Asia. As many are doing today, we were making the case then for intellectuals, policymakers, and government leaders to come to grips with the momentous and wide-ranging changes reshaping the international scene, and the need for fresh thinking to address new problems.[1]

The Trilateral Commission

The ideals and objectives which led me to support *Interplay* remained close to my heart, and I was immediately drawn to the idea of a Trilateral Commission that was laid out for me by Henry Owen and Zbigniew Brzezinski as I was finishing my duties as head of the SALT delegation in 1972. The Trilateral Commission was the brainchild of David Rockefeller, then chairman of Chase International, who was seeking new forums to bring together officials, scholars, and businessmen concerned with the future course of relations and cooperation between North America, Western Europe, and Japan, building on the existing Bilderberg Conferences, which had an Atlanticist focus. Rockefeller convened a meeting of friends from these three regions in the summer of 1972 to discuss his ideas for such an organization. The early groundwork was laid by Rockefeller along with Zbigniew Brzezinski, the well-known international affairs expert, and my old friend and colleague, Henry Owen.

These men shared a growing concern over the rocky state of U.S. relations with Western Europe and Japan, which they felt the diplomacy of Nixon and Kissinger had allowed to deteriorate through inattention. In this sense, the Trilateral Commission was envisaged as the nucleus of a new foreign policy.[2]

Early on, it was decided there should be a chairman from each of the three major areas, and Owen suggested my name as a candidate for the North American chair. (Apparently, I was not the first choice, as I understand that William Scranton had turned the post down.)[3] As a result, in December 1972, Zbig and Henry came on David Rockefeller's plane to meet with me in Geneva, where I was finishing up my duties as head of ACDA and the SALT delegation. After hearing them describe the proposed new organization and its goal of greater political and economic cooperation between North America, Western Europe, and Japan, I readily agreed to be the North American chair, once I had stepped down as head of ACDA in early 1973. Rockefeller's new initiative clearly played into my long-standing concerns, and I saw the Trilateral Commission as a splendid tool for continuing the work I had sought to promote, on a much smaller scale, with *Interplay* in the 1960s.

I felt I should let the administration know of my interest in taking on this new post. So, in one of my talks with Nixon and Kissinger in January 1973 before I left the government, I broached the subject. Both men said they had heard of the Trilateral Commission proposal and indicated they thought the idea of my joining it was great. Kissinger even said he would like to help the Commission as much as possible. I suspect this amicability declined as the Commission turned a critical eye on his foreign policy in the years ahead.

So, after resigning from the Nixon administration, I became the North American chairman of the Trilateral Commission. I served in this capacity for more than four years and attended meetings in Europe, Japan, and North America. My counterparts in these early days were George Berthouin, and Takeshi Wantanbe who had played, and would continue to play, a key role in postwar Japanese international economic policy. The Trilateral Commission came to be quite a prestigious organization, membership in which was sought after by leading figures in industry, politics, and academia of the three regions. Many of its founding members were brought in through the efforts of George Franklin, the Commission's first North American secretary. A Rockefeller in-law and Executive Director of the Council on Foreign Relations, Franklin travelled far and wide and drew upon his vast network of contacts to help select the first members. These members included many future leaders of government and prominent individuals. As an indication of the lack of sexism in the Trilateral Commission, I would point out that one of its earliest members was Mary Robinson, who is now the President of Ireland. Another was Marina Whitman, the daughter of John Von Neumann, the scientist whom many consider the father of the modern computer and who was a key scientific advisor to the AEC and the White House in the 1950s. She went on to become one of the top executives in General Motors Corporation.

Yet, success of the Trilateral Commission was not preordained, and it went through struggles and debates before becoming firmly established as a major voice in foreign policy debates. Its founders clearly had their eyes upon this goal. As stated in a letter sent to prospective members in 1973, the Commission's aims were:

(a) to propose policies which the Member States of the European Community, and the European Community itself, the United States, and Japan could follow in

1. their economic relations;
2. their political and defense relations;
3. their economic and political relations with developing countries;
4. their relations with the countries of Eastern Europe and with China;

(b) to gain acceptance of these policies.[4]

The early organizational meetings of the Commission took place in October 1973 in Tokyo and June 1974 in Brussels. These were not the most auspicious of times for efforts to promote greater allied unity. The renewal of war in the Middle East in October 1973, followed by the Arab oil embargo and subsequent skyrocketing of world oil prices, had brought out the worst in nations. Governments scrambled to secure oil supplies, at the cost of efforts to coordinate a response to the crisis. These troubles had followed upon Kissinger's abortive "Year of Europe," which for many Europeans and the French especially, only deepened their suspicion of any initiative which came with an American label. There were also difficulties with the Japanese, who took issue with the American and European desire to have the Commission become a major voice in policy debates and who feared being outnumbered.[5]

Still, we persevered, and the October 1973 meeting issued a Statement of Purposes stressing interdependence, the prospect of new, nonmilitary threats to security, and the need for greater cooperation among North America, Western Europe, and Japan to meet the challenges posed by this new world. To be effective in meeting these common problems, the Commission called on the trilateral countries to "consult and cooperate more closely, on the basis of equality, to develop and carry out coordinated policies on matters affecting their common interests; . . . [to] refrain from unilateral actions detrimental to other regions; . . . [and to] take advantage of existing international and regional organizations and further enhance their role."[6] A full meeting of the Trilateral Commission was held at the end of 1974, at which the decision was made to hold another in Kyoto in May 1975. Despite the strained political ties between the United States and Western Europe, the venture had taken root, though not without the expenditure of much time and energy in just trying to keep the enterprise afloat.[7]

Zbigniew Brzezinski, who was the first Executive Director of the Commission, was a driving force in pushing the Commission to secure a respected voice in foreign policy debates. Under the Commission's organization, his was an influential post, with authority to set the agenda for discussions at meetings. Zbig possessed a forceful intellect and personality. He was determined to put his imprint upon this new organization. His vision of the Trilateral Commission as a serious player in foreign policy debates produced a serious row during the Commission's early years. Zbig argued for the issuing of agreed statements after each Commission meeting, which would put it on record with clear positions on key foreign policy issues. The Europeans objected to this idea, as did the Japanese. At heart, this was a debate over the raison d'être of the Trilateral Commission: was it to be an international networking group, bringing together statesmen, businessmen, and academics to discuss affairs of state, or was it to be the means to advance a foreign policy agenda as a counter and alternative to what some felt to be misguided U.S. policies? On this score, David Rockefeller, Henry Owen, and I agreed with Zbig's position, which won out, and the Commission went on to produce a lengthy series of Triangle Reports and Papers on a wide range of topics. I would like to think these papers contributed a needed leavening to the debate on U.S. foreign policy, though I will have to leave the question of their actual influence upon this policy to later students of American diplomacy.

Years later, after service in the Carter administration, I was closely involved in the writing of one of these reports which stirred up some controversy within the Commission and beyond it. This occurred in 1982-83, when I, as principal author, joined with Paolo Vittorelli, the chairman of the Nomura Research Institute, to prepare a Triangle Report entitled "Trilateral Security: Defense & Arms Control in the 1980s." We were ably assisted in drafting this report by Christopher Makins, the son of a former British ambassador to the United States, and an expert on defense issues. Makins had worked with the Trilateral Commission during the early days of 1975-76, and was a natural choice to help us deal with the wide range of issues the paper set out to address. We also drew upon a long list of experts in the United States, Western Europe, and Japan.

This report was the first serious effort by the Commission to address military security issues. In earlier years, Japan had resisted such a focus, and the early reports had focused on economic and energy issues. The 1983 report sought to address security issues from a trilateral perspective, and for the most part presented recommendations which were not controversial. A major theme running through the report was the indivisible nature of the trilateral regions' security. The dual-track approach to the Euromissiles problem (continuing deployment while pursuing negotiations with the Soviets on reductions in this class of weapon) was endorsed, as was the need to give greater emphasis and energy to the problem of nuclear nonproliferation.[8]

Given the arrival of nuclear parity between the West and Soviet Union, the report stated anew the principle that the main, and perhaps only, utility of nuclear weapons was deterrence. As this summary stated:

> The heart of trilateral security will continue to rest indefinitely on strong survivable nuclear deterrent forces. This fact must not be underestimated or depreciated. The report considers certain measures to maintain such forces. But with belated recognition of the diminished credibility of the threat of first use in a situation of nuclear parity should come acceptance of the need for some changes in the way the trilateral nations must handle their deterrence and defense arrangement.[9]

It was in the area of these recommended changes in the way deterrence and defense arrangements were handled that the controversy arose. Until this time I had not really tried to advance my views on nuclear issues within the Trilateral Commission. The 1983 report gave me a chance to do this. As it happened, I started work on this report soon after having co-authored, with McGeorge Bundy, George Kennan, and Robert McNamara, an article for *Foreign Affairs* in 1982 which called upon the United States and NATO to adopt a policy of no first use, or NFU, regarding nuclear weapons. This proposal was deemed very controversial and even pernicious in its potential consequences for alliance security and cohesion, striking as it did against the heart of three decades of NATO policy linking deterrence to the threat of the preemptive use of nuclear weapons against an imminent Soviet attack. I firmly believed in the wisdom of the NFU proposal, and so argued for its inclusion in the Trilateral Commission report as well. I met the expected resistance as the established European viewpoint tended to agree with my critics and there were a number of go-rounds on this issue within the authors' circle.

Christopher Makins indicated his sympathy with the European viewpoint that it was dangerous to move precipitously to NFU as a policy, though he was in favor of reducing the significance of nuclear weapons in U.S. and NATO defense policy. I believe that Makins might have included some passages in the first draft to address these European concerns and point out what Europeans (and Makins) saw as the more compelling arguments against adopting NFU as a policy. In fairness to Christopher, I can say in retrospect that he likely wanted the report to reflect European views, not just the views expressed by the so-called "Gang of Four." Still, I stuck to my guns, as I was determined to put the Trilateral Commission report on record in support of a recommendation that I felt on principle was correct. Still, the report did include language that indicated that NFU should be a longer range objective, which would have to be approached carefully. The report also called upon the NATO allies to institute universal military service and to increase the reserves, points which Makins did support as addressing both the need to reduce NATO's nuclear dependency and the recurrent burden-sharing disputes within the alliance.[10]

These ideas were the object of further criticism. Among the critics was Henry Kissinger, by now a member of the Commission. He proposed that the paper not even be considered by a Commission meeting in Rome.[11] I recall saying to several people at the time that, as Galileo had also been suppressed in Rome, I guessed I was in good company. The paper was eventually considered at the meeting, and later published, with no dire consequences for the NATO alliance.

One important objective of the Trilateral Commission was to bring the Japanese members into closer relations with the members from North America and Europe, and so engage Japan more strongly in international affairs, giving them a voice, and responsibilities, commensurate with their growing economic power. To achieve this, it was important to have Japan as an equal partner within the Commission from the outset. I was very keen on this point in particular. In all of the chairmen's meetings, I was concerned to make sure Japan pulled its weight as an equal, and so I put pressure on the Japanese members to this end. I worked to pull Watanabe into discussions and planning. I believe the Trilateral Commission performed a useful and important function in bringing Japanese members into the European-American dialogue. This was not easy because at first the Japanese found it awkward and unfamiliar to engage in the freewheeling exchange of views preferred by the Americans and the Europeans. After the first meetings, though, the Japanese became more at home in this type of international exchange and I think that it proved to be a useful instrument for discussing matters of common interest. As recent developments underscore, ranging from the tensions during the Gulf War to long-standing trade frictions, the effort to engage the Japanese more deeply in international affairs is an ongoing one that remains crucial to U.S.-Japanese relations.

I believe the Trilateral Commission succeeded in the 1974-76 period in articulating the view that common interests must not be lost sight of in light of specific squabbles with U.S. allies. It did have some impact, though not so great as its critics came to argue. For some, the supposed political orientation of the Commission was enough to provoke protest, as when George Bush resigned from the Commission, pronouncing it as "too liberal," a stand no doubt taken with an eye on the 1980 presidential election. Though the Trilateral Commission had little or no real political influence (at first, it had to go to often absurd lengths just to get media attention for its meetings) it was hard to convince certain proponents of conspiracy theories that the Commission was not an evil influence bent on some unspecified internationalization of America. The Commission became the *bête noire* in particular of Lyndon LaRouche, who targeted his band of agitators on the Commission with wild accusations that it was a conspiracy to take over the United States government. In the end, LaRouche ended up in jail for tax violations.

Far from being an international conspiracy, the Trilateral Commission actually debated seriously in 1976 whether it should consider its work done and close up shop after its initial three-year run. The consensus was that the Commission still had important work to do, and as fate would have it, it would have perhaps its greatest impact upon U.S. foreign policy in an indirect manner following the election of Jimmy Carter to the White House in 1976. Carter's election would serve as an entrée to Trilateral Commission associates, largely through the efforts of Brzezinski. Zbig mobilized a cadre of scholars and statesmen to help Carter, and these were naturally the same people he had drawn upon in setting up the Commission.

For a time, the myth circulated that the Trilateral Commission had somehow "chosen" Carter as its candidate for President in 1976. The facts are much more mundane and the outcome much more the result of personal choices, not conspiratorial maneuvering. I met President Carter in 1973 when he became one of the first members of the Trilateral Commission. As North American chairman of the Commission, I, with the help of my colleagues Henry Owen, Bob Bowie, Brzezinski, and George Franklin, was in charge of recruiting new members. We had selected the governor of a northwestern state, Oregon I believe, and sought to match him with a governor from the southeast. I asked George Franklin to visit Georgia and give us a report on Carter, who had received some national attention. Franklin came back with a very high opinion of Carter and when invited to join the Commission, Carter accepted with alacrity. He became an enthusiastic member and later would say that he was obliged to the Commission as it acted as an instrument for his education about foreign policy.

At this time he was not a national figure. I recall that at an early meeting in Tokyo, the press club asked for a member of the Commission to address their luncheon meeting and, when we suggested Carter, the press men said, "Oh, offer us one of your well known members." Carter was a very active member of the Commission and, in subsequent years, he several times said to me that I had been his mentor in foreign policy. Upon becoming President, he selected a number of Trilateral Commission associates to be in his administration. Zbig Brzezinski became his National Security Advisor, Harold Brown became his Secretary of Defense, and Cyrus Vance became his Secretary of State.[12]

I, too, would find myself unexpectedly tapped by the newly elected President to assist him in an endeavor which lay close to my heart. Despite the successful negotiation of the nuclear Non-Proliferation Treaty in the 1960s, there were still a number of nations which were not party to the treaty's commitment not to develop nuclear weapons, or to help other nonnuclear nations develop or obtain nuclear weapons. The problems of combatting nuclear proliferation had become even more difficult. The spread of nuclear power technology had inevitably led to the diffusion of the means to produce nuclear weapons, a dilemma foreseen in the 1950s when I had worked on the creation of the International Atomic Energy Agency. The United States faced issues regarding its agreements to provide nuclear fuel to allies and other customers, and the potential for diversion of nuclear material during the fuel cycle of nuclear power plants. Carter, as a former naval officer specializing in nuclear engineering under Rickover, had a natural interest in these issues. Yet, our common interest in erecting stronger barriers to the proliferation of nuclear weapons would not insure that my efforts were to be strongly supported within the administration.

Special Ambassador for Nonproliferation, 1977-1980

It was in mid-1977 that President Carter appointed me his Special Representative and Ambassador-at-Large for nonproliferation matters. I was sworn in on July 22, 1977. This appointment was not the first job Carter had in mind for his foreign policy "mentor," however. Shortly after taking office, the President telephoned me and said that he wanted me to be his ambassador to Moscow. All I could think to say was, "Oh, Lord. Let me think it over." I asked him for the weekend to ponder the matter, and on Monday morning, knowing of his reportedly very early starts at work, I called him at about 6:00 a.m. I told him that I thought I had better decline his gracious offer. He took it well and said, "Well, I will get you for some other job."

One of my reasons for declining the Moscow post was that, at that time, the Soviets were pumping microwave radiation into the American Embassy. My wife had had an operation for cancer. Needless to say, I did not believe I should expose her to more radiation. In addition I had had enough experience working with ambassadors to know how much of their effort really went into "running a hotel" for visitors from Washington–a role in which I had little interest. The President's view was that someone who had close connections with the White House in addition to practical business experience would be welcomed by the Soviets, and perhaps could be more productive than a member of the Foreign Service. I questioned the realism of this belief. Shortly thereafter, Brzezinski called me to say that my name had gone forward to the President to head up the CIA. I had no interest whatsoever in getting into the intelligence business and few qualifications. I immediately told Zbig to get that paper off Carter's desk. A few weeks later, the White House asked me to take on the task of Ambassador-at-Large, which I accepted.

I believed that I was qualified to take on the complicated issue of nonproliferation in view of the many years I had thought about and worked on this problem. I felt confident that I could make a contribution to the administration's nonproliferation (and arms control) efforts, especially after I was once again able to convince Phil Farley to come back from Stanford and work with me as my deputy.[13] Also, Carter and I enjoyed a special relationship as a result of my association with him on the Trilateral Commission. Of all the presidents I had worked with, I believed that Carter was perhaps the most deeply committed to arms control and preventing the spread of nuclear weapons.

My appointment was generally well accepted by the press and public media. The *New York Times*, for example, reported that "President Carter has again signaled his seriousness in trying to limit the proliferation of atomic weapons" by choosing me as his Special Representative.[14] One exception to this generally favorable treatment I viewed as somewhat ironic. An article by Roger Morris in *Harper's* magazine entitled "Diplomatic Spoils" described me as one of several "relatively junior and minor bureaucrats who ascended due to the extraordinary methods and policies of the Kissinger era." I thought that it was particularly amusing, given my experience and my battles with the former Secretary of State, that I could be characterized as a minor bureaucrat who had achieved his position because of devotion to Kissinger.[15]

Although I was initially optimistic about my new job, my tour of duty during the Carter years ultimately proved to be quite frustrating. The world community, including the United States, had not yet realized what a deadly threat proliferation was and what radical measures would be needed in order to make a dent on the problem. Early on–against a backdrop that included the 1973 oil crisis, increased worldwide attention to nuclear power programs, and the Indian peaceful nuclear explosion of 1974–Carter called for and Congress passed legislation based on the incorrect assumption that, as a major supplier of fuel for reactors, the United States could unilaterally control the international flow of nuclear materials and leverage our policies abroad. The Nuclear Nonproliferation Act

(NNPA) of 1978 gave the United States veto rights over reprocessing of spent fuel it provided to foreign countries, called for renegotiation of existing contracts and agreements, tightened export license criteria, and prohibited U.S. export of fuel to any nation not accepting so-called "full-scope" international safeguards. When we tried to exercise this supposed leverage of export controls, it became clear that foreign nations could and would find other sources of supply for their fuel. A British judge put it correctly in saying, "To cancel a contract is no way to make a new one." I remember wondering at the time, "What if *our* energy requirements depended on some other country's NNPA, for example Saudi Arabia?" When the President signed the bill into law and photos were taken in the White House, I stood to one side despite Brzezinski's protest that I should be in the middle of the picture. I was determined not to be associated with this legislation, although as Carter's Special Representative, I was bound to uphold it.

Handcuffed in large measure by the restrictive and often myopic terms of the 1978 NNPA, much of my time became devoted to what Phil Farley has called "damage limitation and course corrections."[16] I became involved in three primary roles. First, the administration asked me to head up its effort known as the "International Nuclear Fuel Cycle Evaluation," or INFCE. Second, as a strong supporter of the International Atomic Energy Agency (IAEA), I insisted that I serve as the U.S. member of the IAEA Board of Governors. Third, I personally directed negotiations and discussions with governments around the world in an effort to persuade them that it was not in their security or economic interests to develop nuclear weapons or nuclear power plants that might give them that option in the future. In fact, as things developed, I took it as my principal mission to roam the globe trying to cut down on the bitterness about our new policies and to mend fences with both allies and "threshold," or potential nuclear, states.

INFCE was a U.S. inspired and directed multilateral effort to examine the fuel cycle and alternative methods of reprocessing. It involved both major industrial nations and key developing countries in a technical evaluation of nuclear fuel cycle alternatives. According to recently declassified State Department cablegrams, INFCE objectives as seen from the perspective of Washington were

(1) to "enhance international cooperation in dealing with . . . nuclear power for civil purposes and provide a forum for exchange of views and voluntary harmonization of policy," and (2) to "provide information to guide the development of alternative nuclear power systems that minimize potential proliferation."[17] With the aid of an NSC Ad Hoc Group on Nonproliferation and a Management Group of agencies–State, ACDA, and the AEC successor Energy Resources Development Agency (ERDA)–I took charge of coordinating U.S. positions and carrying out negotiations in Vienna.[18]

Although it went on for several years and involved an immense amount of paperwork by reactor engineers and experts from many countries, INFCE was basically a lost cause from the start. Not surprisingly, it produced no earth-shattering results or conclusions. At one point during the proceedings in 1978, the European Community representative pointed out the difficulty in coming to any type of consensus in INFCE. The process, he said, was "becoming a meeting point of three groups of nations with differing objectives: (1) those whose overriding objective is nonproliferation; (2) those who are aware of the importance of strengthening nonproliferation . . . but who must at the same time guarantee their future energy supply; and (3) the third world countries, whose primary motivation is assured energy supply."[19] I understood this dilemma, and stressed that the United States was there not to preach but to listen and learn. The INFCE summary document, produced in early 1980, represented not a consensus but a set of very diverse opinions, what the French representative derisively termed an "à la carte menu for all to choose from."[20] I noted at about the same time that there existed the danger of creating a "political vacuum" in the post-INFCE period. I thought that much of the follow-on work should involve bilateral talks and should be centered in IAEA.[21]

INFCE did make positive contributions to nonproliferation efforts. I circulated early on within the administration a memo that called for "a much heightened sense of alarm about the dangers of nuclear spread. Widespread and long-lasting information programs are needed to dispel present apathy and ignorance."[22] INFCE at the very least initiated a dialogue that proved to be an education for all involved, including the United States. In March 1980, I reported to Secretary of State Vance that the INFCE dialogue had "eased tensions, eliminated misunderstandings regarding U.S. policy, and provided a basis for common approaches." Just as important to my mind, it also indicated that there could be no easy "technical fix" for the proliferation problem.[23]

My work on the Board of Governors of the IAEA was of greater interest than INFCE. It brought back pleasant memories of helping to negotiate the original IAEA charter in the 1950s. But here again, I did not sense that we were making much progress with the IAEA in the 1970s. Unfortunately, a good deal of politics became mixed into substantive atomic energy matters. Much energy, for example, went into rivalry for seats on the Board of Governors. The early hopes that nuclear energy would become a panacea for the economic and energy problems of poor countries never materialized, but the safeguarding functions of the agency were realized from the very beginning. The IAEA's role as nuclear safeguarder was hardly helped in 1981, however, when Israel, not trusting the findings of IAEA inspectors that an Iraqi reactor was for peaceful purposes, destroyed it using U.S. supplies, planes, and bombs. I testified at the time before a Senate Armed Services Committee that such a resort to violence prejudiced the IAEA. But recent events in Iraq have shown that the Iraqis were engaged in a bomb program of substantial proportions. If the circumstances were repeated, I think I would favor what the Israelis did. American support for Israel nonetheless caused tensions a few years later when the IAEA sought to exclude Tel Aviv from its membership, and the United States withheld funding until the issue was settled.

Today, despite its problems, I believe that the IAEA will only have increasing importance in the post-Cold War world, becoming one of the most critical international instruments at our disposal to control proliferation. As demonstrated by its role in dealing with Iraq and North Korea, the IAEA has become a central part of American and world security in tracking down countries that are either violating the Nuclear Nonproliferation Treaty (NPT) or have plans to surreptitiously produce nuclear weapons. It is a great institution which should be nurtured and not made an orphan by foolish attempts at economic savings.

Neither INFCE nor the operations of the IAEA were the main concerns during my tenure as Ambassador-at-Large. Reflecting my fundamental belief that the root cause of nuclear proliferation was insecurity, I tended to focus on the politics of the problem through separate negotiations with most of the major nations involved in nuclear power generation at the time. I believed that an approach emphasizing diplomacy, with some attention devoted to technical safeguards and reasonable restraints on national nuclear programs, had the best chance for success. I attempted to put this philosophy to the test (despite the restraints imposed by our own NNPA) with both our allies in Asia and Europe–Japan, France, Germany, and Britain–and with the recognized threshold states–India and Pakistan, Argentina and Brazil, South Africa, and Israel.

Perhaps the liveliest and certainly the most intense negotiations that I engaged in dealt with the Japanese and their nuclear fuel reprocessing plant at Tokai Mura. Japan had been purchasing enriched uranium for its many nuclear power reactors from the United States under conditions that included the right of Washington to withhold permission for the Japanese to reprocess this fuel. At the beginning of Carter's term in office, the Japanese finished construction of the small pilot reprocessing plant at Tokai Mura. Administration officials initially took the position that this plant should not be allowed to open or operate because of the potential proliferation danger. Japanese officials strongly objected, seeing the American position as a basic threat to their energy integrity. They believed that they needed the reprocessed plutonium that Tokai Mura would produce to fuel the next generation of so-called fast-breeder reactors. Tensions ran very high. One Japanese friend of mine, a leading industrialist, told me in Washington that if we did not ease off on our position, tensions would approach those of December 1941, when we had embargoed the Japanese oil supply.

I went to Tokyo in late 1977 with an interagency group to see what could be done. In discussions with Sosuke Uno, the director general of Japan's Science and Technology Agency, we quickly worked out an arrangement permitting the Tokai Mura plant to operate on a limited basis with the understanding that the emphasis would shift to research on fuel processing that would not produce weapons-grade material. Also, we obtained a promise from the Japanese to participate in INFCE and other bilateral nonproliferation efforts. I was able to get White House permission for this deal on a single long-distance call to Brzezinski.[24] I gather that, since those early days, the Japanese have been having their fuel reprocessed in Europe. The transfer of the resulting plutonium over the high seas to Japan is now a matter of some concern, for fear that some terrorist organization might hijack one of the ships. But the Tokai Mura arrangement was sufficient to diffuse the tension in 1977, and the Japanese seemed very pleased. Many years later, they awarded me the "Grand Cordon of the Order of the Sacred Treasure" for my role in this episode.

A second important set of negotiations involved our NATO allies. I went to Europe a number of times in 1978 and 1979 in an effort to influence the allies' role as emerging nuclear suppliers and to restore confidence in U.S. policies. I was not terribly successful in these efforts. After returning from one trip in February 1978, I reported to President Carter that INFCE was not having a great impact and that a general feeling of resentment over U.S. policy was developing. I noted in my diary that we seemed to be driving the Europeans toward independent energy sources when we actually desired interdependence and that, with the impending NNPA, we gave the appearance of trying to breach international agreements with domestic legislation.[25]

On another trip, President Carter asked me to take along some overhead reconnaissance photographs of the progress that Argentina had made on a plutonium production facility. I showed these pictures to West German Chancellor Helmut Schmidt and French President Valéry Giscard d'Estaing. Neither seemed unduly impressed. Schmidt asked me whether we had similar photos of plants in other countries. I was glad to tell him that I did not know. Giscard seemed much more interested in talking to me about some recent barge trips I had taken through France than in discussing nonproliferation questions.

France in particular appeared very worried that the United States rated nonproliferation concerns ahead of French energy security. Giscard once told me that U.S. nuclear policies were creating the greatest strain on the alliance since the end of the war.

Still, our nuclear relations with Paris remained on basically sound footing. I attributed much of this to the fact that one of the top members of the French atomic commission, Bertrand Goldschmidt, and I were good friends. We had worked together for many years, most notably in helping to set up the IAEA in Vienna. Once, in 1979 I believe, André Giraud, the head of the French atomic energy program, invited me to visit the French uranium enrichment plant at Pierrelatte. Giraud informed me that I was the first non-Frenchman to see this plant.

Yet another set of talks took me to Brazil and Argentina, the potential nuclear rivals in South America. Brazil had concluded a very large contract with the West Germans to set up an extensive reactor program that involved reprocessing to extract plutonium and a uranium enrichment plant. The implications for nuclear weapons development were obvious. In 1978, a high-level U.S. delegation, led by Undersecretary Warren Christopher (President Clinton's Secretary of State) and Joseph Nye of the State Department, unsuccessfully took a very strong position with Brazilian officials. The American mission was so exercised by its lack of success that it left Brazil before the final formal banquet that was to be given in its honor. Carter asked me to see what I could do to improve the situation. I visited with the Brazilian foreign minister and took the position that, of course, Washington could not presume to tell the Brazilian government how to handle its energy problems. But I hoped that, after looking at the matter, Brazil would see that enrichment and reprocessing were neither necessary nor desirable. I pointed out that such a course would almost inevitably lead to an arms race between Brazil and Argentina.

I also went to Argentina and took the same position. The Argentines were actually constructing a reprocessing plan that would serve as an additional stimulant to the Brazilian weapons program. In addition to the leaders of the Argentine nuclear program, I talked with military authorities about nuclear matters. They seemed less than interested. When I talked to them about the Soviet military campaign in Afghanistan, however, and the vulnerability of Soviet helicopters, they showed a great deal of interest. One of the sadder parts of my work in Argentina was to host a meeting of the relatives of the "disappeared" ones who presumably had been murdered by the military government. I assured them that I would report their concerns to President Carter, which I subsequently did.

While at least keeping a viable dialogue open, I do not believe that my visits to Brazil and Argentina had any greater inhibiting impact on their nascent nuclear programs. The South American discussions also had the unfortunate effect of further straining our relations with our European friends. In 1979, Schmidt told me, "You stretched our nerves to the limit" over the Brazil contract problem.[26] In recent years, however, both the Brazilian and Argentine governments have come to recognize the security and economic risks in pursuing a nuclear weapons option. Each has given up aspirations to attain nuclear status, and both now support the 1968 Treaty of Tlatelolco to make Latin America a nuclear weapons free zone.

The personal highlight of my international negotiations during the Carter years was a mission to the Union of South Africa in June 1978. The specific event that triggered my visit to Johannesburg was an intriguing case of Soviet-American cooperation on the nonproliferation front. In 1977, the Soviets approached us with evidence that the South Africans were making preparations to test a nuclear weapon. Soviet reconnaissance satellites had detected a site in the Kalahari Desert that appeared to be an underground test range under construction. The CIA then checked their photography and, to the extreme embarrassment of our intelligence community, found that the Soviet findings were true.[27] As a result of this discovery, which seemingly confirmed long-standing suspicions that South Africa was developing nuclear weapons, several major countries put pressure on Johannesburg to stop. President Carter raised the threat of breaking diplomatic relations if a test took place. The United States thought that it had special leverage because it was supplying highly enriched uranium for a South African research reactor and was going to supply fuel for a power reactor at Koberg.

The South African government responded by sending a communiqué directly to President Carter. The cable suggested that they would receive an American to talk about the entire nonproliferation question–and it specifically mentioned my name as a candidate to fill that position! I believe that nomination stemmed from the fact that I was an acquaintance of A.J.A. (Ampie) Roux, the president of the South African Atomic Energy Board. Roux and I had negotiated back in the early 1950s about obtaining uranium from South Africa, during which time he had actually visited me at Ratcliffe Manor. We also had worked together at the IAEA in Vienna.

The White House went along with the South African government's suggestion. My wife and I flew to Johannesburg in June 1978, and we set up headquarters at the American Embassy in Pretoria. Over the course of about a week, Roux and other atomic energy authorities showed me the South African atomic facilities, none of which had any apparent connection to weapons production. The CIA had a special interest in one complex which they thought to be a uranium enrichment facility. When I asked Roux if I could see this facility, he told me he would have to check with "higher authorities." He came back to me and said, "Why do you want to spoil everything? This visit has been going very smoothly, and you have seen a great deal of our program." He asked how I would feel if he came to the United States and asked to see some specific building at Oak Ridge? To me, this was a clear indication that the South Africans were up to something.

I also visited with South African military leaders and raised the issue of the alleged nuclear testing site. They pleaded ignorance. I then got permission from Washington to provide the exact geographical coordinates of the site as we had observed it. The military quickly explained away this evidence by telling me that the Kalahari site was "just a conventional ordinance testing area." I reported these evasive responses and my strong conviction that a weapons program was proceeding when I returned to Washington.

Needless to say, not many specific results can be attributed to my South African talks. As Roux commented at the time, "All I can say is I think the discussions were very constructive—constructive in the sense that both sides had the opportunity of making clear things that were previously unclear."[28] In part because of the meeting, we decided not to supply the South African reactors with fuel, but I believe that the French took over the supply contract. Yet our efforts in Pretoria did make the South Africans stop and think, and may have made a tiny contribution toward the eventual abandonment by the government of its nuclear aspirations. They never proceeded with development of the Kalahari site, for example, and in 1992 they signed the NPT. More recently, the government admitted to having produced a few nuclear weapons, but committed to destroying them and stopping all further work on such weapons.

By late 1979, the lack of any concrete results from my globetrotting on behalf of the Carter administration and the inflexibility of our policies had led to a growing frustration on my part. Many of my diary notations for this period reflected my pessimism, in particular about the counterproductive approach embodied in the NNPA. On one occasion I lamented, "Is our policy in a shambles? Probably. Does pres. know how much resentment our N.P. policy/*law* has caused?" Another time, I noted that in the evolution from Atoms for Peace to the IAEA to the NPT and the London Suppliers Group, the 1978 legislation clearly was an "anomaly." The United States, I concluded, was now considered "unreliable" and "unpredictable" in international circles. On INFCE I wrote, "We have gotten attention, but what else?" I was tempted to quit, suspended as I was between the White House, the State Department, and Congress.[29]

A number of immediate issues or crises–including South Africa, Argentina-Brazil, Euratom, post-INFCE, and the upcoming NPT Review Conference–precipitated my private concerns. But the particular case of Pakistan served as perhaps the most important catalyst in my thinking, and, I hoped, in that of the government as well. Pakistan was a classic instance where an inflexible, generic approach to nonproliferation could not work. Pakistan was a near-nuclear state experiencing a great deal of internal political turmoil, but which nonetheless remained a key ally for the United States, especially in light of the December 1979 Soviet invasion of Afghanistan. All of this complicated any effort to use sanctions or controls with regard to Pakistani nuclear development.

My private hope was that the Pakistani situation could be used to "leverage a change in our whole policy," which I thought was long overdue. "Has Pak case shocked us enuf," I wrote in my diary in August 1979, "to consider more radical ideas?" A Pakistani bomb would have a "spiraling" effect on India, and create ripples in the Soviet Union and Europe. The stakes were indeed high, as I alluded to another time: "Great energy release from religion (Moslem) joined to great energy release from nuclear fission = disastrous, catastrophic world tragedy."[30] I once suggested facetiously to Carter that we should develop an Islamic interpretation that the Koran prohibits nuclear weapons. But in a more serious vein, the Pakistani case prompted me to work on a set of policy recommendations that I had been thinking about for a long time.

In October 1980, I submitted my own assessment of U.S. nonproliferation policy to the government. Marked "confidential," the report stressed that the United States should adopt a "more balanced approach" that utilized diplomacy and persuasion as much as threats and constraints. I recommended that proliferation problems should be treated as security problems, and that we focus on specific countries that posed the greatest risks. I argued for increased flexibility, especially with our major allies. Finally, I put forward several measures that I believed could enhance our reliability as a supplier and build international consensus on nonproliferation. I urged that we support an international plutonium storage system, increase support for IAEA safeguards, and amend the NNPA by eliminating certain automatic sanction provisions and transferring the export license function from the independent Nuclear Regulatory Commission (NRC) to the executive branch. Ultimately, I concluded that "the best hope—indeed, the only real long-term hope—of slowing proliferation lies less in constraints . . . than in reducing motivations to acquire nuclear weapons—primarily through resolving international disputes, providing security guarantees, and reducing the prestige value of nuclear weapons."[31]

During my final months with the Carter administration, another episode underscored what I viewed as fundamental weaknesses in our nonproliferation policy. During 1980, Congress and the White House clashed over whether we should continue with a commitment to supply India with low-enriched uranium for its reactors at Tarapur. The NNPA required that the United States export only to countries which had accepted "full-scope" safeguards—*i.e.*, IAEA safeguards over existing and future nuclear facilities. The law did provide a two-year grace period to work out new contracts. Since

India continued to resist full-scope safeguards, many in Congress–led by Representatives Jonathan B. Bingham of New York, Clement Zablocki of Wisconsin, and Edward J. Markey of Massachusetts–believed that we should support an NRC decision of June 1980 to not ship the fuel for Tarapur. Congressman Bingham, who had been a classmate of mine at Yale, and others had been chiding the administration for several years about potential backsliding on the NNPA. During the INFCE discussions, for example, Bingham warned against any "softening" of the U.S. attitude or position.[32] He and Zablocki then called for a "full-scale review" of U.S. policy in January 1980.[33]

The administration responded that the Tarapur sale should go forward for two reasons. First, the shipments fell within the grace period, under the White House interpretation. Second, and more important, nonproliferation goals would be best served by living up to our earlier (1963) commitments to ship the fuel. On my recommendation and that of State,[34] Carter demonstrated unusual flexibility in this instance. Warren Christopher and I defended this position before Zablocki's House Committee on Foreign Affairs in June. We argued that it would be counterproductive to draw a line in the sand with regard to India. As I testified, "Affording the Indians now bound by partial safeguards an opportunity to reduce them hardly seems a good way to advance toward our goal of full-scope safeguards." It was better to maintain some leverage "instead of overturning the whole applecart." Moreover, cutting off the fuel would have possible geopolitical ramifications, opening the way for the Soviets to fill the supply vacuum and perhaps leading to a major weapons competition on the Indian subcontinent. I also used my prepared statement as a vehicle to promote a diplomatic approach to the entire question:

> There are two main approaches that the United States uses in trying to constrain proliferation–export controls and diplomacy–using influence and leverage to dissuade nations from going toward a nuclear explosive capability. There is a tension between these two approaches–overuse of one may render the other ineffective. With India we have been pursuing both approaches. Now if we resort to the most extreme export control–embargo–we will effectively

> destroy any chance of progress in the second approach—diplomacy. It seems clear to me that an embargo will have no positive effects in India and just as clear that a number of negative results will follow.[35]

The committee did not support shipment of the fuel, but Congress eventually did. Still, the Tarapur incident further damaged our reputation abroad as a reliable supplier and reduced our influence on nonproliferation matters.

At about this time, I finally decided to quit my post as Ambassador-at-Large. On July 7, 1980, I wrote to Zbig with my intention to resign. "As a known advocate of some adjustment in our policy, I doubt that my departure will cause a ripple," I noted. "In fact it would probably be greeted with pleasure in certain quarters. . . ."[36] As a favor to the administration and to Carter, I delayed my departure until after the November election. In my letter to Carter, I regretted "not having been able to do more to help reduce this [proliferation] danger."[37]

Once out of government, I felt free to go public with my misgivings about our nonproliferation policy. I did this in a *Foreign Affairs* article published in the spring of 1981. My co-author on this piece was George Rathjens, an MIT political science professor and my deputy for INFCE matter in 1979-80. Rathjens was an international affairs specialist and veteran of discussions with the Russians. He since has become recognized as an expert in nuclear arms control and problems of the post-Cold War world. The article echoed most of the same points I had made in the October 1980 internal reassessment. It reiterated the shortcomings of the Carter policy and made many of the same policy recommendations, for example to establish an International Plutonium Storage System and to expand IAEA safeguards. We again emphasized that the "best hope of stemming nuclear proliferation lies in dealing effectively with the motives that lead nations to want to have nuclear weapons."[38]

Elaborating on a point that I only alluded to in the 1980 document, Rathjens and I also stressed the special responsibility of the United States in the arms control arena. I had long believed that one of the reasons that U.S. policy had been less than effective was that, while we were trying to get other nations to change their policies, we were not willing to do very much in the way of sacrificing our own freedom of action.[39] We had not (nor had the Russians) paid enough attention to the proliferation implications of our own nuclear posture. The article made a strong pitch for a CTB and SALT II as important nonproliferation measures.[40]

Although we did not always agree, Carter must have thought that my efforts had been of some value during his administration. Before finishing his term, the President awarded me the Medal of Freedom, the highest honor open to a civilian in the U.S. government. I was never sure, however, whether this award was because I introduced Carter to the intricacies of foreign policy or whether he believed that I had had a constructive effect in limiting the spread of nuclear weapons. The citation was ambiguous: "Gerard C. Smith has represented our country in many capacities–as the first U.S. Chairman of the Trilateral Commission and as Chief U.S. Delegate to the Strategic Arms Limitation Talks in 1969. In helping formulate our national security policy, in promoting a better understanding of foreign relations, he has helped us all to perceive that, in this nuclear age, security and peace are indivisible."

Chapter Seven

Final Reflections

Termination of government service did not end my engagement in nuclear policy. I continued to be active in a number of private endeavors, most notably the Arms Control Association, serving as its chairman until 1992. This association continues the labor of public education regarding international arms races and nuclear nonproliferation. Through collaboration with colleagues and the ACA, I remained active in national dialogue on these issues.

These years also brought deep sadness with the illness and death in 1987 of my wife, Bernice, ending 46 years of profound and loving companionship. She had been at my side literally and figuratively throughout my career. In spite of health problems, she kept me company through long weeks in hotels in Helsinki, Vienna, and Geneva. Her adept management of the family and personal details spoiled me while greatly adding to the time I had available for professional pursuits.

Upon leaving government, I helped start an international consulting firm, Consultants International Group, where I worked until 1989. A special satisfaction of my involvement with Consultants International Group was that I was joined by Henry Owen. In 1989 I took up full-time residence on the Eastern Shore of Maryland. Since my rustication, despite bouts of ill health, I have had time for further reading and reflection about the previous four decades and about the sudden and extraordinary end to the Cold War that had provided the rationale for development of this nation's nuclear arsenal.

This closing chapter offers some personal reflections on lessons that may be drawn from fifty years of the "nuclear era." Over many years of professional collaboration and personal friendship,

Henry Owen, and Robert Bowie, my predecessor as Assistant Secretary of State of Policy Planning, have had large influence on my thinking about the broader implications of nuclear weapons in our nation's foreign and security policy. Some of the reflections that I offer in this final chapter are the fruit of patient teaching by these two friends.

My thinking on this all-important topic has also been shaped by the events and persons described in this memoir. They have given me insights from varying perspectives. Indeed my own views changed over the course of decades. As a relatively young aide to a Commissioner of the AEC, I did not much question the necessity or wisdom of the nation's buildup of its nuclear arsenal. Later in the 1950s, I witnessed and shared the initial doubts of men like Eisenhower and Dulles regarding the practical utility of nuclear weapons, even as they propounded a policy of massive retaliation. Beginning at this time and extending into the 1960s, I was engaged in the important issues of how we could guarantee the security of our NATO allies against a perceived Soviet threat without undue reliance on a threat of use of U.S. nuclear weapons. The development of independent nuclear forces by the United Kingdom and France may have indicated that our allies doubted our resolve to put the United States directly at risk of a Soviet nuclear strike in the event of a Soviet attack in Europe. It also was early evidence that the United States and the Soviet Union were setting bad examples in their development of nuclear arsenals. Other countries now felt that to be "first-class powers" and to ensure their security, they needed nuclear weapons.

Beginning in the Nixon administration, I had a chance to address the dilemmas of the nuclear era by direct negotiation with Soviet counterparts. I remain convinced that the willingness of the United States and Russia to reduce radically their nuclear arsenals is a necessary first step in resolving problems of nuclear proliferation–itself a precondition to large powers someday forswearing maintenance of nuclear arsenals of any size. The important achievements of SALT I, in particular the ABM Treaty, have helped stabilize the arms race, but our failure to address MIRVs kept the race alive.

My responsibilities during the Carter administration for nonproliferation reinforced my view that preventing the spread of nuclear weapons was as important as curbing the U.S.-Soviet arms competition, but that the two processes were interdependent. We were less likely to persuade others to forswear nuclear weapons when we ourselves declared them central to our national security, continued their testing, and continued to expand and upgrade our arsenal. The arms agreements of the late-1980s and the sudden demise of the Soviet Union finally make it possible for such meaningful reduction of our nuclear arsenal–long a commitment of the United States and Russia under Article VI of the Non-Proliferation Treaty of 1968.

My endeavors as diplomat and lawyer have been at the level of the practical rather than the theoretical. They have included efforts to make treaties and quietly to persuade other nations that acquisition of nuclear weapons will detract from their security. I have largely left to others the broader intellectual debates about grand strategy and deterrence theory. Nevertheless, in sober hindsight, I am struck by the extent to which myths and misjudgments fueled the nuclear arms race.

We pursued the initial atomic bomb based upon an erroneous intelligence judgment that if we did not quickly acquire this capacity, Hitler's Germany would soon do so. In the early part of the Cold War, our domestic political discourse soured by McCarthyism, our political leaders fell into the habit of exaggerating Soviet conventional and nuclear military capacities. Most dangerous of all, perhaps, was the view held by some that nuclear weapons differed in degree, but not in kind, from conventional weapons.

Ignorance about these issues persisted–from Truman's Secretary of Defense, Louis Johnson, who reputedly stated that all he needed to know about atomic weapons was "that they go boom," to Ronald Reagan who, in his first administration, believed that after SLBMs had been launched they could be recalled. American citizens, who attended school in the 1950s, have sobering memories of nuclear air raid drills, when they crouched in school basements. Nevertheless, most put this terror out of mind, at least until the early-1980s when a "nuclear freeze" effort, stimulated by the callousness of Reagan's early actions, briefly appealed to the political mainstream. Indeed, there still appears little appreciation by the American people of the significance of the fact that the end of the Cold War and the ongoing arms reductions of the United States and Russia are significantly reducing the risks of a general nuclear war. Having long put these risks out of mind by a collective process of "denial," the public fails adequately to realize the extraordinary significance of recent events.

While I acknowledge the intellectual zeal and rigor that civilian strategists have employed in analysis of the balance of terror, a tendency existed to over-intellectualize. Civilian planners, most of whom had never seen a nuclear explosion, spun elaborate hypotheses as to how to fight limited nuclear war. Even when such a limited war appeared extremely implausible, planners moved on to discern political advantage to be obtained from maintaining the appearance of being able to wage limited nuclear war. Thus, they justified acquisition of weapons systems with which to give the appearance of being able to fight nuclear war as a way of trying to achieve "stability" to ensure that such a war would never occur.

The zenith of this abstract line of thinking was reached in the 1980s, when the Reagan administration affirmed the existence of a "window of vulnerability." This "window" was first discovered in 1977 by the Committee on the Present Danger, spearheaded by Paul Nitze and Eugene Rostow. They argued that, even if it were inconceivable that any rational leader of the Soviet Union would launch a nuclear first strike against the United States, the United States could not allow an international *perception* that, should such an event occur, we could not prevail by means of a strategic nuclear response. They posited that the Soviet's "advantage" in heavy ICBMs made conceptually possible a disabling first strike by Russian MIRVs that, by eliminating the U.S. land-based deterrent, would force a U.S. President to confront the choice of either capitulating or launching of a second-strike using SLBMs against Soviet cities at the risk of a counter strike against our own. Proponents of the "window of vulnerability" theory argued that the United States was at a geopolitical disadvantage so long as our land-based deterrent remained hypothetically vulnerable, since other countries would perceive the United States as being at a "disadvantage" in the nuclear arms race.

I was never persuaded that the "window of vulnerability" was real. I suspect the Soviet Union was similarly unpersuaded. Ironically, those who propounded these elaborate hypotheses were potentially harming, rather than improving, the nation's geopolitical standing. Their pronouncements contained elements of self-fulfilling prophecy. If they were right that there existed a "window of vulnerability" that the Soviet Union could exploit to obtain geopolitical advantage, it was curious behavior for American leaders to draw attention to this point of weakness.

Closing this imaginary "window of vulnerability" became one of the rationales for President Reagan's sudden and ill-conceived 1983 proposal for a Strategic Defense Initiative, discussed in chapter 5. The myth that nuclear or nonnuclear defensive technology, such as SDI, can end the nuclear arms race has been one of the most persistent of the nuclear era. I recognize that there is intuitive and even moral appeal to investment in defense as a way of solving nuclear arms dilemmas. Nevertheless, I remain persuaded that the ABM Treaty helped limit the offensive arms race and that there is no defensive, technological "fix" to the arms race. Indeed, history teaches that pursuit of strategic defense simply stimulates investment in offensive systems. I am certain that the fruits of Reagan's SDI would have been a more dangerous world. Rather than attempting to compete with us in the development of expensive and highly sophisticated defenses, the Soviet Union could have expanded its already vast offensive potential. The notion advanced by President Reagan that we would share SDI technology with the Soviet Union struck me as laughable.

Another important myth of the nuclear era that enjoyed wide public and political support was that the Soviet Union could be expected systematically to cheat with respect to its international treaty obligations. Some used this theory to depreciate the likely benefits of nuclear arms control agreements. During the first Reagan administration, the myth of the inherent untrustworthiness of the Soviet Union enjoyed special potency. A controversy centering on a large radar facility under construction at Krasnoyarsk, which by its location and orientation appeared to violate provisions of the ABM Treaty, added credence to this myth. Indeed, Gorbachev ultimately conceded the point. With the exception of the Krasnoyarsk radar, however, I know of no occasion of Soviet breach of arms control treaty obligations. In retrospect, the Soviets' technical violation with this radar pales by comparison to the massive breach of our ABM Treaty obligations that would have been necessitated by further pursuit of SDI.

I have often wondered whether military officers had the time or the patience to read the extensive academic writings on nuclear weapons strategy. Indeed, generals and admirals who had actually served in combat showed a sober appreciation for the confusion and uncertainty that characterize large-scale armed conflict. Many were, therefore, deeply skeptical of the nation's ability to maintain the necessary command, control, and communications to limit nuclear war should one ever begin. (The *New York Times* of April 18, 1994, describes termination of a program initiated in the Reagan years to help secure national command authority to allow nuclear war fighting over a 180-day period. Active in the initiation of this program was a military man, who perhaps didn't share the skepticism of his colleagues–Lt. Col. and White House aide Oliver North. Reportedly, this highly classified program consumed $11 billion.) There was, nevertheless, a range of views within the uniformed military. No one would question General Curtis LeMay's zeal for nuclear weapons, although even this fierce hawk reportedly became skeptical in his latter years.

Of course, the development of the nation's nuclear arsenal was deeply affected by interservice rivalry. The Navy's maintenance of its SLBM systems helped keep it from playing second fiddle to the Air Force with its missiles and bombers. The persistence of the nation's aspirations for antiballistic missiles can be explained in part by the Army's desire to be a factor in the strategic nuclear equation. (The Army had long had battlefield nuclear weapons in its arsenal.) Even though our military leaders tended toward common sense on the issue of the utility of nuclear weapons, they have been tempted to endorse the hypotheses of civilian planners when doing so would enhance the stature of their particular service.

Throughout my professional career, I was concerned by the apparent lack of comprehension by public officials and by American citizens of the true peril that we confronted as we, our allies, and the Soviet Union acquired ever more potent nuclear arsenals. The slowness with which the nation realized the futility of the nuclear arms race and the complacency with which most viewed its risks resulted in part from abdication of responsibility by various parties. There were few experts in nuclear diplomacy to match the expertise of scientists and engineers in the creation of nuclear weapons. With some notable exceptions, scientists have viewed weapons decisions to be the responsibility of political and military leaders. Military leaders, while skeptical about the utility of nuclear arms, properly have looked to civilian leaders for ultimate decisions (while competing among services for a proper place in the nuclear game). Civilian and political leaders at the highest levels have been relatively ignorant of the risks of nuclear weapons, and have been disposed to defer to scientists and military officers–completing a circle of failed accountability.

As early as the mid-1960s, realization began to emerge that nuclear weapons were potentially useless. Battlefield or tactical nuclear weapons could inflict so many casualties on our own forces and upon civilian populations of allied countries as to be unacceptable. Use of strategic nuclear weapons risks sacrifice of our nation and potentially the planet. True, the presence of these arsenals may have given the leadership of the United States, the Soviet Union, and other nations cause for prudence and hesitation. But a suicide threat cannot indefinitely shape relations between nations.

At the beginning of the 1980s, realization of the uselessness of nuclear weapons was neither immediate nor universal. However, during the decade there was wide and open debate on issues of nuclear strategy. This debate, coupled with extraordinary changes within the Soviet Union, foreshadowed the end of the nuclear arms race between the United States and Russia.

The Reagan administration entered office in 1981 claiming that the United States was at a military and strategic disadvantage that justified significant new expenditures on both conventional and strategic arms. There was renewed discussion of the feasibility of limited use of nuclear weapons, if necessary, to stop Soviet conquest of Western Europe. These developments brought back into focus the fact that the United States had long declared itself willing to be the first to use nuclear weapons in the event of conflict between NATO and the Warsaw Pact. In contrast, the Soviet Union had consistently asserted that it would never be the first to use these weapons. (The Chinese have similarly said that they would not be the first to use these weapons.)

As mentioned in chapter 6, in 1982 I joined with George Kennan, McGeorge Bundy, and Robert McNamara in publishing an article in *Foreign Affairs* urging the United States and its allies to take steps to strengthen conventional deterrence in Europe so as to be able to adopt a policy of "no first use." With the sudden end of the Cold War, such a policy no longer seems radical. In 1982, however, the article caused wide comment. The four of us were pleased to receive recognition for this article in the form of a $50,000 award and designation as "peace laureates" by the Einstein Foundation for World Peace.

With the widening of public debate regarding the nuclear arms race in the early 1980s, the Bishops of the Catholic church in the United States undertook to prepare a "pastoral letter" on this topic. I was honored to be one of many individuals consulted. Bryan Hehir, an exceptionally able and hard working priest, did much of the staff work for preparation of the Bishops' letter. The Bishops' effort to place the nuclear arms race in moral and religious context was both important and challenging.

Though a practicing Catholic, in my professional career I had not squarely confronted the question of whether it is moral for a nation to maintain a nuclear deterrent. I recall once being invited to make a speech about the "moral use of nuclear weapons." I declined the invitation, replying that I knew of none. Indeed, I still cannot conceive any moral, prospective use of nuclear weapons. As Father Hehir and the Bishops discerned, this situation raises the central question of whether, in the name of deterrence, a nation may threaten to use nuclear weapons, the actual use of which would be immoral due to vastly disproportionate effects on innocent lives and risks to future generations. Yet, having defined this issue, the Bishops confronted a dilemma. Stating categorically that it is immoral to threaten use of nuclear weapons as part of deterrence could erode the legitimacy of deterrence, potentially adding to the risk of conventional and even nuclear war.

In an effort to find their way out of this thicket, the Bishops approved continuing declaration of willingness to use nuclear weapons, but only under limited circumstances. The United States should never be the first to use such weapons. There could never be deliberate targeting of civilian populations. Nuclear weapons could only be used in a limited second strike against military targets, subject to tightly defined criteria. The Bishops further predicated their approval of maintenance by the United States of its nuclear arsenal on the condition that the country was in good faith striving for accords that would lead to mutual reduction by the United States and the Soviet Union of such weapons systems.

While I welcomed the thoughtful, and perhaps overdue, engagement by the Bishops of my church on this all-important issue, I was somewhat troubled by the implications of their recommendations. In trying to resolve the moral conundrum posed by maintenance of a nuclear deterrent by prescribing criteria for use of nuclear weapons, the Bishops implied that limited use of such weapons for purely military purposes could be acceptable. I respectfully disagree.

The Bishops' labors confirmed my career-long intuition that the dangers of nuclear weapons must be addressed by realistic and practical endeavor. Nuclear weapons cannot be wished out of existence, any more than they can be used to direct geopolitical advantage. Even though these weapons are not rationally useable and cannot purchase any genuine leverage for national leaders, the maintenance of nuclear arsenals by nations carries an ever-present risk of miscalculation or accident. Greater still perhaps is the risk that control of nuclear weapons could fall to a deranged leader. The disconcerting political rise of Mr. Zhirinovsky in Russia demonstrates that this risk is not merely hypothetical. For these reasons, reduction of nuclear arsenals and prevention of further proliferation of nuclear arms capacity remain imperative.

The end of the Cold War has created opportunities and risks that we are only beginning to understand and appreciate. Early focus has been upon risks–with four nations controlling the former Soviet Union's arsenal–and with uncertainty about internal control over weapons-grade materials and scientific competence. Nevertheless, the Cold War's end should eliminate the justification for the nuclear arms race. Challenges abound for a new generation of diplomats and policy makers.

First, nuclear arsenals need dramatic further reduction. The steps embarked upon by the United States and Russia pursuant to SALT II and the START Agreements, including on-site inspection and technical assistance in dismantling nuclear weapon systems, are heartening first steps, but much remains to be done. My current thinking is that maintenance by the United States of 100 survivable nuclear warheads should suffice, provided no other country or potentially hostile coalition of countries in aggregate has significantly more deliverable weapons. Also, I favor formalizing the current, informal moratorium on nuclear weapons testing by adoption and wide ratification of a comprehensive test ban. Even maintenance of this small arsenal should be viewed as an interim expedient pending creation of some form of international trusteeship for all remaining nuclear weapons and, some day, their abolition from the planet.

International trusteeship for nuclear technology was proposed by the United States in the Baruch Plan in 1947. While the international system would have to mature quite a bit more, and Russia and the other new countries of the former Soviet Union would have to stabilize, international trusteeship, such as by the United Nations, deserves renewed consideration.

In any event, further reduction of the nuclear arsenals of the present nuclear states and adoption of a comprehensive test ban should be important means to prevent further proliferation. In urging others not to acquire this awesome capacity, the United States and Russia may persuasively say that they have found it expensive, dangerous and, ultimately, useless.

In fact, in reflecting on this memoir, I have determined that of all the dimensions of the "arms control" problem, the most important is the number of individual states possessing nuclear weapons. The more apparent, immediate risks of the nuclear arms race between the United States and the Soviet Union have, for much of the past four decades, diverted our energies from the risks posed by acquisition of nuclear weapons by other countries. Iraq's efforts to obtain the bomb were sobering. North Korea's apparent efforts are now the focus of world concern. Yet, we have long indulged Israel in the development and maintenance of a significant nuclear arsenal. (In 1989, I published an article in *Foreign Affairs* highlighting the risks of the double standard that we have applied with respect to Israel's nuclear arsenal.)

With the end of the Cold War, the problem of third-country proliferation has become unequivocally the major challenge. There are reasons for hope, if not for complacency. South Africa, having covertly achieved a nuclear weapons capacity, has become the first state so situated to forswear continued possession. With lessons learned in Iraq, the world supports a strengthening role for the Vienna-based IAEA in attempting to assure that civilian nuclear power programs are not diverted to military uses. More broadly, experience in the United States during the past fifteen years demonstrates that civilian nuclear programs, with their attendant risk of spreading availability of weapons-grade nuclear materials, are less cost-effective than originally thought–especially if conducted with adequate attention to protection of health, safety, and the environment.

States with nuclear technology should continue and reinforce efforts to deny maverick nations, such as Libya, Iraq, and North Korea, the technologies with which they may acquire a nuclear weapon. It should remain the highest priority of intelligence services to detect efforts of would-be proliferators or of supplier nations aiding such states. The United Nations should authorize heavy sanctions, including military intervention if necessary, to avert further proliferation. Where absolutely necessary, and even in the absence of U.N. approval, the United States should be prepared to intervene on its own.

In the late 1940s, possession by the United States of the "bomb" seemed a robust guarantee of the Nation's security. During ensuing decades, the nuclear arms race between the United States and the Soviet Union, coupled with proliferation of nuclear weapons capacity or aspirations in less stable countries, emerged as the principal danger to the security not only of the United States but also of the planet.

At present, I believe that the world should be striving to rid itself of these weapons. While we cannot suppress the scientific knowledge that made them possible, we can seek to eliminate nuclear weapons from the military arsenals of all nations. I am under no illusions regarding the difficulty of such abolition. Yet as one who has witnessed their awesome force firsthand, and who has long thought about their implications for national and international security, I conclude that abolition of nuclear weapons is the only sensible, ultimate policy objective.

Notes

Chapter One
The Atomic Energy Commission, 1950–54

1. Truman quote in David Alan Rosenberg, "The Origins of Overkill: Nuclear Weapons and American Strategy, 1945–1960," *International Security* 7 (Spring 1983), 21–22. On the Soviet nuclear program, see David Holloway, *The Soviet Union and the Arms Race.*

2. Richard G. Hewlett and Jack M. Holl, *Atoms for Peace and War, 1953–1961: Eisenhower and the Atomic Energy Commission* (Berkeley: UC Press, 1989), 5–9.

3. Ibid., 13.

4. Thomas E. Murray, *Nuclear Policy for War and Peace* (Cleveland: World Publishing Company, 1960), 47.

5. GCS Diary, January 14, 1953.

6. Ibid., April 7, 1952.

7. Ibid., April 24, 1952.

8. See Lewis L. Strauss, *Men and Decisions* (Garden City, NY: Doubleday, 1962); Richard Pfau, *No Sacrifice Too Great: The Life of Lewis L. Strauss* (Charlottesville: University Press of Virginia, 1984).

9. GCS Diary, January 2, 1952.

10. "The Opening Doors: A Remarriage of Religion and Science," *Vital Speeches of the Day*, 560.

11. *Congressional Record*, January 7, 1953, 239.

12. David Alan Rosenberg, "U.S. Nuclear Stockpile, 1945–1950," *Bulletin of Atomic Scientists* 38 (May 1982), 25–30.

13. Richard G. Hewlett and Francis Duncan, *Atomic Shield, 1947–1952*, Vol. II, *A History of the United States Atomic Energy Commission* (University Park: Penn State University Press, 1969), 547.

14. SIPRI, *Tactical Nuclear Weapons: European Perspectives* (London, 1978), 10; David C. Elliot, "Project Vista and Nuclear Weapons in Europe," *International Security* 11 (Summer 1986), 163–83.

15. GCS diary, January 22, 1952.

16. Ibid., July 1, 1952.

17. Memo, Lovett to James S. Lay (executive secretary of the NSC), December 11, 1951, quoted in Hewlett and Duncan, *Atomic Shield*, 572.

18. Herbert F. York, *The Advisors: Oppenheimer, Teller and the Superbomb* (Stanford, Calif.: Stanford University Press, 1976), 128–30.

19. Hewlett and Duncan, *Atomic Shield*, 568–71.

20. Thomas B. Cochran et al., *Nuclear Weapons Databook*, vol. II (Cambridge, Mass.: Ballinger, 1987), 152–53.

21. Thomas E. Murray, *Nuclear Policy for War and Peace*, 166–68; Thomas B. Cochran et al., *Nuclear Weapons Databook*, vol. II (Ballinger, 1987), 153.

22. Ibid., 213.

23. Ibid., 20–21.

24. Ibid., 198–99.

25. GCS diary, January 25, 1954.

26. Smith to Owsley, Dec. 19, 1956, Weapons Testing-Eleventh General Assembly, Oct. 1956–Feb. 1957, Box 6; Smith, Draft Note to the Soviet Union, April 22, 1957, Francis O. Wilcox to Smith, April 26, 1957, Nuclear Weapons Tests, April-May 1957 (3), Box 6, Stassen Records, DDE Library.

27. Thomas B. Cochran et al., *Nuclear Weapons Databook*, vol. II, 154.

28. Robert A. Divine, *Blowing on the Wind* (Oxford University Press, 1978), 7–8.

29. Ibid., 4–6.

30. Gregg Herken, *Cardinal Choices: Presidential Science Advising from the Atomic Bomb to SDI: A Twentieth Century Fund Book* (Oxford University Press, 1992), 83.

31. Ibid., 83–84.

32. Ibid., 186.

33. GCS diary, September 11, 1952.

34. Ibid., October 19, 1953.

35. Norman Polmar and Thomas B. Allen, *Rickover* (New York: Simon & Schuster, 1982), 252–53.

36. GCS diary, April 22, 1953.

37. Ibid., April 27, 1953.

38. Ibid., June 17, July 2, 1953.

39. Polmar and Allen, *Rickover*, 606–07.

40. Hewlett and Holl, *Atoms for Peace and War*, 194–95.

41. Ibid., 130–40.

42. Thomas E. Murray, *Nuclear Policy for War and Peace*, 194–98.

43. Richard Pfau, *No Sacrifice Too Great*, 203–4.

44. Thomas B. Cochran et al., *Nuclear Weapons Databook*, vol. II, 2.

45. J. Robert Oppenheimer, "Atomic Weapons and American Policy," *Foreign Affairs* (July 1953), 530.

46. McGeorge Bundy, *Danger and Survival* (Santa Rosa, Calif.: Vintage 1990), 288–93.

47. Hewlett and Holl, *Atoms for Peace and War*, 48.

48. Richard Pfau, *No Sacrifice Too Great*, 140–41.

49. My thanks to Ben Huberman for passing on this recollection to me.

50. Gregg Herken, *Cardinal Choices*, 77.

51. Hewlett and Holl, *Atoms for Peace and War*, 261–62.

52. Ibid., 210.

53. GCS diary, March 16, 1954.

Chapter Two
Special Assistant for Atomic Energy Affairs, 1954–57

1. Richard G. Hewlett and Jack M. Holl, *Atoms for Peace and War 1953–1961: Eisenhower and the Atomic Energy Commission* (Berkeley: University of California Press, 1989). I have found this book valuable for refreshing my memory about these long-ago issues and events.

2. John Lewis Gaddis , "The Unexpected John Foster Dulles," in Richard H. Immerman, ed., *John Foster Dulles and the Diplomacy of the Cold War* (Princeton, N.J.: Princeton University Press, 1990), 51.

3. Ibid., 54–58, 67–72.

4. Gerard C. Smith, "Take Nuclear Weapons into Custody," *Bulletin of the Atomic Scientists*, December 1990, 12.

5. Gerard C. Smith, "The Unexpected Dulles," *Arms Control Today*, May 1991, 29.

6. Memorandum from State Department to embassy of the Soviet Union, July 9, 1954, in *Foreign Relations of the United States, 1952–1954*, vol. II, 1475.

7. Hewlett and Holl, *Atoms for Peace and War*, 245; Letter from Dulles to Special Assistant to the President Nelson Rockefeller, May 2, 1955, based on a memorandum of April 29 from the author to Dulles, in *Foreign Relations of the United States, 1955-57*, Vol. XX, 71-72.

8. Hewlett and Holl, *Atoms for Peace and War*, 229-230.

9. Letter from James J. Wadsworth to John Foster Dulles, April 23, 1956, in John Foster Dulles papers, Seeley G. Mudd Library, Princeton University.

10. Wadsworth to Dulles, October 26, 1956, GCS private papers.

11. Hewlett and Holl, *Atoms for Peace and War*, 320–322.

12. Ibid., 232-234.

13. Ibid., 234-235. Whitman told me in 1958 that Strauss's concern over the security risks in allowing U.S. scientists to meet with their Soviet counterparts had led Whitman in 1955 to leave a sealed letter explaining his motives in going, against Strauss's wishes, to a scientific conference in Moscow in 1955.

14. Memorandum from Smith to Hoover, January 19, 1955, in *Foreign Relations of the United States, 1955-57*, Vol. XX, 9–10.

15. Joint State Department–AEC press release of February 23, 1955, in *Department of State Bulletin*, March 14, 1955, 444.

16. Hewlett and Holl, *Atoms for Peace and War*, 308–309.

17. Ibid., 310–313.

18. Ibid., 313–314.

19. Ibid., 314–315.

20. Ibid., 317.

21. Ibid., 278–279, 293.

22. Ibid., 285.

23. However, President Bush was to revive this so-called gimmick in 1989, and in 1992 a treaty was signed by 25 nations—the sixteen NATO states, the former Warsaw Pact satellites, and the republics of Russia, Belarus, Ukraine, and Georgia. Since the United States and Russia already gain much data from their satellite reconnaissance programs, the agreement is expected mainly to benefit smaller countries, and to promote arms control

agreements in Europe. See "Open Skies Treaty Signed," *Arms Control Today*, April 1992, 15.

24. See in this connection Eisenhower's statement during a meeting with Admiral Radford, General Taylor, and General Goodpaster on May 24, 1956, at which the President said he would like to see a test of the new NIKE system, but "had been unable to do so because of the need to give psychological support to peaceful rather than military things."

25. Telephone call, Eisenhower to Strauss, February 23, 1955, Phone Calls(3), Diary Series, Eisenhower Library.

26. On this shift in Dulles's views, see G. Allen Greb and Gerald Johnson, "The Test Ban Treaty Reconsidered: Arms Control in the Eisenhower Administration" (unpublished paper). That Dulles underwent a basic change in his views is also attested to by Hewlett and Holl: "By spring 1957, . . . Dulles, despite his recent bout with cancer, emerged as the President's most dependable disarmament champion. While Stassen and Strauss increasingly voiced the extremes of disarmament and international nuclear policy, Dulles, under the shrewd tutelage of Gerard Smith, kept to the middle road occupied by the President"; Hewlett and Holl, *Atoms for Peace and War*, 385.

27. Memorandum of conversation by Dulles, December 14, 1954, in *Foreign Relations of the United States, 1952–54*, vol. II, 1584–85.

28. Letter from Murray to Eisenhower, March 14, 1955, *Foreign Relations of the United States, 1955–57*, vol. XX, 56–57.

29. *Foreign Relations of the United States, 1955-57*, vol. XX, 62–64.

30. Robert A. Divine, *Blowing on the Wind* (New York: Oxford University Press, 1978), 70–71.

31. Gregg Herken, *Cardinal Choices*, 94.

32. GCS Diary, October 17, 1956.

33. Department of State Bulletin, April 8, 1957, 562.

34. Radio and television speech, July 22, 1957, in Department of State Bulletin, August 23, 1957, 270–71.

35. *Foreign Relations of the United States, 1955-1957*, vol. XX, 566–73.

36. Ibid., 575–77.

37. I am indebted to Lawrence Weiler for sharing his recollections of this episode with me.

38. *Foreign Relations of the United States, 1955–1957*, vol. XX, 665.

39. Hewlett and Holl, *Atoms for Peace and War*, 456–457, 459–460.

Chapter Three
The Policy Planning Staff, 1957–60

1. Information in this and subsequent paragraphs concerning my duties as head of PPS draws in part upon my testimony before the Senate Committee on Foreign Relations in 1958; see Hearing held before the Committee on Foreign Relations, the United States Senate, August 7, 1958, 60–91.

2. *New York Times*, June 26, 1958, 16.

3. See Memorandum for Dr. Killian from Minshull, September 23, 1958, "Policy Decision re Terms of Reference for Surprise Attack Delegation"; NSA files.

4. See chapter 2, pp. 33–37. See also my "The Unexpected Dulles" (Review of *John Foster Dulles and the Diplomacy of the Cold War*, edited by Richard H. Immerman), *Arms Control Today* (May 1991), 28–29.

5. Fred Kaplan, *The Wizards of Armageddon* (New York: Simon and Schuster, 1983), 141–145; the quotation is on page 142.

6. 343rd Meeting of the NSC, November 7, 1957.

7. 363rd Meeting of the NSC, April 24, 1958.

8. Kaplan, *Wizards of Armageddon*, 149–152. The NSC discussion and the report itself can be found in *Foreign Relations of the United States, 1955-1957*, Volume XIX, 630–661.

9. Ibid.

10. The Gaither Committee endorsed spending as much as $22 billion over five years on fallout shelters, but actually assigned this a secondary priority to the buildup of offensive forces.

11. I can take some comfort in knowing that Eisenhower made the same mistake more than once.

12. Murray, *Nuclear Policy for War and Peace*, chapter 3, especially pp. 60–61, 89.

13. Memorandum of April 9, 1958, by Gen. Andrew Goodpaster, in John Foster Dulles papers, Seeley G. Mudd Library, Princeton University.

14. Robert Cutler, Conference Memorandum, June 17, 1958, in the Eisenhower Library.

15. Maxwell Taylor, *The Uncertain Trumpet* (New York: Harper & Brothers, 1959), 56–65.

16. Memorandum for the Secretary from Gerard C. Smith, October 29, 1959, Subject: Force Cuts Discussion with DOD on October 24, 1959; NSA collection.

17. John Foster Dulles, "Challenge and Response in United States Foreign Policy," *Foreign Affairs*, October 1957, 32–33.

18. McGeorge Bundy, *Danger and Survival* (New York: Vintage, 1990), 488.

19. Declaration and communiqué, December 19, 1957, Department of State Bulletin, January 16, 1958, 14. The IRBMs had been developed because we thought our ICBMs might not come on line soon enough. When this fear proved unfounded, a search was begun to find some use for these weapons, and SACEUR's nuclear requirements seemed to provide a good fit. During one discussion on what to do with the IRBMs, I heard President Eisenhower say, "Why don't we throw them into the sea." Since it was these weapons in Turkey and Greece that caused a great deal of anxiety during the Cuban Missile Crisis, in hindsight that might not have been such a bad idea.

20. "Nuclear Policy," background paper, December 4, 1957, declassified June 20, 1986.

21. GCS Diary, December 8, 1957.

22. I remember in particular the case of "Penney's Bang Meter." This was a device to measure an explosion's yield, put together by William Penney, one of the leading lights in Britain's nuclear weapons program at Aldermaston, which at the cost of less than a dollar provided readings equal in accuracy to those provided by a U.S. instrument costing thousands of dollars.

23. Richard G. Hewlett and Jack M. Holl, *Atoms for Peace and War* (Berkeley: University of California Press, 1989), 467.

24. I have discussed this subject at greater length in "The French Temptation," *Interplay*, Volume 2, Number 7 (February 1969), 48–49.

25. John Newhouse, *De Gaulle and the Anglo-Saxons* (New York: Viking, 1970), 60.

26. Stephen Ambrose, *Eisenhower: The President* (New York: Simon and Schuster, 1984), 462–463.

27. Ibid., 463–466.

28. Memorandum of a conference with the President by Gen. Andrew Goodpaster, July 14, 1958, in *Foreign Relations of the United States:1958-1960*, Volume XI, 211–13; Memorandum, Subject: United States Military Intervention in Lebanon (The White House, Morning of July 14, 1958), and Memorandum, Robert Cutler to John Foster Dulles, July 14, 1958, Documents Nos. 159–160 in Microfiche Supplement to the above *Foreign Relations* volume; Ambrose, *Eisenhower: The President*, 469–471.

29. Ambrose, *Eisenhower: The President*, 472; Cable, JCS 945198, July 21, 1958, in CCS 381 Lebanon (5-13-58)(section 3), and Cables JCS 945598, July 28, 1953 and EC9-3874, July 25, 1958, both in CCS 381 Lebanon (5-13-58)(section 4), all three in RG 218, National Archives, Washington, D.C.

30. See the discussion of the 1958 Quemoy-Matsu crisis in Gordon H. Chang, *Friends and Enemies: The United States, China, and the Soviet Union, 1948-1972* (Stanford, Calif.: Stanford University Press, 1990), 182–194.

31. Most of this new information has been collected and analyzed by a team of U.S., British, European, and Soviet scholars under the leadership of David Rosenberg and Wolfgang Krieger, with the support of the Nuclear History Program at the University of Maryland. The studies produced by

this group were presented at a conference in the spring of 1993 and will be published. I have found some of these studies quite useful for refreshing my recollections about the Berlin Crisis, particularly the roles of Eisenhower and Dulles in dealing with it.

32. McGeorge Bundy, *Danger and Survival* (New York: Random House, 1988), chapter 8; and Marc Trachtenberg, *History and Strategy* (Princeton, N.J.: Princeton University Press, 1991), chapter 5.

33. Michael A. Guhin, *John Foster Dulles* (New York: Columbia University Press, 1972), 302.

34. I have refreshed my memory of my role in the State Department's handling of the Berlin Crisis by examining a number of documents collected by the National Security Archive in Washington, D.C., on the crisis. Many of these have been published in a valuable microfiche collection with a useful accompanying index and guide; see *The Berlin Crisis, 1958–1962* (Alexandria, Va.: Chadwyck-Healey, Inc., 1992).

35. GSC Diary entries: December 2, 6, 9, and 11, 1958.

36. See for example Memoranda of Conversation, Subject: Berlin Contingency Planning, March 9 and 14, 1959, both in National Security Archives, Washington, D.C.

37. William Burr, "Dwight D. Eisenhower and American Policy During the Berlin Crisis, 1958–1960" (unpublished paper, 1993), 43.

38. Gerard Smith, Memorandum for the Secretary, June 15, 1959; NSA collection.

39. David Bruce Diary entry, May 19, 1959, NSA collection.

40. Hewlett and Holl, *Atoms for Peace and War*, 384.

41. See, for example, draft speech before World Order Study Conferences of the National Council of Churches, November 15, 1958, Dulles—November 1958, Box 8, Dulles-Herter Series, Ann Whitman File, DDE Library.

42. Memorandum of Conversation, "Meeting with Disarmament Advisors, April 26, 1958," April 28, 1958, Dulles–April 1958(1), Box 8, Dulles-Herter Series, Eisenhower Library.

43. James R. Killian, Jr., "The Origins and Uses of a Scientific Presence in the White House," in William T. Golden, ed., *Science Advice to the President* (New York: Pergamon Press, 1980), 30; James R. Killian, Jr., *Sputnik, Scientists and Eisenhower: A Memoir of the First Special Assistant to the President for Science and Technology* (Boston: MIT Press, 1977), 227–229.

44. Dulles to Eisenhower, August 21, 1958, Dulles-August 1958, Box 8, Dulles-Herter Series.

45. Dulles to Eisenhower, June 18, 1957, Dulles-June 1957, Box 7, Dulles-Herter Series; public address, "Disarmament and Peace," July 22, 1957, DPC Note #158, July 23, 1957, DPC Notes [121-159](7), Box 2, Stassen Records, Eisenhower Library. See also my piece, "The French Temptation," *Interplay*, 2 (February 1969), 48–49.

46. I have addressed these issues at greater length in the following: Gerard C. Smith and James F. Leonard, "Nuclear Club Needs to Confront Proliferation Issues," *Baltimore Sun*, July 18, 1993, 4C; and in a letter sent to David Hamburg of the Carnegie Corporation, January 27, 1993.

47. Killian, *Sputnik, Scientists and Eisenhower*, 296–297.

48. See Killian to Dulles, July 10, 1958, Disarmament–Surprise Attack, July-December 1958(1), Box 2, Killian-Kistiakowsky Records, Eisenhower Library; Ad Hoc Working Group on Surprise Attack, meeting of August 14, 1958, Disarmament–Surprise Attack, July-December 1958(1), Box 2, Killian-Kistiakowsky Records; W.H. Minshull to Killian, Policy Decision re: Terms of Reference for Surprise Attack Delegation, September 23, 1958, NSA.

49. See my recollections about the Geneva Surprise Attack Conference imparted to historian Gregg Herken in his *Counsels of War* (New York: Knopf, 1985), 123.

50. Herter to Eisenhower, July 9, 1959, Herter—July 1959(2), Box 9, Dulles-Herter Series.

51. GCS Diary, September 22, 1959.

52. See, for example, Dulles to Stassen, September 27, 1957, Disarmament Talks, Box 12, Administration Series; Dulles, News Conference of October 16, 1957, No. 579, Dulles-October 1957(2), Box 7, Dulles-Herter Series; Memorandum of Conversation, Eisenhower, Dulles, Soviet

Ambassador Menshikov, March 3, 1958, Dulles–March 1958(2), Box 7, Dulles-Herter Series; Dulles, News Conference of March 4, No. 104, Dulles–March 1958(2), Box 7, Dulles-Herter Series, all in Eisenhower Library.

53. Smith to Kohler, September 10, 1959, NSA. See also Smith to Secretary of State, March 9, 1959, NSA.

54. Memorandum, President Eisenhower's Talks with Chairman Khrushchev at Camp David, undated, NSA.

55. Herter, "National Security with Arms Limitation," *Department of State Bulletin* (March 7, 1960), 354–358.

56. GCS Diary, May 3, 1960.

57. Michael Beschloss, *Mayday* (New York: Harper and Row, 1986), 276.

58. Senate Committee on Foreign Relations, "Events Incident to the Summit Conference, May 27," June 1–2, 1960, 26–27, 95–96.

59. Ibid., 7–8, 37, 46.

60. Dwight D. Eisenhower, *Waging Peace* (New York: Doubleday, 1965), 580.

61. ACDA, *Arms Control and Disarmament Agreements* (Washington, D.C.: GPO, 1990), 3, 314–315.

Chapter Four
Alliance Diplomacy and the NATO Multilateral Force

1. A number of recent works have detailed the renewal of the Berlin crisis during Kennedy's first year in office. See for example Michael Beschloss, *The Crisis Years: Kennedy and Khrushchev, 1960–1963* (New York: Harper Collins Publishers, 1991). A forthcoming collection of essays by American, British, French, German, and Soviet scholars, drawing on the latest releases of declassified documents and edited by David Alan Rosenberg and Wolfgang Krieger, should shed much new light on the Berlin Crisis.

2. My memory of the work of this Berlin Task Force has been refreshed by the helpful recollections of Raymond Garthoff, as well as by a number of documents; *see* Berlin Task Force, Minutes and Assignments of Meeting for September 19, 20, 28, October 3 and November 15, 1961, National Security Archives, Washington, D.C.

3. This memorandum, dated March 3, 1959, and related memoranda by Secretary Herter and Loftus Becker, the Department's Legal Advisor, can be found in the National Security Archives. One of my last acts as head of Policy Planning was to urge serious reconsideration of this idea by the Joint Chiefs; *see* Memoranda, Smith to Merchant, February 10, 1960, National Security Archives.

4. Arthur Krock, "In the Nation" column entitled "A Maritime Deterrent to the Communist Threat," the *New York Times*, November 21, 1961, 38. Efforts to secure a copy of the "Minos" paper have proved unavailing, and so this column is a key source for information on this paper. Another source, which is a later reworking of the same themes, is a paper which I circulated at the Washington Center of Foreign Policy Research in November 1961 entitled "Oceanic Control and Community" (copy in author's personal papers).

5. Letter, Dean Acheson to GCS, December 13, 1961, GCS Papers.

6. George C. Lowe, "Deterrence, Sea Power and Cuba," *Navy Magazine* (November 1963), 24–29, 47–53.

7. There are a number of scholarly works which discuss the origins and troubled history of the MLF, and I have consulted a number of them to refresh my memory. Among the more useful are: John D. Steinbrunner, *The Cybernetic Theory of Decision: New Dimensions of Political Analysis* (Princeton, N.J.: Princeton University Press, 1974); David N. Schwartz, *NATO's Nuclear Dilemmas* (Washington, D.C.: The Brookings Institution, 1983); Glenn T. Seaborg, with Benjamin S. Loeb, *Stemming the Tide: Arms Control in the Johnson Years* (New York: Free Press, 1987); Jane E. Stromseth, *The Origins of Flexible Response: NATO's Debate Over Strategy in the 1960s* (New York: St. Martin's Press, 1988); McGeorge Bundy, *Danger and Survival: Choices About the Bomb in the First Fifty Years* (New York: Random House, 1988); and George Bunn, *Arms Control by Committee: Managing Negotiations with the Russians* (Stanford, Calif.: Stanford University Press, 1992).

8. On these points, see the discussion in Schwartz, *NATO's Nuclear Dilemmas*, as well as in Robert A. Wampler, "Ambiguous Legacy: The United States, Great Britain and the Foundations of NATO Strategy, 1948–1957" (Harvard University, Ph.D. Thesis, 1991).

9. For an extended analysis of Norstad's proposed MMRBM force and proposals to share U.S. ballistic missile technology with selected NATO allies, *see* Schwartz, *NATO's Nuclear Dilemmas*, 75–83.

10. This and following paragraphs draw upon Robert Bowie's recollec-tions about the Bowie Report, as well as the report itself, as published in "The North Atlantic Nations Tasks for the 1960s" [A Report to the Secretary of State, August 1960], by Robert R. Bowie (Nuclear History Program Occasional Paper 7, Nuclear History Program, University of Maryland, 1991).

11. Bowie, "The North Atlantic Nations Tasks for the 1960's," iv–v.

12. The preceding two paragraphs draw heavily upon ibid., pp. v–vii.

13. Bundy, *Danger and Survival*, 489. For the relevant text of Kennedy's speech, *see* Schwartz, *NATO's Nuclear Dilemmas*, 88.

14. Ibid.

15. Schwartz, *NATO's Nuclear Dilemmas*, 88–89.

16. Standard accounts include Steinbrunner, *The Cybernetic Theory of Decision*, chapters 8 and 9; Schwartz, *NATO's Nuclear Dilemmas*, chapter 5; and Seaborg, *Stemming the Tide*, chapters 9, 10, and 12.

17. Apparently the proponents of aiding the French had more impact than once thought, in light of the revelations about long-standing U.S. assistance to the French nuclear weapons program revealed in a recent article; see Richard Ullman, "The Covert French Connection," *Foreign Policy*, Number 75 (Summer 1989), 3–33.

18. For a good discussion of the debate over the French offer and Owen's paper, see Steinbrunner, 225–227; and Schwartz, 90.

19. On these points, see Admiral John Marshall Lee, "The NATO Multilateral Force, 1960–1964," in *Gerard C. Smith: A Career in Progress*, edited by Henry Owen and John Thomas Smith II (Lanham, Maryland: University

Press of America, 1989), 32–33. I have found this piece especially useful in reconstructing my role in the MLF.

20. "NACNA," undated memorandum, GSC papers.

21. Lee, "The NATO Multilateral Force," 34; *The Eisenhower Administration and NATO Nuclear Strategy* [transcript of oral history session directed by Robert A. Wampler and David A. Rosenberg, May 10, 1989]. Seaborg, 86–87.

22. The voyage of the U.S.S. *Claude V. Ricketts* is documented in *The Mixed Manning Demonstration 1964–65*, the cruise book of the tour. (Copy in possession of the author).

23. Examination of my private papers reveals a long list of draft memoranda, talking points, and papers rehearsing the arguments pro and con for the MLF written during 1962–1965. Usually, these papers delved into detailed analysis of various contingencies—for example, trying to track what the Soviets would do if the NATO allies did X or Y in response to the U.S. proposing A, B, or C with regard to the MLF, or the range of alternatives to the MLF and their relative strategic merits and demerits. I have spared the reader detailed discussion of these efforts to get my thoughts in order and to assay the contending political winds within NATO, as in the end, I always came to the conclusions I am sketching in these pages.

24. Ironically, the security-control system for handling nuclear information within NATO was code-named "CABAL," which I suppose could have inadvertently fed suspicions that such a group of conspirators existed.

25. This and the following paragraphs draw largely upon an address I made to the U.S. Naval Academy Foreign Affairs Conference in April 1964, as well as memoranda found in my private papers; see "The Nuclear Defense of NATO," by Gerard C. Smith, in *Department of State Bulletin*, May 18, 1964, 783–790.

26. Smith, "The Nuclear Defense of NATO," 784–785.

27. In addition to ibid., 787–788, see "Outline of Remarks for Kissinger Seminar," n.d. (ca. June 1963), Smith private papers.

28. Lee, 34–35.

29. Untitled memorandum re meeting with British officials, September 13, 1962, Smith Papers.

30. Seaborg, 85–86.

31. This paragraph draws upon and summarizes rather severely the detailed analysis of these issues found in Seaborg, 101–105.

32. Seaborg, 99, 105–107.

33. Cited in Richard Reeves, *President Kennedy: Profile of Power* (New York: Simon & Schuster, 1993). 546.

34. Seaborg, 88–90.

35. Ibid., 92, 101–102, 105.

36. Ibid., 90–91; the quote is from p. 90.

37. Ibid., 92.

38. Ibid., 95–97.

39. Draft Memorandum of Conversation, January 16, 1964 [Merchant, Ricketts, Goodpaster, Smith, Iler and Eisenhower], attached to Letter, GCS to Eisenhower, January 20, 1964, GCS Papers.

40. Seaborg, 97–101.

41. Seaborg, chapter 12 (121–130) discusses these events quite well. On the subsequent establishment of the Nuclear Planning Group, see Schwartz, *NATO's Nuclear Dilemmas*, 179–186; and Stromseth, 182–186.

42. Letter, GCS to Dean Rusk, December 15, 1964, GCS Papers.

43. Seaborg, 129.

44. Letter, GCS to Finletter, December 15, 1964, GCS Papers.

45. Letter, McGeorge Bundy to GCS, December 26, 1964, GCS Papers.

46. Letter, Dean Rusk to GCS, December 22, 1964, GCS Papers.

47. Letter, Henry Kissinger to GCS, December 29, 1964, GCS Papers.

48. Letter, GCS to Henry Owen, December 4, 1967; and undated note, Owen to GCS, both in GCS Papers.

49. Letter, GCS to Henry Owen, April 26, 1965, GCS Papers.

Chapter Five
ACDA and the Salt Negotiations, 1969–72

1. Gerard C. Smith, *Gerard Smith on Arms Control* (Lanham, Md.: University Press of America, 1987), Kenneth W. Thompson, ed.

2. A sampling of the extensive literature on SALT would include the following: John Newhouse, *Cold Dawn: The Story of SALT* (New York: Holt, Rinehart and Winston, 1973); Mason Willrich and John B. Rhinelander, eds., *SALT: The Moscow Agreements and Beyond* (New York: Free Press, 1974); Thomas W. Wolfe, *The SALT Experience* (Cambridge, MA: Ballinger, 1979); Raymond Garthoff, *Detente and Confrontation: American-Soviet Relations from Nixon to Reagan* (Washington, D.C.: Brookings, 1985); Philip J. Farley, "Strategic Arms Control, 1967–1987," in Alexander George, Philip Farley, and Alexander Dallin, eds., *U.S.-Soviet Security Cooperation* (Oxford: Oxford University Press, 1988).

3. JFK Library. Owen to Mac Bundy (NSC) May 10, 1961. Other Owen recommendations were Joseph Johnson, head of Carnegie, and James Perkins, chairman of Council on Foreign Relations panel on military matters.

4. GCS on Arms Control, 58; Smith, "The Arms Control and Disarmament Agency: An Unfinished History," *Bulletin of Atomic Scientists* (April 1984), 13–17.

5. Farley, "Strategic Arms Control," 224–25.

6. Gerard C. Smith, *Doubletalk: The Story of SALT I* (Lanham, Md.: University Press of America, 1985), 16.

7. Gromyko statement, in Farley, "Strategic Arms Control," 226–27.

8. Lori Esposito, "The Selling of SALT," *Foreign Service Journal* 59 (February 1982), 22.

9. *Interplay*, November 1968.

10. GCS to Gregory Smith, Dec. 6, 1969. Along these lines, one unofficial Soviet source described Semenov at the time as having an "original mind," acquitting himself "better in cocktail party banter than most Soviets." Quoted in Anthony Astrachan, "Delegates Are Clue to Arms Attitudes," *Washington Post*, November 24, 1969.

11. Bernard Weintraub, "In Vienna, SALT Means Tourists, Delegates, Secretaries and Security Men," *New York Times*, April 16, 1970.

12. I first made this analogy during the negotiations, in a letter of April 28, 1971, to Henry Owen, who was then at the Brookings Institution.

13. Smith, *Doubletalk*, 84.

14. See also account of Garthoff, "Negotiating with the Russians," *International Security*, 1 (1977).

15. John Newhouse, *War and Peace in the Nuclear Age* (New York: Knopf, 1989), 221.

16. Newhouse, *War and Peace*, 210.

17. Paul H. Nitze, with Ann M. Smith and Steven L. Rearden, *From Hiroshima to Glasnost: At the Center of Decision* (New York: Grove Weidenfeld, 1989), 198–99; Newhouse, *War and Peace*, 220.

18. Bunn, *Arms Control by Committee*, 110.

19. Smith, *Doubletalk*, 225–26.

20. Henry Kissinger, *White House Years* (Boston: Little, Brown, 1979), 822.

21. Smith, *Doubletalk*, 76.

22. "Chronology of Principal Developments on the Strategic Arms Limitation Talks (Part I)," drafted by R.W. Lambert, September 11, 1973, 4.

23. See *e.g.*, Dobrynin's July 1969 report to the Politburo on opening the back channel. Recently declassified from Soviet archives, this document is reproduced in full in the *Cold War International History Project Bulletin* (Fall 1993), 63–67. It also contains a revealing portrait of Kissinger by Dobrynin. Noting that Kissinger had a "dominant influence . . . in the area of foreign policy," Dobrynin described him as both "smart and erudite" and "at the same time extremely vain" and "not averse to boasting about his influence."

24. Seaborg, *Stemming the Tide.*

25. Recently declassified documents in the SALT collection at the Johnson Library reveal that both the President and Rostow tried to keep the idea of SALT alive even after Czechoslovakia. See especially "Strategic Missile Talks" folder, Box 11, National Security File, Files of Walt W. Rostow, Lyndon Baines Johnson Library.

26. Smith, *Doubletalk*, 187.

27. "Chronology of Principal Developments," 6 passim; R. W. Lambert, "Forward-Based Systems and the Non-Circumvention Formula in the First Phase of SALT (1969–1972)" [Historical Division, Bureau of Economic Affairs, U.S. Arms Control and Disarmament Agency, June 6, 1973]; and R.W. Lambert, "Chronology of Vienna Discussions on Forward-Based Aircraft, MR/IRBMs, and Third-Country Problems," April 17–July 7, 1970 [Historical Division, Economics Bureau, U.S. Arms Control and Disarmament Agency, July 10, 1970]; both in National Security Archive.

28. Smith, *Doubletalk*, 92.

29. See "Chronology of Vienna Discussions," 8.

30. Ibid., 31.

31. See discussion of vulnerability issue in Herbert York and Allen Greb, "MIRV," in Bernard Brodie, Michael Intriligator and Roman Kolkowicz, eds., *National Security and International Stability* (Cambridge, Mass.: Oelgeschlager, Gunn and Hain, 1983), 407–22; George Rathjens, "ABM Debate," in ibid., 386–87; and Ted Greenwood, *Making the MIRV: A Study of Defense Decision Making* (Lanham, Md.: University Press of America, 1988).

32. Press release, Dec. 3, 1974, quoted in *Doubletalk*, 177.

33. Smith, *Doubletalk*, 156. See also my letters to Nixon of May 22, 1969, and Dec. 3, 1969, in ibid., 479–82.

34. Information from Doty, Ruina, other principals. Seymour Hirsch, *Price of Power*. Kissinger does *not* mention the meetings with the Doty group in his memoirs.

35. Rathjens to Kissinger, June 2, 1969, with report; Rathjens to Kissinger, April 13, 1970. Made available by author.

36. On public and congressional support for MIRV ban, see Newhouse, *Cold Dawn*, 123–30, 173–90; Newhouse, *War and Peace*, 216–17; Alton Frye, "U.S. Decision-making for SALT," in Willrich and Rhinelander, *SALT*, 78–87.

37. Nixon's stance on the "SWWA" proposal was perhaps bolstered by Nitze's opposition to it; see Nitze, *From Hiroshima to Glasnost*, 302.

38. Seaborg, *Stemming the Tide*, 436–37.

39. Memorandum of conversation of July 14, 1969 with Robert Kleiman, GSC Papers. See also Nitze, *From Hiroshima to Glasnost*, 291–92, 307–08.

40. Smith, *Doubletalk*, 175.

41. "Reassessment of the U.S. Position During the Second Session of the Strategic Arms Limitation Talks," ACDA Historical Division, March 1971, 16–17; the National Security Archive.

42. GSC letter to editor, *Issues in Science and Technology* (Winter '85), 4.

43. Smith, *Doubletalk*, 456.

44. Ibid., xvii.

45. York, *Making Weapons*; Wiesner, *Where Science and Politics Meet*; Kaplan, *Wizards*, 344–45.

46. York, *Race to Oblivion*, 194; *Making Weapons*; Seaborg, *Tide*, 414–15; Kaplan, *Wizards*, 346.

47. Greb discussion with Doty. On Pugwash, see J. Rottblatt, *Scientists in Quest for Peace*; Helen Hawkins, Allen Greb and Gertrud Weiss Szilard, eds., *Toward a Livable World: Leo Szilard and the Crusade for Nuclear Arms Control* (Cambridge, Mass.: MIT Press, 1987), 153ff.

48. Quoted in Sanford Lakoff and Herbert York, *A Shield in Space?: Technology, Politics, and the Strategic Defense Initiative* (Berkeley: University of California Press, 1989), 185.

49. Remarks originally made November 4, 1985, and reprinted in *Gerard Smith on Arms Control*, xvii–xviii.

50. See *e.g.*, Abraham D. Sofaer, "The ABM Treaty and the Strategic Defense Initiative," *Harvard Law Review* (June 1986), 1972–1985, and

Sofaer, "The ABM Treaty: Legal Analysis in the Political Cauldron," *Washington Quarterly* (Autumn 1987), 59–75.

51. In memoirs, Shultz implies he was misled by Judge Sofaer; see *Turmoil and Triumph: My Years as Secretary of State.* See also Raymond Garthoff's review of Shultz's memoirs in *Arms Control Today* (October 1993).

52. Nitze, *From Hiroshima to Glasnost*, 467–73. In this annex, Nitze still maintains that "the broad interpretation is fully justified." 473.

53. GCS, "A Dangerous Dream: Why Reagan's Plan Threatens the Nuclear Balance," *Baltimore Sun*, March 24, 1983.

54. *Foreign Affairs* (Winter 1984/85), 277–92.

55. GCS diary, January 14, 1985.

56. Abram Chayes and Antonia Handler Chayes, "Testing and Development of 'Exotic' Systems Under the ABM Treaty: The Great Reinterpretation Caper," *Harvard Law Review* (June 1986), p. 1956.

57. Raymond Garthoff, *Policy Versus the Law* (Washington, D.C.: Brookings, 1987).

58. *Washington Post*, July 15, 1993.

59. I used the "aura of jubilee" term in *Doubletalk*, 453. On the overselling phenomenon more generally, see Esposito, "Selling of SALT."

60. For one example during the talks, see recently declassified "Warnings Against Undue Optimism on SALT," ACDA, Sept. 14, 1970. NSA.

61. Smith, *Doubletalk*, 452.

62. Speech on "Arms Control and the Rule of Law," NY Law School, Aug. 17, 1982 in *GCS on Arms Control*, 76.

63. Smith, *Doubletalk*, 96.

64. For one of a few instances in which this episode has been mentioned, see Newhouse, *War and Peace*, 223–24.

65. Beschloss, *The Crisis Years*, 623–26.

66. For details of Accidents and Hot Line negotiations, see *Doubletalk*, 139–44, 280–98.

67. On overhead reconnaissance and arms control, see Gaddis, *Long Peace*, chapter 7.

68. Article in *Journal of International and Comparative Law*, in *GCS on Arms Control*, 12.

69. "Non-Proliferation: The Forgotten Issue," *Washington Post*, Oct. 26, 1969.

70. GCS Diary, Oct. 25 1972.

71. Greb interview with Johnson; Duncan Clarke, *Politics of Arms Control: The Role and Effectiveness of the U.S. Arms Control and Disarmament Agency* (New York: The Free Press, 1979).

72. Information provided by J.T. Smith II, who was Executive Assistant to Secretary of Defense Elliot Richardson at the time.

73. GCS Diary, Oct. 27, 1972.

Chapter Six
New Ventures in Diplomacy: The Trilateral Commission and Special Ambassador-at-Large for Nonproliferation under Carter

1. "Reason for Being," Anthony Hartley, *Interplay*, Volume 1, Number 1 (June-July 1967), 5.

2. The following discussion of the Trilateral Commission has benefited from the help of Henry Owen and Max Kohnstamn, who graciously shared their memories of these times with me. In Max's case, his recollections were printed in *Gerard C. Smith: A Career in Progress* (edited by Henry Owen and John Thomas Smith II) as part of his contribution, "The European Connection." I have also drawn upon David Rockefeller's reminiscences when he introduced Paul Volcker as his successor as North American Chairman of the Trilateral Commission; see "Remarks of David Rockefeller," November 7, 1991, in Trilateral Note.

3. Supposedly, there was some controversy in Japan over my selection. Stephen Gill reports that "Rockefeller's importance was reflected in the threat, later withdrawn by the Japanese establishment, to pull out of the negotiations to set up the commission upon learning that Gerry Smith and not Rockefeller was to become the first North American chairman." I had not heard of this report before. Perhaps it is as accurate as this author's earlier statement, referring to "Smith, a Rockefeller in-law. . . ." Sometimes I wish I were. See S. Gill, *American Hegemony and the Trilateral Commission* (New York: Cambridge University Press, 1990), 138, 143.

4. Kohnstamn in "A Career in Progress," 83.

5. Richard Harroran, "U.S.-Japanese-European Body Off to a Shaky Start in Tokyo," *New York Times*, October 24, 1973, 4.

6. *Trialogue: A Bulletin of American-European-Japanese Affairs*, No. 2, November, 1973.

7. Kohnstamn, 83–84.

8. Gerard C. Smith, Paolo Vittorelli, and Kiichi Saeki, *Trilateral Security: Defense & Arms Control Policies in the 1980s* (New York: The Trilateral Commission, 1983).

9. Ibid., ix.

10. These issues are discussed at length in chapter 3, "The Search for Greater Security," of the report; Trilateral Security, in particular 37–71.

11. To get the flavor of the discussion and criticisms surrounding the draft report, consult the "Summary of Discussion at Trilateral Commission Plenary, Rome—April 18–19, 1983" appended to the report; Trilateral Security, 89–106. As this summary notes, ". . . several members thought the draft report came too close to advocating a policy of no first use of nuclear weapons and took the occasion to argue against such a policy." p. 89.

12. A good source of information on the ties between the Carter Presidency and the Trilateral Commission, albeit written from a critical leftist position, is Laurence H. Shoup, *The Carter Presidency and Beyond: Power and Politics in the 1980's* (Palo Alto, Calif.: Ramparts Press, 1980), especially chapter 2.

13. This discussion of my tenure as Ambassador-at-Large owes a great deal to Phil Farley, whose recollections are recorded in Henry Owen and John Thomas Smith II, eds., *Gerard C. Smith: A Career in Progress* (Lanham, Md.: University Press of America, 1989), 87–102.

14. "Mr. Smith Is Chosen Again to Talk Arms," *New York Times*, June 5, 1977.

15. John T. Smith II to the editor, *Harper's*, Nov. 15, 1978.

16. Farley, "Nuclear Nonproliferation, 1954–57 and 1977–80," *A Career in Progress*, 100.

17. State Department cable, "The Objectives of the International Nuclear Fuel Evaluation (A Possible Approach)," June 1977. I am indebted to the NSA for providing me with this and several other documents on INFCE.

18. "Management of INFCE: Policy and Program Coordination," no date, NSA.

19. State Department cable, "Nuclear Non-proliferation—Ambassador Smith and the EC," February 1978, NSA.

20. "Rouget's Concern About INFCE Summary," February 1980, NSA.

21. "Smith-Hauff Discussions on INFCE and Post-INFCE," October 1979; "Smith-Eckluynd Telcon, November 7, 1979, Regarding Post-INFCE Follow-on," November 1979, NSA.

22. See James Reston, "The Ticking Bomb," *New York Times*, Feb. 12, 1978.

23. Memo, GCS to Secretary of State Vance, March 5, 1980, NSA. I had made the same point earlier in my diary. On September 15, 1979, I wrote that we should recognize that there is no "technical fix" to the problem. "It must be *political* and turn the pol. engineer loose." I added, "Another case like weapons control where political devel. falls behind technical." GCS Diary, Sept. 15, 1979.

24. See Andrew H. Malcolm, "U.S. and Japan Agree on Tokyo's Opening of Atom Fuel Plant," *New York Times*, Sept. 2, 1977.

25. GCS Diary, Feb. 27, 1978.

26. Officially, the Argentines reported that my talks with them had been "clear and frank," described by the *New York Times* as "terms generally used in

diplomatic notes to indicate disagreement." Juan de Onis, "Argentina Is Nearing Nuclear Deal for Reactor that Makes Plutonium," *New York Times*, March 27, 1980.

27. I worried in my diary, "If the Soviets go public first [with the news of a possible South African bomb], what effect will that have on our image as intelligence collectors?" I thought the entire episode should be "left fuzzy." GCS Diary, Oct. 12, 1977.

28. "U.S. and South Africa End Talks on Nuclear Energy," *New York Times*, June 30, 1978.

29. GCS Diary, Sept. 12, 24, 26, 1979; Oct. 1, 29, 1979; Jan. 26, 28, 1980.

30. GCS Diary, Aug. 12, 1979; Sept. 6, 14, 17, 1979.

31. "U.S. Non-Proliferation Policy and Programs: An Assessment," Report and Executive Summary, October 30, 1980. Quote on p. 8.

32. Jonathan B. Bingham and Paul Findley to Sec. of State Cyrus R. Vance, November 14, 1978; Vance to Bingham, February 3, 1979, NSA.

33. Bingham and Clement J. Zablocki to Vance, January 29, 1980; Walter L. Cutler (acting assistant secretary for congressional relations) to Bingham, April 2, 1980, NSA.

34. Harold H. Saunders and Thomas R. Pickering to Dep. Sec. Warren Christopher, "SCC April 9 Meeting on Tarapur," April 8, 1980; GCS to Sec. State, May 22, 1980; GCS to President Carter, May 23, 1980, NSA. See also David Burnham, "Restraint of Nuclear Panel's Power over Exporting Is Reported Urged," *New York Times*, Feb. 11, 1980; Burnham, "Nuclear Unit Keeps Export Review Role," *New York Times*, March 23, 1980.

35. House Committee on Foreign Affairs, *Resolutions of Disapproval Pertaining to the Shipment of Nuclear Fuel to India* (96th Cong., 2d Sess.), June 26, July 23, September 10, 1980, 19–26, 44–46. See also my letter of June 25, 1980, "India Should Keep Getting U.S. Nuclear Fuel," *New York Times*, July 2, 1980, and Congressman Edward Markey's response of July 11, 1980, "Time to Stop U.S. Nuclear Cooperation with India," *New York Times*, July 25, 1980.

36. GCS to Brzezinski, July 7, 1980; Brzezinski to GCS, July 11, 1980.

37. GCS to President Carter, Oct. 20, 1980.

38. GCS and George Rathjens, "Reassessing Nuclear Nonproliferation Policy," *Foreign Affairs*, 59 (Spring 1981) 875–94. Quote on p. 888.

39. During the Pakistani crisis, for example, I wrote in my diary, "Should we not be stressing with the Joint Chiefs, et al., the importance now of getting the Comprehensive Test Ban as a way to stave off the Pakistani development?" GCS Diary, Aug. 24, 1979.

40. GCS and Rathjens, "Reassessing Nuclear Nonproliferation Policy," 889–90.

Index

Index

About the Author

The late Gerard C. Smith, a graduate of Yale College and Yale Law School, devoted most of his professional life to nuclear arms control. His service under six presidents, Truman through Carter, included leading the U.S. delegation to the first Strategic Arms Limitation Talks (SALT I).

He is the author of *Doubletalk: the Story of SALT I* (Lanham, Md.: University Press of America, 1985) and numerous articles and essays on national security issues.